Mediterranean Diasporas

Mediterranean Diasporas

Politics and Ideas in the Long 19th Century

**EDITED BY
MAURIZIO ISABELLA AND
KONSTANTINA ZANOU**

Bloomsbury Academic
An imprint of Bloomsbury Publishing Plc

B L O O M S B U R Y
LONDON · NEW DELHI · NEW YORK · SYDNEY

Bloomsbury Academic

An imprint of Bloomsbury Publishing Plc

50 Bedford Square	1385 Broadway
London	New York
WC1B 3DP	NY 10018
UK	USA

www.bloomsbury.com

BLOOMSBURY and the Diana logo are trademarks of Bloomsbury Publishing Plc

First published 2016

© Maurizio Isabella, Konstantina Zanou and Contributors, 2016

British Library Cataloguing-in-Publication Data

A catalogue record for this book is available from the British Library.

ISBN:	HB:	978-1-4725-7665-1
	PB:	978-1-4725-7664-4
	ePDF:	978-1-4725-7667-5
	ePub:	978-1-4725-7666-8

Library of Congress Cataloging-in-Publication Data

A catalog record for this book is available from the Library of Congress.

Typeset by RefineCatch Limited, Bungay, Suffolk
Printed and bound in India

In memory of
Christopher Alan Bayly, 1945–2015

CONTENTS

ACKNOWLEDGEMENTS

This volume originated in a series of workshops and conferences in Nicosia and London on *The Patriotism of the Expatriates: Diasporas and national consciousness between Europe, the Mediterranean and beyond in the long 19th century*, organised under the auspices of the University of Nicosia, Cyprus and Queen Mary, University of London (2011–12). Funding was provided by the Research Promotion Foundation of Cyprus (National Framework Programme for Research and Technological Development 2008–11, DIDAKTOR Programme), the University of Nicosia, the School of History and the Centre for the Study of the History of Political Thought and Intellectual History, Queen Mary University of London. We are particularly grateful to the President of the University of Nicosia Nicos Peristianis for embracing this project, and for contributing to its funding and organisation. Without his warm encouragement much of this would have been impossible. Special thanks should go also to John Mavris (University of Nicosia) and Kyriakos Georgiou (Cyprus Centre for European and International Affairs, University of Nicosia) and the Association for Historical Dialogue and Research of Cyprus, who helped organise the Nicosia meetings. Jeremy Jennings, then director of the Centre for the Study of the History of Political Thought, Queen Mary University of London and the Istituto Italiano di Cultura assisted with the organisation of the meeting in London. We are greatly indebted to all participants at these gatherings, and wish to express our gratitude to them for sharing their research with us and contributing to the debate, even though their papers regrettably could not be included in the volume: Gregorio Alonso, Olga Augustinos, Catherina Bregianni, Antonio D'Alessandri, Ada Dialla, Daniele Fiorentino, Mathieu Grenet, Paschalis M. Kitromilides, Ilham Khuri-Makdisi, Dessislava Lilova, Nicos Peristianis, Vivi Perraky, Panayiotis Persianis, Irene Pophaides, Jordi Roca Vernet, Anthony Santilli, Vaso Seirinidou, Michael Sotiropoulos and Nassia Yakovaki. We are also thankful to Michalis Attalides, Antonis Hadjikyriacou, Niyazi Kizilyürek, Daphne Lappa and Emilios Solomou, who chaired sessions at these meetings. Antonis Liakos, Axel Körner, Georgios Varouxakis, Joanna Innes and Mark Philp at various stages kindly agreed to act as discussants. Joanna Innes, Mark Philp, Ilham Khuri-Makdisi and Sakis Gekas read the introduction and parts of the volume and offered precious advice. Finally, Thomas Gallant enthusiastically supported the project and accepted our invitation to write an afterword to this collection.

Martin Thom did much to improve the quality of the English of several chapters. At Bloomsbury Academic, we thank Claire Lipscomb for being always so responsive and helpful. Last but not least, the two anonymous reviewers thoroughly read the proposal and the individual chapters and offered valuable insights.

During the final stages of the project Maurizio Isabella benefited from the support of the Leverhulme Foundation, which awarded him a Research Fellowship in 2013–14, while at various stages of the project Konstantina Zanou benefited from the support of fellowships from the Research Promotion Foundation of Cyprus, the Fulbright Foundation, the Centre for Advanced Studies Sofia and the British School at Athens.

LIST OF CONTRIBUTORS

Andrew Arsan is University Lecturer in Modern Middle Eastern History in the Faculty of History, University of Cambridge, and a Fellow of St John's College. He was previously a British Academy Postdoctoral Fellow at Cambridge, and has held positions at Princeton and Birkbeck, University of London. His first monograph, *Interlopers of Empire: The Lebanese Diaspora in Colonial French West Africa*, was published in 2014.

Grégoire Bron is a postdoctoral researcher at the University of Neuchâtel (Switzerland), where he also teaches. He completed his Ph.D. in 2013 on '*Révolution et nation entre l'Italie et le Portugal. Les relations politiques luso-italiennes de la fin des Lumières à l'Internationale libérale de 1830*' (Ecole Pratique des Hautes Etudes, Paris and Lisbon University Institute, Portugal).

Ian Coller is Senior Lecturer in the History Program at La Trobe University in Melbourne, Australia. His book *Arab France: Islam and the Making of Modern Europe 1798–1831* (University of California Press, 2010) was the recipient of the W.K. Hancock Prize of the Australian Historical Association, and recently appeared in French as *Une France Arabe 1798–1831: Histoire des origines de la diversité* (Alma éditeur, 2014). He has held fellowships at the University of Melbourne, the European University Institute in Florence, and the University of Paris 8.

Thomas W. Gallant holds the Nicholas Family Endowed Chair in Modern Greek History at the University of California, San Diego. He has written twelve books and over fifty articles. His most recently published or forthcoming books are *Experiencing Dominion: Culture, Identity and Power in the British Mediterranean, 1817–1864* (in Greek, 2014), *The Edinburgh History of the Greeks, 1768–1913* (2015), *Murder on Black Mountain: Love and Death on a Nineteenth Century Greek Island* (2015), and *Modern Greece: From Independence to the Present* (2016). Among his best known previously published books are *Modern Greece* (2001) and *Experiencing Dominion: Culture, Identity and Power in the British Mediterranean* (2001).

Maurizio Isabella is Senior Lecturer in Modern History at Queen Mary University of London. He has written on the political culture and economic thought of the Risorgimento, and on its connections with European and extra-European national movements. His *Risorgimento in Exile. Italian Émigrés and the Liberal International in the Post-Napoleonic Era* (2009) is a study of exile liberalism and patriotism in the European and Transatlantic context. He is currently working on a history of the revolutions of the 1820s in Southern Europe in a global context.

Vangelis Kechriotis earned his Ph.D. in 2005 from the Program of Turkish Studies, University of Leiden, the Netherlands. He is Assistant Professor in the Department of History, Boğaziçi University, Istanbul, Turkey, where he is also sponsored by the Onassis Foundation. He is also a member of the editorial committee of the journals *Historein* and *Toplumsal Tarih* as well as member of the board of the History Foundation (Tarih Vakfı). His research interests focus on late Ottoman imperial ideology, political and cultural history, Christians and Jewish communities, and nationalism in the Balkans. He has published many articles related to these topics.

Dominique Kirchner Reill received her Ph.D. from Columbia University and is currently Associate Professor in Modern European History at the University of Miami. Her first monograph, *Nationalists Who Feared the Nation: Adriatic Multi-Nationalism in Habsburg Dalmatia, Trieste, and Venice,* was published by Stanford University Press in 2012 and was awarded the Austrian Studies Book Prize as well as an Honorable Mention from the Smith Award. Currently she is completing her new monograph tentatively titled *Rebel City: Fiume/Rijeka's Challenge to Wilson's Europe.* Research for this project was sponsored by the ACLS grant in Eastern-European Studies and the American Academy's Rome Prize.

Gabriel Paquette is Professor of History at The Johns Hopkins University. He is the author of *Imperial Portugal in the Age of Atlantic Revolutions* (2013) and author of articles published in *Journal of Latin American Studies, The Historical Journal,* and *European Historical Quarterly.*

Artan Puto holds a Ph.D. in History from the European University Institute (Florence, Italy). He teaches at Tirana University, Faculty of History and Philology. His fields of interest are the period of Albanian national movement (1878–1912), the Albanian interwar period (1912–39) and the communist regime (1944–90).

Juan Luis Simal (Ph.D. 2011, Miguel Artola Prize) teaches at the Universidad Autónoma de Madrid, Spain. He has been a Postdoctoral Research Fellow of the Alexander von Humboldt Foundation at the Historisches Institut – Universität Potsdam, Germany. He has written several academic articles and book chapters, and is the author of *Emigrados. España y el exilio internacional, 1814–1834* (2012) and co-editor of *Exils entre les deux mondes. Migrations et espaces politiques atlantiques au XIXe siècle* (2014).

Konstantina Zanou is a visiting fellow at the Institut d'Études Avancées, Paris. She is joining Columbia University in Fall 2016 as an assistant professor of Mediterranean Studies in the Department of Italian. She has previously held fellowships at the University of Nicosia (Research Promotion Foundation of Cyprus), New York University (Fulbright), Centre for Advanced Studies Sofia Bulgaria, Queen Mary University of London (British School at Athens grant) and Université Paris-Est Créteil. She has published articles on expatriate intellectuals and national consciousness in the post-Venetian Adriatic. Her book in progress is tentatively titled *Stammering the Nation. Transnational Patriotism in the Mediterranean, 1800–1830.*

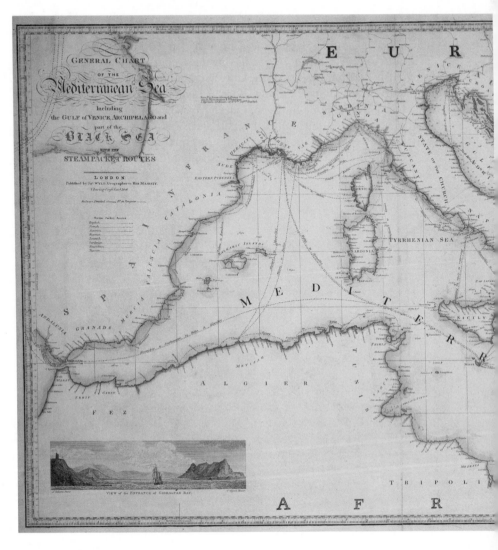

Map of the Mediterranean

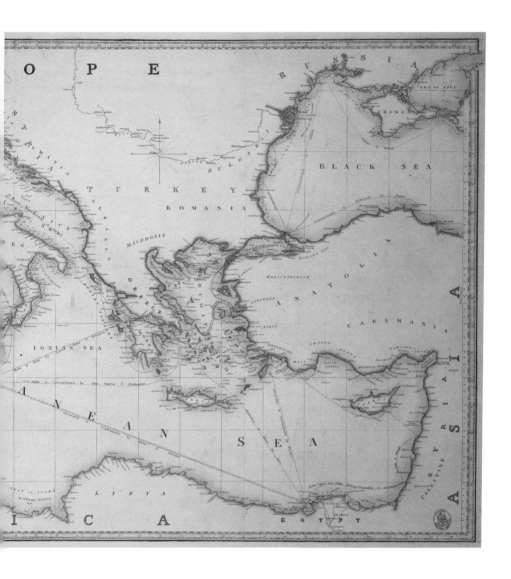

INTRODUCTION

The Sea, its People and their Ideas in the Long Nineteenth Century

Maurizio Isabella and

Konstantina Zanou

The Mediterranean as a category of historical analysis

Recent years have seen a flurry of exciting works in the field of Mediterranean history. These publications have revisited in new and creative ways the Mediterranean as a category of historical analysis, disturbing the fifty-year peace in which the sea had been resting since Fernand Braudel's monumental treatment of its history.[1] This 'new thalassology' of the Mediterranean (as it was labelled by two of the scholars who have done most to constitute it) has questioned the traditional ways of perceiving the history of the sea, by challenging both the concept of 'unity' and its contrary 'fragmentation'.[2] On the one hand, the Braudelian idea of the natural and cultural 'unity' of the Mediterranean space has been abandoned in favour of an approach that sees the Mediterranean as a 'fragmented topography of microregions'.[3] Against the static image of the sea developed by Braudel, historians now view the Mediterranean as a space of dynamic and multiple interconnections, as a fragmented world which is nonetheless united by its very connectivity. On the other hand, the new trend in Mediterranean history has been to overcome the chronic fragmentation of national and regional studies and to question the borderlines between east and west and north and south. In their recent contributions, scholars such as, for example, Julia Clancy-Smith, and Manuel Borutta and Sakis Gekas, have attempted to reconstruct interactions, entanglements and shared experiences between Western and Eastern Europe, the Maghreb and the Middle East, abandoning not only the constricting national frameworks of modern Mediterranean history but also its occidentalist narratives.[4] In this sense, they have transformed the Mediterranean into a domain where established historiographical notions are being challenged. By putting together histories that are usually examined individually, recent historians have made of the sea the theatre of trans-national and trans-imperial experience; sometimes also of colonial experience.[5]

As a result, the Mediterranean of the historians has been pluralized, both by division and by multiplication. By division, because the 'Classic Mediterranean' is now broken down into a series of sub-Mediterraneans: the Adriatic Sea, the Aegean, the central Mediterranean corridor, the Eastern Mediterranean, are all considered to be 'miniature Mediterraneans'.[6] The sea is thus understood as a set of interconnected seas, which can be studied together or as separate environments in their own right.[7] Even smaller units, such as port cities or islands, are gradually claiming a place among the categories of historical analysis.[8] Yet recent historical imagination has also multiplied the Mediterranean. For David Abulafia and other historians, the Mediterranean is not simply one, nor is it necessarily made of water. Any space that can function like a 'middle sea', with its waters fostering links between different cultures, societies and economies, can be considered to be a Mediterranean. A desert can, for example, be a Mediterranean.[9] What is more, these Mediterraneans are far from being closed worlds. In fact, one theme that is increasingly addressed by historians is the relationship between the different Mediterraneans that flowed into one another, carrying goods, people and ideas.[10] Accordingly, the geography and limits of the Mediterranean have become a matter of scholarly inquiry. Where exactly does the Mediterranean end? The answer to this question is no longer taken for granted. Historians would appear now to agree that the Mediterranean is much larger than its geographical bounds suggest. The flux of peoples, cultures and ideas is such that its borders can at times be reckoned to extend as far as the Baltic Sea or Latin America. As this volume shows, the ties created between the Mediterranean and its surrounding lands, from Portugal, to Russia and Anatolia, could at times leave observers with the sense that the basin bordered on regions beyond itself.

This is the way, then, that we understand the Mediterranean in this collection: as a malleable space of contact, encounter, entanglement and interaction among its diverse and heterogeneous peoples. Its history is a history of interconnections and of their multiple forms: among them, diasporas and intellectual exchange. Our Mediterranean history is all about contacts, as much peaceful as violent; it is a dynamic, interactive, trans-Mediterranean history.

For all the work that has already been done in Mediterranean history, there remains much to explore, not least in the period under investigation here, the nineteenth century, and in our chosen field of inquiry, intellectual history and the history of ideas. Since Braudel, the Mediterranean has been studied mostly by ancient, medieval and early modern historians.[11] With the exception of Abulafia, who extends his narrative into the twentieth century, the authors of such sweeping, all-inclusive histories give the impression that the Mediterranean ceases to exist as a category of historical analysis when we enter modern times.[12] In this collection, however, we endeavour to show that the Mediterranean can serve as a useful framework of historical analysis until well into the nineteenth century. Furthermore, the handful of works that have dealt with the modern Mediterranean have done so from a different perspective to the one proposed in this volume. The nineteenth-century Mediterranean has hitherto been narrated either in terms of an all-embracing factual history, as colonial history, or as economic history and history of trade.[13] By contrast, the originality of this volume lies in the fact that it sees the Mediterranean, first and foremost, as a place of intellectual communication.

The need to restore the one element overlooked by Braudel, namely human beings, has been repeatedly addressed by historians.[14] Yet, what remains still to be restored is the circulation of ideas: what did the people crossing the Mediterranean shores or travelling beyond them carry in their heads? Attention to this question is the defining feature of the present collection, which brings together essays addressing intellectual history, and for the most part through the lens of biography. If the heroes of Braudel are principally inanimate objects or agencies operating at the level of macro-reality (the sea, the climate, the landscape), our heroes are individual men and women and their fractured micro-lives: intellectuals, patriots, political exiles, travellers, adventurers, revolutionaries, diplomats, merchants, students, migrants and refugees, people who shaped their ideas on the move or far away from the country they were imagining as homeland. The protagonists of these global micro-histories were, in Francesca Trivellato's words, 'individuals who embodied geographical and cultural dislocation'.[15] They were tiny fragments of a gigantic mosaic formed by the Mediterranean diasporas in the long nineteenth century.

From the Diaspora to the diasporas

The Mediterranean had been a place of migration since Antiquity. Pre-modern diasporas settled on one or other shore of the Mediterranean, establishing arteries through which flowed not only commodities but also seamen, merchants, fleeing peasants, missionaries, corsairs, captives and slaves. From the fifteenth to the eighteenth centuries, islands like Corsica, Malta and Corfu saw ships and people come and go every day, sailing from or headed for Genoa, Venice, Livorno, Cagliari, Rome, Otranto, Naples,

Algiers, Constantinople, Seville, Valencia – and especially Marseilles. Sixteenth-century Venice, with its Greek, Albanian, Armenian, Turkish and Vlach communities, and seventeenth-century Cairo, with its Armenian, Greek, Christian Syrian, Jewish and Muslim cohorts from the Maghreb and the Levant, bear witness to the sheer extent of population movement in the early modern Mediterranean.[16] Within this glittering and complex tapestry of the pre-nineteenth century Mediterranean diasporas, diverse segments from three populations, namely the Jews, the Greeks and the Armenians, were particularly mobile. After their expulsion from the Iberian peninsula in 1492, a large number of Jews found refuge in the Ottoman Empire, while in the seventeenth and eighteenth centuries many resettled in Morocco, Tunis and the Italian peninsula – especially in the port of Livorno and in the wider region of Tuscany.[17] Along with the Greeks and the Armenians, they were the only people to develop trade diasporas within the Muslim world. Indeed, from the mid-fifteenth century, and especially from the eighteenth century onwards, we find Greek settlements nearly everywhere: in the Black Sea and the Sea of Azov (the Russian Crimea and Novorossiya), in Budapest, Vienna, Trieste, Bucharest, Iasi, Venice, Livorno, Marseilles, Ancona, Naples, Amsterdam, Alexandria, even in Corsica and Minorca.[18]

Not only did these ethnic trade diasporas not disappear in the nineteenth century, but many of them followed the same routes as they had done in the early modern period, retaining by the same token several of their older characteristics. However, some new elements made their appearance during the nineteenth century. First, new types of migration and migratory paths emerged, while others disappeared. The imperial expansion of certain powers, such as Britain, France and Russia, and the collapse or gradual decline of others, such as the Venetian, the Habsburg and the Ottoman Empires, substantially altered the political, economic and demographic parameters of the Mediterranean, at the same time establishing new trade routes and economic centres. This was the period when Britain created its Mediterranean Empire, through the occupation of Sicily between 1806 and 1815, the possession of Malta in 1800, the Ionian Islands in 1809 and Corfu from 1815 to 1864, the seizure of Cyprus in 1878, the temporary occupation of Palestine in 1840 and the creation of the 'veiled British protectorate' of Egypt in 1882. France also spread its wings, starting with the invasion of Egypt in 1798–1801, the possession of the Ionian Islands from 1809 to 1814, and the occupation of Algeria in 1830 and Tunisia in 1881. The opening of the Suez Canal in 1869 brought more competition between the two colonial powers and, together with the Eastern Question and the Crimean War (1853–6), it weakened the Russian influence. The Russians, who had, at the turn of the eighteenth century, encroached upon the Eastern Mediterranean by instigating revolts in the Aegean and occupying the Ionian Islands (1800–9), were now forced to retreat. The same happened to the Ottomans and the Habsburgs, who by the end of the nineteenth century had relinquished the majority of their Adriatic possessions, due to the establishment and expansion of the Kingdoms of Greece (1830) and Italy (1861), and to the recognition of the independence of the Principality of Montenegro by the Congress of Berlin (1878). The Ottoman Empire lost all territories along the Adriatic following the First Balkan War and the subsequent 1913 Treaty of London that established an independent Albania. Imperial readjustment brought about the demise of some old diaspora communities and the emergence of others. Together with the circulation of goods, colonialism also reinforced the circulation of human beings (especially officials, soldiers and settlers), imposing new trade and mobility routes across the sea and creating newly flourishing port-cities: Alexandria, Beirut, Izmir, Tunis, Algiers are only some of the formerly languishing ports which were transformed into boom-towns thanks to direct or indirect colonial rule.[19]

Second, where migration was concerned, the nineteenth century became the century of Africa and the Atlantic. If immigration to Europe was the rule for the twentieth century, the opposite was true for the nineteenth: the transformation of North Africa from 'Barbary' into a place where one 'could make it' led, during the period from the Napoleonic era to the Great War, tens of thousands of people to cross the sea from north to south and from west to east, towards Africa and the Levant.[20] On the other hand, a revolution in transport, which dramatically lowered costs, made movement within the Mediterranean and across the Atlantic easier and more accessible to ever greater numbers. Indeed, if there was one thing that changed in this period it was surely the nature and scale of migration. Whereas before migrants had tended in the main to be itinerant traders, workers, sailors and soldiers, now, and especially after 1850, emigration to the large Mediterranean cities and to the Americas became a mass phenomenon: some historians have calculated that in the nineteenth century roughly one third of the entire population of Europe was on the move.[21]

But what was new about the nineteenth century was also the association of migration with the territorial state. This was the century of imperialism and colonialism, but it was also the century of nation-states. State frontiers and control processes had already appeared in the seventeenth century, but they only assumed a major political significance in the course of the nineteenth.[22] The expanding regulatory reach of the modern state and the need to place under surveillance any potential nuclei of political subversion in a Europe hard hit by the Napoleonic Wars, created, in the first half of the nineteenth century, a new type of itinerant figure in the Mediterranean: the political exile. Flight into political exile, although not uncommon earlier, loomed larger during this period, and especially after the Congress of Vienna (1814–15). The Vienna settlement had brought about the geopolitical recasting of the European continent after the fall of Napoleon, while the Congresses of Troppau (1820) and Laibach (1821) suppressed revolutionary movements in Southern Europe and proscribed their leaders.[23] The revolutions in the European South and the Ottoman Empire in the first half of the nineteenth century engendered, in addition, another kind of migration:

the war refugees. We have in mind here Cypriot families who sought refuge in Marseilles, Venice and Trieste in 1821, Christian families from Asia Minor and the islands of the Aegean who fled to the coasts of the Black Sea during the 1820s, and Druze notables deported from Mount Lebanon by the Egyptian forces in 1831–40, but there were many others.[24]

Whether political exiles, refugees displaced by war, expatriate intellectuals or itinerant merchants, persons caught up in the diasporas were usually accustomed to travelling, being men – and, more rarely, women – who lived their lives on the move: across states, empires and seas.[25] However (as Dominique Kirchner Reill argues in this volume), the actual limits of 'displacement' are hard to imagine in an era of such constant geographical and political change. In a world of vast empires, customs unions, miniature city-states and semi-independent principalities, the frontiers of which were continually shifting, it is unclear what 'home' and 'abroad' really meant. On the one hand, travelling from one city to another, or from one state to another, might represent for many a circulation within a familiar space where they could feel at home no matter where they laid their heads. On the other hand, the delineation and consolidation of new frontiers (cultural, national, linguistic and religious) transformed many individuals into liminal beings, obliged to divide their allegiance between societal units which now came to be seen as separate and distinct. More and more persons were found thus to live in the margins of new empires and nation-states, transforming themselves into trans-imperial and trans-national subjects.[26] If multiple political, cultural and linguistic affiliations were typical of the pre-national era and of early modern diasporas, this collection shows that they in fact continued to exist in the nineteenth century. If this was the century of national boundaries, it was also a century in which these same boundaries were all too permeable.

Until recently, scholarship defined diasporas in relation to a centre (usually national, but also regional, continental, religious or ethnic) from which they were considered to be dispersed and to which ideally one day they would return. In actual fact, until the mid-twentieth century the word 'Diaspora' (usually spelled with a capital *D*) referred to Jews only, or had a predominantly religious connotation.[27] Nevertheless, a recent historiographical trend has reversed the terms of how we understand the relationship between centres and diasporas, abandoning the notion of 'national diasporas' for that of 'diasporas as such'. According to this new reading it is not the centres that produce their diasporas, but rather the diasporas that reinvent their centres.[28] Building on these new approaches, this collection understands diasporas not as extensions of the homeland, but as sites where collective or individual consciousnesses were originally shaped. Thus the Italian-, Greek- or Albanian-speaking patriots discussed here first developed new notions of nationhood or empirehood in this 'mobile space' of the diasporas, often combining them with other allegiances (Zanou, Bron, Puto and Isabella, Kechriotis, Kirchner Reill).[29] Moreover, in this collection diasporas are viewed as spaces of communication, as 'contact zones', as 'social spaces where cultures meet, clash, and grapple with each other' – according to the celebrated formulation of the concept by Mary Louise Pratt – but also as spaces where, perhaps, cultural influences may be rejected.[30] From being an emblem of the unity of a dispersed people with an imagined homeland as a point of reference, diasporas thus become in this book an expression of fragmentation, of the multiplicity of loyalties and belongings. They come to stand as a synthesis of everything that operates *through* empires and nation-states, and we hope thereby to offer modern historians a vantage point from which to survey the shifting and polycentric world of the nineteenth century.

Revolutionary Mediterraneans

The nineteenth century was not only the age of new and intense migratory waves precipitated by colonialism or by economic exchanges in the Mediterranean. It coincided also with the age of revolutions. Its chronology, however, while overlapping with that of Western Europe, traditionally centred around 1789 and 1848, differs substantially from it and manifests its own characteristic features. Extending from the French Revolution's shock waves to the Italian peninsula, the Ionian Islands and Egypt, to the Turkish Revolution of 1908, it displays a peculiar intensity, variety and frequency of events, since it includes anti-imperial and anti-colonial uprisings, military *pronunciamientos*, peasants' rebellions and civil wars, all events in which external pressures and foreign interventions interacted with internal social and political dynamics.[31] It comprehended the simultaneous and army-led uprisings of the 1820s that brought together Portugal, Spain, Turin, Naples, Sicily, Greece and the Atlantic; the revolutions of 1830 and 1848 that in turn associated the Mediterranean and the Italian peninsula in particular with Western and Central Europe, as well as with the Balkans. It was beset by counter-revolutionary movements and civil wars, such as those dividing Portugal between 1832 and 1834, Spain, with the Carlist wars of 1833–9, 1846–9 and 1872–6, and Southern Italy in the years after the birth of the Italian state in 1860.[32] It also included a Sicilian revolution in 1837, the Greek military *pronunciamiento* of 1843 which gave rise to a new constitutional regime, as well as a number of rebellions within the Ottoman world, from the anti-reform movements of 1807–8 in Constantinople, and the 1840 Rebellion of Lebanon against Ali Pasha, to the uprising against the bey of Tunis in 1864, the Cretan revolution of 1866–9, and the Egyptian Arab revolution between 1879 and 1882.[33] These revolutions were often either directly influenced by, or the outcome of diasporic activities, and produced multiple waves of emigration and displacement that added new links or reinvigorated existing ones between countries and revolutionary episodes unfolding at the same time or one after the other. Nineteenth-century revolutionary cultures took shape through the very fact of movement: there were no revolutions unaffected by voluntary or enforced emigration and exile, or uninfluenced by intellectual diasporas. Historiography has increasingly recognized the importance and intensity of such phenomena in the age of revolutions. Greek revolutionary culture, for instance, was the product of the interactions of the Greek intellectual diaspora, which was dispersed across the Habsburg Empire, France, the Italian peninsula and the Balkans and was in contact with the centres of intellectual production within the Ottoman Empire.[34] But this is the case with a number of different revolutionary traditions. As Ian Coller has recently observed, the French Revolution has to be understood not only in terms of its Southern European dimensions, that included territories occupied directly by the French armies or affected by war, but also as a phenomenon that involved people scattered around the sea: French residents in the Ottoman coastal cities drawn there by the expansion of trade embraced revolutionary principles, as did those Muslims and Christian Ottomans whose aspirations for autonomy were enhanced by the new political and ideological context.[35]

Later revolutions produced similar phenomena, to such an extent, indeed, that we can talk about the consecutive formation of 'multiple revolutionary Mediterraneans' across the nineteenth century. The 1820s *pronunciamientos* in Spain, Portugal, Greece, Naples and Sicily drove patriots in large numbers towards France and Britain, but also towards the Ionian Islands, Malta, as well as North Africa, where conspirators reorganized secret societies and plots and maintained contact across the sea. Conversely, after 1848, Constantinople and other port cities of the Middle East and the North African littoral became centres of attraction for exiles coming from Western and Southern Europe as well as from the Balkans.[36] As many of the contributions to this volume show, exile allowed the defeated revolutionaries to ponder the reasons for their defeat, to revise earlier beliefs and to imagine new political projects (Paquette, Simal, Bron). What connected the different parts of the Mediterranean among themselves and with northern Europe was also a culture of volunteerism that led consecutive waves of officers and soldiers to support foreign revolutions in the name of the principles of solidarity, 'Mediterranean brotherhood' and internationalism.[37] Therefore, if we take into account these people crossing the sea in all directions, our narrative of the age of revolutions in this region is decentred and assumes an entirely new guise. This book, by so doing, adds to a growing literature that is more sensitive to the global, multi-regional dimension of the period, and has abandoned a focus on France and America as unique centres of radiation of revolutionary culture.[38]

The Mediterranean as an imaginary political and civilizational space

If the intense circulation of individuals across the basin facilitated the formulation of new ideas, doctrines and debates, what brought the region together was also the fact that intellectuals, whether in Sicily, the Adriatic or in Egypt, had to grapple with a similar set of questions. The nineteenth century was marked by the rise of Orientalism, with its formulation of notions of a 'backward Islamic Orient' as the polar opposite of Western or European Christian civilization and progress. In this respect, the sea space was the imaginary territory in which increasing cultural polarizations, ideological fractures and distinctions between East and West, North and South were acted out. Western European intellectuals employed the Mediterranean as a rhetorical device serving to reinforce geopolitical hegemonies and to develop intellectual notions of superiority that applied, although generally with different sets of arguments and with different political and intellectual objectives, to Southern Europe, the Balkans and North Africa alike. In some cases, in fact, notions of backwardness were employed to justify colonial rule, whether in the Ionian Islands, Sicily, or in North Africa and the Middle East. This placed intellectuals around the basin in similar predicaments, as they were all forced to engage with these Western representations at a time when geographies of civilization were being crystallized.[39] Late Ottoman intellectuals, for instance, ended up responding with equally antithetical definitions of Muslim civilization, based on ethnicity and religion and an increasingly entrenched notion of irreconcilable values.[40] As this book demonstrates, diasporic intellectuals at times accepted and at times challenged the cultural stereotypes coined in Western Europe and applied to these extra-European peripheries. For instance, it was in response to European travellers' notions of Muslim backwardness and fanaticism that the Ottoman-Albanian writer Sami Frashëri drew a distinction between Muslim Albanians, viewed by him as intrinsically European, on the one hand, and the Turks, on the other, to legitimize Albanian nationalism in the eyes of European public opinion (Puto and Isabella). As the Italian and North African liberals discussed by Maurizio Isabella and Ian Coller show, patriots from both shores of the sea criticized European colonial rule, condemning the hypocrisy and inconsistency of European civilizational discourse.[41]

Besides, during the nineteenth century, the Mediterranean region was reimagined as a geographical and civilizational space. It was primarily the Saint-Simonians and their followers who first saw the Mediterranean in such terms, but their vision was subsequently adopted and reinvented by thinkers native to the region. So far as the latter were concerned, this was the century that would put the Mediterranean back again at the centre-stage of the world after a long decline: the commercial exchanges facilitated by the opening of the Suez Canal and the railway networks along its coasts would connect it to global links and the sea would become once again, as it had been in Antiquity, the cradle of modern civilization. The sea could by turns be conceived as a French, an Italian or an English space, in which one or the other nation should dominate, either because of its geographical position within it, or because of its civilizational mission, or because of the 'natural' bond existing between coastal regions (as was argued for the case of Syria, construed as a part of France).[42] In the late nineteenth century, the Adriatic was re-appropriated by both Italian and Albanian nationalists as 'their own' sea, while Greek nationalists dreamt about the reconstruction of a Byzantine Empire.[43]

The sea and its civilization was likewise historicized, and its ancient past was revisited by intellectuals in both Northern and Southern Europe, as well as in the Eastern Mediterranean, for multiple and at times conflicting purposes, invariably associated with ideas about the political and economic modernity the Mediterranean world should by rights acquire.[44] While during the early decades of the century some Italian liberals looked back to the pre-Roman Mediterranean populations as models of peaceful colonialism in order to criticize contemporary European conquest around the sea, the Phoenician past was employed by Christian Lebanese writers to recover and celebrate the Eastern Mediterranean origins of a civilization that had been brought from there to the West, or to provide historical justification for the current mass experience of emigration to the Americas. In the second half of the century Italian intellectuals retrieved memories of the Venetian Empire to support the colonial ambitions of the new state.[45] In general, by connecting the present and future of the Mediterranean to its glorious past, intellectuals aimed at giving it a new centrality in the transformations of the modern world.

An intellectual history *in* the Mediterranean and beyond?

This project has brought together intellectual and cultural historians, as well as historians of emigration and exile from a variety of regions and subject areas who, in spite of the geographical proximity of the countries they study, tend to work separately, either because of the predominance of national historiographical frameworks or because of a lack of communication between historians of Europe and Ottomanists, historians of the Balkans and those of Southern Europe. They have all shared a commitment and determination to rethink the boundaries of their various disciplines, and have welcomed the opportunity to explore new and often neglected connections, parallels and similarities that suggest a revision both of the way in which the Mediterranean is perceived, and of the manner in which political imagination and ideas were shaped in its different areas. By so doing, this enterprise is inspired by, and in turn hopes to represent, an original contribution to the recently established but rapidly growing field of transnational and global intellectual history. In this vein, we have tried to go 'beyond familiar geographical boundaries', and have provided space to voices in intellectual history and experiences that are generally ignored or considered to be marginal, peripheral, and therefore irrelevant. Unlike more conventional histories of ideas, this collection is concerned with ideas in motion, the trans-national and trans-regional crossing of borders and circulation of culture and the imagining of political communities that are today all but forgotten.[46]

The nineteenth century has traditionally inscribed the Mediterranean within the narratives of the age of nationalism. It is the century of the birth of the Italian and Greek states, in which national movements began to threaten the integrity of the Ottoman Empire. In relationship to this narrative and interpretative framework this collection offers new perspectives. The emphasis on movement across space and time, and the study of ideas through the interaction between individual trajectories and geopolitical transformations offered by the essays collected here help to break down the paradigm of the rise of the nation-state in a variety of different ways. First of all, the contributors show that the nation was by no means incompatible with political systems other than those modelled upon the nation-state, and in particular with empires (Isabella, Coller, Arsan, Zanou and Kechriotis). In fact, a Mediterranean perspective makes various forms of imperial nationalism or patriotism a common, if not the most common, type of political community conceived in the nineteenth century. What was at stake for most diasporic patriots coming from all the shores of the Mediterranean was the accommodation of aspirations towards autonomy, self-government and constitutional guarantees, or administrative modernization within the existing Ottoman or Habsburg empires, or in the newly expanding French and British colonial empires. Cultural and linguistic notions of nationality could readily be reconciled with imperial allegiances. This happened on all sides of the sea, from the Adriatic and Sicily to North Africa, from the Ionian Islands to Anatolia. Italian-speaking writers like Ugo Foscolo or Vittorio Barzoni considered British hegemony in the Mediterranean and British protectorates compatible with local freedoms (Isabella), as did other Ionian patriots, for example Ioannis Kapodistrias (Zanou). The Anatolian Greeks studied by Vangelis Kechriotis saw in a modernized and constitutional Ottoman Empire the best guarantee for the protection of their rights against the rising Balkan nationalisms, and so too did the Albanian intellectuals Girolamo de Rada and Sami Frashëri, who remained loyal to the Empire until the end of the century, while devoting their lives to the Albanian language, literature and history. The Ionians discussed by Konstantina Zanou considered their Greek patriotism and attachment to their islands as perfectly compatible with service to the Russian Empire and Russian imperial hegemony in the Adriatic and over Greece. Finally, these case studies show how a shift from empire to nation was not always a foregone conclusion for Mediterranean liberals. Some might turn their back on earlier plans for 'national' emancipation and consider that political modernity would stem from imperial reformism, rather than the other way round. As Coller showed, in the 1820s the North African Hassuna D'Ghies first advocated the full independence of the Tripoli regency under a constitutional government, and supported the autonomy of Algiers under a French protectorate, but in the 1830s he decided to put all his hopes for change in a reformed Ottoman administration. Thus the Italian *Risorgimento*, the Greek *Epanastasis* and the Arab *Nahda* that emerge from the following pages reveal their intrinsic complexity, a range of different possibilities being envisaged, the nation-state representing only one.

Second, in the devising of their imagined political communities, diasporic intellectuals often took issue with the premise that nations had to be conceived as single and separate cultural, ethnic, religious and linguistic units. They might, for example, reject cultural or linguistic homogeneity on the grounds that linguistic and cultural pluralism were perfectly compatible with ideas of emancipation and freedom; indeed, they represented a better choice for the survival of regions that were transitory spaces between different cultural worlds.[47] But the opposite might happen also. As the case of the Portuguese liberal Almeida Garrett scrutinized by Gabriel Paquette shows, the experience of exile and displacement could at the same time give rise to more intolerant forms of patriotism and to ideas of a national culture hostile to external influences.

Emphasis on the interaction between shifting political and geopolitical contexts and individual or collective intellectual biographies helps us to understand how some political and cultural options became gradually marginalized. It shows how the birth of new polities and the demise of older ones rendered it more difficult to sustain allegiances to different states, or to a plurality of languages and cultures, forcing individuals to choose between them. This is what happened, for example, to the Adriatic patriots studied by Kirchner Reill. The post-Venetian imperial space in which they moved, partly inherited by the Habsburg Empire, and characterized by the coexistence of different languages and different cultures, was increasingly threatened by essentialist notions of nationhood deemed to be at odds with pluralistic values.[48] In the case of Niccolò Tommaseo and his circle the turning point seems to have been the revolutionary wave of 1848, when more xenophobic and mutually exclusive ideas of the Italian and the Dalmatian nation became dominant. In the case of the Ionian intellectuals studied by Zanou, it was the creation of the Greek state that made the Ionian openness to different languages and cultures unfeasible.[49] Within the Ottoman Empire, the intellectual and political leaders of the Karamanlı Greek community of Anatolian origin based in Smyrna, explored here by Kechriotis, exemplified the resilience of a peculiar sense of Greekness that was compatible with the Ottoman Empire, thrived during the constitutional phase of the Empire, but was inexorably marginalized and rendered unsustainable by the Balkan Wars, the First World War and the collapse of the Empire itself.[50] In other instances, however, ways of conceiving links beyond the local or the national, rather than disappearing, were continuously rethought and adapted to new circumstances and through new intellectual means. Forms of trans-national Mediterranean solidarity and internationalism first developed in the 1820s

6   David Abulafia, 'Mediterraneans', in W.V. Harris (ed.), *Rethinking the Mediterranean* (Oxford: Oxford University Press, 2005), pp. 67–75.

7   For example, the Adriatic: Pierre Cabanes et al., *Histoire de l'Adriatique* (Paris: Seuil, 2001); Emilio Cocco and Everardo Minardi (eds), *Immaginare l'adriatico. Contributi alla riscoperta sociale di uno spazio di frontiera* (Milan: Franco Angeli, 2007); Francesco Bruni and Chryssa Maltezou (eds), *L'Adriatico: incontri e separazioni (XVIII–XIX secolo)* (Venice-Athens: Istituto ellenico di studi bizantini e postbizantini di Venezia, 2011).

8   Biray Kolluoğlu and Meltem Toksöz (eds), *Cities of the Mediterranean from the Ottomans to the Present Day* (London and New York: IB Tauris, 2010); Edhem Eldem, Daniel Goffman and Bruce Masters (eds), *The Ottoman City Between East and West: Aleppo, Izmir, and Istanbul* (Cambridge: Cambridge University Press, 1999); Sakis Gekas and Mathieu Grenet, 'Trade, politics and city space(s) in Mediterranean ports', in Carola Hein (ed.), *Port Cities. Dynamic Landscapes and Global Networks* (London and New York: Routledge, 2011), pp. 89–103; Nicolas Vatin and Gilles Veinstein (eds), *Insularités ottomanes* (Paris-Istanbul: Institut français d'études anatoliennes, 2004); Antonis Hadjikyriacou, 'Local intermediaries and insular space in late-18th century Ottoman Cyprus', *Journal of Ottoman Studies* 44 (2014), pp. 427–56.

9   Abulafia, 'Mediterraneans'; David Armitage and Alison Bashford, 'Introduction: The Pacific and its Histories', in idem (eds), *Pacific Histories: Ocean, Land, People* (London-New York: Palgrave Macmillan, 2014), pp. 1–28.

10 Leila Tarazi Fawaz, C.A. Bayly and Robert Ilbert (eds), *Modernity and Culture, From the Mediterranean to the Indian Ocean* (New York: Columbia University Press, 2002); Donna R. Gabaccia and Dirk Hoerder, *Connecting Seas and Connected Ocean Rims: Indian, Atlantic and Pacific Oceans and China Seas Migrations from the 1830s to the 1930s* (Leiden-Boston: Brill, 2011); Luigi Mascilli Migliorini and Mirella Mafrici, *Mediterraneo e/è Mar Nero. Due mari tra età moderna e contemporanea* (Naples: Edizioni scientifiche italiane, 2012).

11 On the early modern Mediterranean: Molly Greene, 'Beyond the Northern Invasion: The Mediterranean in the Seventeenth Century', *Past & Present* 174/1 (2002), pp. 42–71; idem, *Catholic Pirates and Greek Merchants: A Maritime History of the Early Modern Mediterranean* (Princeton: Princeton University Press, 2010); idem, *A Shared World: Christians and Muslims in the Early Modern Mediterranean* (Princeton: Princeton University Press, 2000); Adnan A. Husain and K.E. Fleming (eds), *A Faithful Sea, The Religious Cultures of the Mediterranean, 1200–1700* (Oxford: Oneworld, 2007).

12 David Abulafia, *The Great Sea, A Human History of the Mediterranean* (New York: Oxford University Press, 2011). Another exception is the popularized version of history offered by John Julius Norwich, *The Middle Sea: A History of the Mediterranean* (London: Vintage Books, 2007). See also Peregrine Horden and Sharon Kinoshita (eds), *A Companion to Mediterranean History* (Oxford: Wiley Blackwell, 2014), which hands the pen to anthropologists when it comes to modern times.

13   Luigi Mascilli Migliorini (ed.), *Storia del Mediterraneo moderno e contemporaneo* (Naples: Guida, 2009); Faruk Tabak, *The Waning of the Mediterranean, 1550–1870: A Geohistorical Approach* (Baltimore, MD: John Hopkins University Press, 2008); Sakis Gekas, 'The merchants of the Ionian Islands between East and West. Forming local and international networks', in M.S. Beerbuhl and J. Vogele (eds), *Spinning the Commercial Web. International Trade, Merchants, and Commercial Cities, c. 1640–1939* (Frankfurt-New York: Peter Lang, 2004), pp. 43–63; Gelina Harlaftis, 'Mapping the Greek Maritime Diaspora from the Early Eighteenth to the Late Twentieth Centuries', in I. Baghdiatz-McCabe, G. Harlaftis and I. Pepelasis Minoglou (eds), *Diaspora Entrepreneurial Networks: Four Centuries of History* (Oxford-New York: Berg, 2005), pp. 147–71.

14   David Abulafia, *The Mediterranean in History* (Los Angeles: J. Paul Getty Museum, 2003), p. 13.

15   Francesca Trivellato, 'Is There a Future for Italian Microhistory in the Age of Global History?', *California Italian Studies* 2/1 (2011), retrieved from: https://escholarship.org/uc/item/0z94n9hq. On 'global microhistory' see also: Tonio Andrade, 'A Chinese Farmer, Two Black Boys, and a Warlord: Towards a Global Microhistory', *Journal of World History* 21/4 (2011), pp. 573–91; John-Paul A. Ghobrial, 'The Secret Life of Elias of Babylon and the Uses of Global Microhistory', *Past and Present* 222 (2014), pp. 51–93.

16   Claude Liauzu, *Histoire des migrations en Méditerrannée occidentale* (Brussels: Complexe, 1996); Julia Clancy-Smith, 'Mediterranean Historical Migrations: An Overview', in Dirk Hoerder and Donna Gabaccia (eds), *Encyclopedia of Global Human Migration* (London: Wiley Blackwell, 2012), pp. 1–19; Jan Lucassen and Leo Lucassen, 'The mobility transition revisited, 1500–1900: what the case of Europe can offer to global history', *Journal of Global History* 4 (2009), pp. 347–77.

17   Natalia Muchnik, 'Ibériques en exil: marranes et morisques aux prises avec le référent-origine', in Jocelyne Dakhlia and Wolfgang Kaiser (eds), *Les musulmans dans l'histoire de l'Europe*, Volume 2: *Passages et contacts en Méditerranée* (Paris: Albin Michel, 2013), pp. 165–89; Francesca Trivellato, *The Familiarity of Strangers: The Sephardic Diaspora, Livorno, and Cross-Cultural Trade in the Early Modern Period* (New Haven: Yale University Press, 2012); Mercedes García-Arenal and Gerard Wiegers, *A Man of Three Worlds: Samuel Pallache, a Moroccan Jew in Catholic and Protestant Europe* (transl. Martin Beagles) (Baltimore: Johns Hopkins University Press, 2003).

18   Sebouh Aslanian, *From the Indian Ocean to the Mediterranean: The Global Trade Networks of Armenian Merchants from New Julfa* (Berkeley: University of California Press, 2011); Ioannis Chassiotis, Olga Katsiardi-Hering and Evridiki Ambatzi (eds), *Oi Ellines tis Diasporas, 15os–21os aionas [Greeks in the Diaspora, 15th–21st centuries]* (Athens: Greek Parliament, 2006); Artemis Xanthopoulou-Kyriakou, *I Elliniki Koinotita tis Venetias, 1797–1866 [The Greek Community of Venice, 1797–1866]* (Thessaloniki: Aristotelian University of Thessaloniki, 1978); Olga Katsiardi-Hering, *I Elliniki Paroikia tis Tergestis, 1751–1830 [The Greek Community of Trieste, 1751–1830]* (Athens:

53   On Khodja's liberalism see also Jennifer Pitts, 'Liberalism and Empire in a Nineteenth Century Algerian Mirror', *Modern Intellectual History* 6/2 (2009), pp. 287–313.

54   Clancy-Smith, *Mediterraneans*, p. 315ff.

55   Christopher Bayly, 'Rammohan Roy and the Advent of Constitutional Liberalism in India, 1800–1830', *Modern Intellectual History* 1/4 (2007), pp. 25–41.

56   Maurizio Isabella, 'Entangled patriotisms: the Italian diaspora and Spanish America', in Gabriel Paquette and Matthew Brown (eds), *Connections after Colonialism: Europe and Latin America in the 1820s* (Tuscaloosa, Alabama: Alabama University Press, 2013), pp. 87–107; Eugenio Biagini and Christopher Bayly (eds), *Giuseppe Mazzini and the Globalisation of Democratic Nationalism 1830–1920* (Oxford-New York: Oxford University Press for The British Academy, 2008).

57   Khuri Makdisi, *The Eastern Mediterranean and the Making of Global Radicalism*, quotation from p. 54; Juan Luis Simal, *Emigrados: España y el exilio internacional, 1814–1834* (Madrid: Centro de Estudios Políticos y Constitucionales, 2012); Christopher Bayly, *Recovering Liberties: Indian Thought in the Age of Liberalism and Empire* (Cambridge: Cambridge University Press, 2012).

58   To borrow the definition by Dipesh Chakrabarty in his *Provincializing Europe: Post-Colonial Thought and Historical Difference* (Princeton: Princeton University Press, 2007).

CHAPTER ONE

Letters from Spain:
The 1820 Revolution and the Liberal International

Juan Luis Simal[*]

Introduction

The reestablishment in Spain in 1820 of the Cadiz Constitution (1812) received extensive attention throughout Europe. The agent in Spain of the Austrian chancellor, Prince Metternich, wrote in a report a month after Rafael del Riego's *pronunciamiento* of January 1820: 'At the cry of revolution that has recently resounded in Spain, the eyes of all Europe have turned to this country, and considering the attention it receives, we can readily acknowledge that the latest events have aroused concerns, revived many hopes, and that many interests even if foreign, are linked to the fate of the Spanish Monarchy.'[1] In the following months, the spread of the revolutionary impulse to Portugal, Naples and Piedmont – where the Spanish constitution was claimed as the inspiration for revolution and directly adopted or adapted – confirmed the event as a turning point for European politics. In October 1820 the Danish representative in Madrid considered that 'the immediate effect of the Revolution on this side of the Pyrenees cannot be felt on the shores of the Sund [the strait between Denmark and Sweden], but it has inaugurated a new European political era'.[2]

[*] I would like to express my gratitude to the editors of the volume and to Fernando Durán for their comments and suggestions on earlier drafts of this text.

Indeed, many revolutionaries and counterrevolutionaries throughout Europe shared the belief, or fear, that the Spanish events had ushered in a new era. Facing the possibility of a continent-wide revolution, the reactionary powers took immediate action. After the Austrian interventions in Naples and Piedmont in 1821, hundreds of Italians fled to Spain and Portugal, which remained the only constitutional powers on the continent.[3] However, in 1823 a French intervention put an end to the second constitutional experience in Spain, sending thousands of liberals into exile.[4]

For three years – the period known in Spanish history as the Liberal or Constitutional Triennium, or *Trienio*, with a parallel development in Portugal – the news coming from the South of the continent was the news of the day. Newspapers all over Europe covered the events and many books were written and quickly published. Many of these publications were presented as 'histories' of the revolution, although they nevertheless had pronounced ideological leanings. Others were controversial pieces written with explicit political goals, either to celebrate or to condemn the Iberian events. Among these publications of the early 1820s, several consisted of compilations of letters written from Spain and Portugal by eyewitnesses, many of them exiles. They were translated and published in different European countries in numerous editions.

This chapter analyses the letters published in these books, focusing on what their authors, addressees, topics and editorial features reveal about the interconnections between liberals scattered across Europe in the wake of the revolutions of the early 1820s. In addition, the letters tell us much about the networks established in exile by Italian, Spanish and French émigrés and their sympathizers. The chapter also considers the authenticity and accuracy of the published correspondences, and examines their contested status in the political polemics surrounding the question of the 'failure' of the constitutional regimes in Southern Europe, as they presented diverse opinions, allocated responsibilities and highlighted errors. However, they also provide unequivocal evidence of the discourse and practice of international liberal solidarity. Overall, the chapter seeks to draw attention to the ways in which the events in Southern Europe, and notably Spain, shaped the political agenda of the rest of the continent during the 1820s, and how they lent impetus to the circulation of ideas and to transnational connections.

The epistolary genre and its politics

There existed in Europe a venerable tradition of travel literature published in the form of private letters sent home by the traveller, developed intensely in the age of the Grand Tour. The genre came with its own conventions. Readers were well aware that the letters were not always meant to be completely genuine. They were part of a game between author and reader, in which the boundaries between fiction and documentary reality were porous, although modifications were kept to a minimum. As a rule, the letters were presented as having been originally written for private purposes, and published only afterwards. Sometimes they were presented anonymously, and on many occasions the addressees were also left unnamed, frequently with only their initials being given. This was meant to add an air of authenticity to the content of the letters. As they were private letters not written for publication, they were supposed to be sincere and to offer a raw, unmediated image of the foreign land that was being visited. They supposedly captured a real experience as it was unfolding, one that had not been reconstructed afterwards from the comfort of home. Nevertheless, even when they were completely genuine, the letters were normally edited, corrected and adapted for publication.

The epistolary form was also extensively used in the daily and periodical press. The journals of the eighteenth and nineteenth centuries included letters serving both analytic and informative purposes, sent by 'foreign correspondents'. A particular case that gave a twist to the epistolary genre, bringing it closer to fiction, were the letters written by European authors passing as exotic foreigners commenting on the mores and institutions of their own countries. Consider, for example, Montesquieu's celebrated *Lettres persanes* (1721) and Cadalso's *Cartas marruecas* (1789), regarded by most as works of fiction. Novels written in the epistolary form were all the rage in this period in Europe, and included Samuel Richardson's *Pamela* (1740), Rousseau's *Julie, ou la nouvelle Héloïse* (1761), Goethe's *Die Leiden des jungen Werthers* (1774) and Laclos' *Les liaisons dangereuses* (1782). The genre continued to flourish in the nineteenth century, as the case of Mary Shelley's *Frankenstein* (1818) attests. The reading public became familiarized with this literary technique, an accepted trope that blurred the lines between reality and fiction, but that also laid claim to historical, anthropological and geographical accuracy.

Before the Spanish revolutionary years that produced the 1812 constitution and the Liberal Triennium, various books of letters dealing with Spain had been published. Since the Iberian peninsula was of marginal importance for the Grand Tour, most of the travellers, who were predominantly British or French, visited Spain for strictly professional reasons. So far as the British – men like Edward Clarke, Henry Swinburne, Alexander Jardine or Robert Southey – were concerned, their emphasis was all upon the chronic shortcomings of a country that had been the enemy of England for centuries and that in their view was ruled by monarchical despotism and Catholic bigotry. Some authors showed a genuine interest in Spain, although never completely abandoning their prejudices or their innate sense of superiority.[5] These collections of letters were presented as genuine and, indeed, as reliable sources for the understanding of the foreign countries they dealt with. Accuracy was of the utmost importance for these enlightened travellers. Southey, for example, presented his work as an impartial view of what he had witnessed: 'In the following letters I have related what I have seen. ... I have given facts, and the Reader may comment for himself.'[6] Likewise Clarke, in order to give his letters a proper context and a more than merely incidental relevance, prefaced them with a historical introduction. Neither book featured an addressee, not even one identified by their initials. Far from seeming to undermine the reliability of the claims contained in the letters, this obfuscation was understood by the readers to be proof positive of the authenticity of the letters, which would never have been published with real names.

In the transition from Enlightenment to Romanticism the focus of travel books upon erudite observations gave way to a stronger emphasis on political and moral issues. The commencement of the revolutionary events that shook the Atlantic world had led to an increasingly extensive use of the epistolary genre for political purposes. As with other revolutionary events, the Spanish revolution became one of the scenarios to which the genre was widely applied. Cultural, artistic and ethnographic descriptions yielded more and more to narratives outlining the courses of wars and political claims and counter-claims.

The Peninsular War (1808–14) had a tremendous impact on European consciousness and on the development of Romanticism.[7] In Britain, it fostered the publication of many travel and epistolary books and the inclusion in the press of letters sent from Spain and Portugal – for example, John Allen's private correspondence published by the *Morning Chronicle* in 1808–9.[8] The British passion for Spain continued after the end of the Napoleonic Wars, and the Spanish liberal exiles who took refuge in London after 1814 obtained the sympathies of local public opinion.[9] Interest in Spain revived in 1820. Press coverage of the revolutionary episode in Spain was intense, and many books were published, some containing letters describing the earlier hostilities, while others were based on recent travels and contemporary events – such as Michael J. Quin's *A Visit to Spain*, whose observations had previously appeared in instalments in the *Morning Herald*.[10] Among these books there were also quickly-penned historical pieces and explicitly political works, many published in France, where events on the other side of the Pyrenees received widespread attention.[11] Some of the authors who published compilations of letters were already well-versed in the genre. Edward Blaquiere, one of the most fervent British supporters of the revolutions in Southern Europe, had published in 1813 *Letters from the Mediterranean*. In his editorial activities in the 1820s he combined the writing of a history of the Spanish revolution with the publishing of correspondences and other personal writings, which he treated as historical documents, thus blurring the lines between strictly historical accounts, political statements and private impressions. He thus edited and wrote the introduction to the English version of two books by the Milanese Count Giuseppe Pecchio, a central figure in the conspiracies in Lombardy and an exile in Spain and Portugal in the early 1820s. In these books, a compilation of letters and a journal, Pecchio recollected his experiences in the revolutions of the Iberian peninsula, prior to his arrival in England in 1823.[12]

In his published letters, Pecchio assured his addressee, an anonymous English Lady, that she should anticipate nothing else but a political account: 'I promise to be guided by truth and sincerity, in the opinions I may give on their [the Spanish people] character, manners, and institutions. Do not, however, expect a description of those ancient monuments or picturesque sites, which may present themselves; it being impossible for me to think of anything now but politics.'[13]

As the case of Pecchio serves to show, it was the letters of revolutionaries that were most widely read. The French Bonapartist Guillaume de Vaudoncourt had participated in the Piedmontese revolution before arriving in Spain in 1821 as an exile. He later published *Letters on the Internal Political State of Spain*. In the introduction, the editor of the book, or maybe Vaudoncourt himself, assured his readers that the letters presented were 'a selection from his correspondence with his friends, and several Spaniards of distinction'. Furthermore, the author had chosen the 'epistolary form' as the best way to reproduce 'the method and fidelity of an historian'.[14] The historical approach was further bolstered by the inclusion of documents. As with other books of the same genre, Vaudoncourt's volume included an appendix that reproduced several of the documents to which he had referred in his letters.

The epistolary genre was not the only one used to transmit immediate first-hand accounts of the Spanish events. Other publications were composed as memoirs or diaries, among them Fiorenzo Galli's *Memorias sobre la guerra de Cataluña*, or Pecchio's *Journal of Military and Political Events in Spain during the Last Twelve Months*.[15] Of course, many of the protagonists of the events would later in their lives – some posthumously – publish their complete memoirs, including accounts of their participation in the revolutions and their years of exile. This was the case with the Neapolitan and Spanish revolutionary leaders Guglielmo Pepe and Francisco Espoz y Mina.[16]

Letters on the Spanish revolution were also published by Spanish authors, who produced in exile a rich and vast bibliography that touched upon each and every literary genre, including political and historical writings. Many of these books and journals were prepared in London for the Spanish American market, and were mainly in Spanish, following the initiative of the German editor Rudolf Ackermann.[17] The veteran Spanish exile José Blanco White published in 1822 *Letters from Spain*. It was not a book on recent events, but rather a ferociously critical account of Spanish culture, an appraisal of its 'moral state' pivoting around the Catholic despotism which, according to the Spanish émigré of Irish origin, who had converted to Anglicanism, held sway in his native country. Blanco White, being only too well aware of the intricate nature of the epistolary genre – rendered still more intense in his own case through his sheltering behind the pseudonym Leucadio

Doblado – acknowledged in the preface that 'the slight mixture of fiction which these Letters contain might raise a doubt whether the sketches of Spanish manners, customs, and opinions ... may not be exaggerated by fancy, and coloured with a view to mere effect'. Yet he assured 'the Public of the reality of every circumstance mentioned in his book'.[18]

Likewise, the Spanish press in London published many letters received from Spain describing the dreadful predicament of the country under absolutist rule and the terror still being inflicted upon the liberals. Supposedly, it was private correspondence, and the authors and addressees retained their anonymity, yet the letters were normally annotated and commented by the editors. Whether they were authentic or just a literary device used to transmit a political message is unclear, but the editors were evidently adept at exploiting the genre.[19] This press also published letters written by Spanish exiles, like the anonymous 'Cartas hibérnicas', which narrated the experiences of a Spanish liberal in Ireland. Joaquín Lorenzo Villanueva subsequently claimed their authorship in his autobiography published in 1825.[20] The fluid relationship between the epistolary and the historical genres was evident in the works of a number of Spanish exiles. Thus in London Pablo Mendíbil transformed the *Cuadro histórico de la Revolución mexicana* by the Mexican Carlos María Bustamante, a book originally written in the form of letters, into an abbreviated *Resumen histórico de la Revolución de los Estados Unidos Mejicanos*. Mendíbil abandoned Bustamante's 'epistolary style', which had allowed him more 'liberties', and adopted a historical narrative technique, using the original as a 'text of reference'.[21]

Euroamerican networks and the different faces of liberalism

The letters published in these books depicted dense networks of contacts, delineating connections among liberals throughout Europe. The writings of the exiles and liberals, translated into different languages, contributed to the reinforcement of a Europe-wide public sphere through the use of a genre that belonged to a shared literary tradition. They were a public demonstration of the contacts existing among revolutionaries of all nations, while at the same time they served as evidence for those conspiracy theorists who discerned an interconnection between all the European revolutions.

The reactionaries were not entirely mistaken, yet the origins of the individual revolutions were nonetheless to be found in internal dynamics. However, from the very beginning the discourses of the revolutionaries were dominated by strong universalistic references. The Spanish liberals were accused by European reactionaries of constitutional proselytizing, not least after the revolutions in Portugal and Italy had adopted the 1812 constitution. Yet no actual evidence for these subversive manoeuvres could be produced, and not until the Italian and French exiles started to arrive in Spain and Portugal did the events in the Iberian peninsula appear to be intrinsically linked to events taking place elsewhere in Europe. Thus Pecchio, once in Spain, could note 'the analogy of circumstances which gave rise to it [the Spanish revolution] with those of Piedmont'.[22] Repression and exile would bring the revolutionaries together, uniting them against a common enemy – embodied in the Holy Alliance – and facilitating their contacts.

Pecchio's works offer an excellent example of the widespread interest that epistolary books on the Iberian revolutions aroused, and illuminate the connections that their publication might foster among European liberals. Pecchio's compilation in several different volumes of the letters sent from Spain and Portugal to an English Lady identified as J.O. (Giannina Oxford) were arguably the most widely circulated example of this literary genre in Europe at the time. The first Italian edition appeared in Madrid in 1821 as *Sei mesi in Spagna nel 1821*. It was followed by *Tre mesi in Portogallo nel 1822*.[23] These two works were swiftly translated into French, English and German, and published in different editions enhanced by additional comments and observations by other members of the 'liberal international', whether Spanish or English. They included the aforementioned Blaquiere, a radical close to Jeremy Bentham, and Juan Corradi, editor of the minutes of the Spanish *Cortes* (Parliament) who was expelled from France by the Paris police in November 1822.[24] The French version was soon followed by a second edition, featuring a piece on the first Spanish revolution written by Count Toreno, also translated into French.[25] The English edition was published in London in 1823 by Blaquiere as *Anecdotes of Spanish and Portuguese Revolutions*, incorporating into a single volume the letters sent from Spain and Portugal. This complete version was soon translated into German.[26]

As in the case of the publication of Pecchio's letters, intellectual contacts were made public through epistolary books. The most celebrated Spanish liberal poet of the period, Manuel José Quintana, living in internal exile in Extremadura after 1823, wrote a number of letters to Lord Holland, a major figure in the Whig party and a convinced Hispanophile, who was the main benefactor of the Spanish and Italian exiles in England. These letters were, however, not published in full until 1852.[27]

Public letters were both interventions in a debate held by European liberal networks supportive of the Spanish revolution, and direct contributions to the public life of liberal Spain. The publications of the English political philosopher Jeremy Bentham are a case in point. Bentham got involved in the legislative debates of the Iberian peninsula through his *Letter to the Spanish Nation* and *Letter to the Portuguese Nation*, which were also translated into Spanish.[28] He also published *Letters to Count Toreno on the proposed Penal Code*, in which he formulated his proposals for the modification of the Spanish penal code being drafted at that time.[29] But these were also a reflection of the engagement of Bentham's circle with an extensive network of Southern European liberals. Toreno had first approached

Bentham with a letter of introduction from their mutual friend John Bowring, an English merchant who lived in Spain during the *Trienio* and who, as Bentham's executor, would later edit his complete works. In 1824 Bowring became a member of the 'City Committee for the relief of the Spanish and Italian refugees' formed in London.[30] Bentham's epistolary contacts with the Southern liberals were intense, and he maintained a wide-ranging correspondence with other Spaniards, Spanish Americans, Portuguese and Greek revolutionaries.[31]

Such published letters also show the close connection between Spanish and Spanish American revolutionary circles and audiences. Mora's *Cartas sobre la educación del bello sexo*, published anonymously, in which a Spanish American woman exiled in Europe writes to her sister a series of letters regarding female education, was republished in many American republics. This book was probably requested by Bernardino Rivadavia, who in 1826 would become president of the United Provinces of the River Plate and invite Mora to join him on the other side of the Atlantic.[32]

The liberalism of the era was marked by a serene optimism regarding the invincible advance of enlightened reason, progress and political freedom. In 1821 Pecchio opined that 'the spirit of the age, which has an inevitable tendency towards freedom', would guarantee the success of the Spanish constitutional regime.[33] This optimism and confidence in the triumph of liberalism through solidarity across nations was part of the creation of an international liberal imaginary. The Spanish *Trienio* loomed large in this imaginary, and its constitution was claimed as a model by liberals elsewhere in Europe. It was adopted in Naples, Piedmont and Portugal, although not without argument.[34] In France, Britain, Germany and other European regions the political debate featured constant reflections on the Spanish model that were essential to the delimitation and refinement of political positions. The legendary Spanish text crossed the entire continent, reaching even Russia, where the Decembrists considered it a model.[35]

Solidarity was a paramount element in international liberalism. Constitutional Spain served as a haven for hundreds of Italian and French liberals persecuted in their home countries. At first Pecchio 'had chosen the mountains of Switzerland for [his] retreat', but after the Spanish diplomat Bardaxí offered him protection in Spain, he 'did not hesitate to change a doubtful hospitality for a certain asylum'.[36] Vaudoncourt praised the generosity of the population of Tarragona that received him and the Piedmontese exiles with open arms: 'every thing has been done to alleviate their distress'. At a banquet held in their honour, they together raised a glass to 'The liberty of Europe forever!'[37] The Spanish *Cortes* had passed a law in September 1820 that, in Pecchio's words, accorded 'the greatest protection to strangers' while declaring 'the Spanish territory an inviolable asylum', and stipulated 'that no person who takes refuge in Spain for political offences or opinions, shall ever be given up'.[38] When the exiles started to arrive, and after some debate in the *Cortes*, the government voted measures in their favour, including the granting of subsidies. However, the question of the refugees divided the Spanish liberals, and some among the more moderate distrusted them, even if they showed their commitment to the Spanish regime.

Several of the exiles joined the Spanish army, and were then involved in skirmishes against the local counterrevolutionaries who had initiated an insurrection in the Northern provinces.[39] When a French army invaded Spain in April 1823, following the Congress of Verona, the aggression was denounced in the press and the parliaments of Europe – especially in Britain and France – and international volunteers took up arms to defend the constitutional regime.[40] The authors of the published letters celebrated these military volunteers in the name of the international cause of freedom. Blaquiere had considered it necessary that Spain, 'exhausted by the despotism of ages – torn by intestine divisions, and unable, from dilapidated finances, to conduct an offensive war on an extended scale', should create 'isolated corps', 'whether native or Cosmopolite', to support the regular army. The 'Cosmopolite Corp ... should exact no other qualification for enrolment, than a detestation of tyranny, and a sufferance in the cause of freedom'.[41] Vaudoncourt proposed to the Spanish government 'the necessity of forming a foreign legion, composed of the French and Italian refugees, of the deserters who might be collected in Spain, and the foreigners whose assistance might be called'.[42] The French, most of them participants in the domestic conspiracies of the early 1820s, formed squadrons that confronted the French army when it crossed the border.[43] The British radical MP Robert Wilson, a veteran of the Peninsular War, landed in northern Spain and formed a battalion of volunteers that joined the Spanish army. Finally, at the beginning of 1823, the Spanish government formally accepted the offers of assistance made by the international volunteers and passed a decree creating the Foreign Legions, reproduced by Vaudoncourt in his book. Hundreds of exiles rallied to the cause.[44]

However, the French invading army prevailed in Spain, and thousands of liberals had to flee the country. The fight for liberty in Spain was followed in the international liberal imaginary by the Greek cause, the fight for independence from the Ottoman Empire initiated in 1821, and by the construction of republics in the independent Spanish American nations. The Greek struggle was equated by many liberals with their own endeavours in Western Europe, and comparisons between the *despotic* and *barbarous* Turks and the Holy Alliance were common. For Blaquiere, 'the preservation of European freedom, and the stability of British power, depend on the stand which the Peninsula and Greece shall make against the Holy Alliance'.[45] Several Italian and French exiles expelled from Spain – yet not many Spaniards – were among the hundreds of European philhellenes who joined the fight for Greece's liberty.[46]

After the defeat of their liberal projects in Europe, some liberals turned their attention to America. Several of them travelled to the United States and/or to the new Latin American nations, where they pursued their political activities.[47] The prospect of the American continent as the land of regenerated politics in a republican guise found its reflection in the epistolary genre. In *Cartas de un americano sobre las ventajas de los gobiernos republicanos federativos*, published anonymously in London in 1826 by the press of a Spanish émigré, the Spanish exile José Canga Argüelles collaborated with Vicente Rocafuerte, who was in the Mexican diplomatic service. Using the 'conciseness of the epistolary style', the letters argued for the establishment in Spanish America of federal republics following the example of the United States.[48]

Yet the letters sent from Spain before the regime fell and those published in the following years were also redolent of disappointment and conflict. After all, Greece and America were nothing but the last causes of a community of European liberals that had been repeatedly defeated and persecuted. The very same letters transmitted contradictory reflections. Pecchio, who praised Spanish generosity towards the exiles, affirmed that after his arrival no one even once asked him about the events in Italy: 'not a soul has yet condescended to interrogate me on the revolution of Piedmont'. Interest was so slight, he continued, that Spaniards confused Piedmont with Naples.[49]

But limited knowledge of similar foreign events was not the only mistake attributed to the revolution. 'The errors, which can never fail to attend a transition from centuries of slavery to a state of liberty, have been most abundantly felt throughout the Peninsula', Blaquiere affirmed.[50] After the French invasion of Spain, many Italians claimed that one of the reasons for the failure of its constitutional regime had been its refusal to help the liberals of Naples and Piedmont when they had been attacked by the Holy Alliance, on this occasion in the form of Austrian bayonets.[51] The Lombard Pecchio declared in 1821 that 'as an Italian' he could 'never forgive' the Spanish minister Argüelles 'for suffering Naples to perish, without a firm and resolute intervention at the Congress of Laybach. The whole of Europe will perhaps one day pay for the terrible consequences of this homicidal prudence'. There was not only resentment in Pecchio's opinion towards Spain, but also regret that Spain had missed the opportunity to become a major European power, to acquire 'the most glorious supremacy' and to regain its place in the balance of power as leader of all the constitutional regimes. But after acknowledging the generous reception granted to the Italian exiles in Spain, his verdict on the issue was bold: 'The Spaniards have acted toward Italy like him who allows his friend to be knocked down without coming to his assistance, and then runs to raise him up, overpowering him with the most generous care and sympathy.'[52] Vaudoncourt thought also that things could have turned out differently: 'ten thousand Spaniards in Italy would probably have rescued Naples from slavery'.[53]

Some also condemned the Iberian constitutional regimes for their failure to assist Greece. Blaquiere, an active philhellene who wrote extensively on the Greek revolution,[54] considered that Spain and Portugal should recognize its independence. In his view, this 'criminal omission' was 'among those errors most deeply to be regretted by the friends of freedom and humanity'. The benefit would be mutual: 'At all events, the experience of the last two years must have convinced the Ministers of Spain and Portugal that there is but ONE nation in Europe from whose cooperation and support they might derive more efficient aid, than from the Hellenic Confederation'.[55] Similar connections between the revolutions of the Mediterranean peninsulas were made by other exiles, in the hope that the constitutional regimes would reinforce each other. Thus Vaudoncourt lamented that 'the speedy and unhappy termination of the two revolutions in Italy, has had a fatal influence on public opinion in Spain' since the 'Spanish patriots ... depended much on the promised success of the Italian revolution, as a new source of strength to the constitutional edifice in Spain'.[56]

Several of the authors, reproducing a widely shared opinion, considered the disunion among Spanish liberals as one of the main causes of the demise of Spanish constitutionalism. Admittedly, they were divided over what brand of liberalism and what liberal party to support. Vaudoncourt and Blaquiere sided with the *exaltados*, the most radical party, which considered mass participation and the involvement of the Patriotic Societies to be a crucial element in constitutional life, while Pecchio had a positive opinion of the government of the *moderados*, who were more hostile to direct political participation and mass politics, declaring for 'the vigour of the executive, and maintenance of order'.[57] The preservation of the original Cadiz text or its modification was the more controversial issue dividing *moderados* and *exaltados*, and was mentioned by almost all commentators. Quin's analysis of the Spanish factions was among the most nuanced of all foreign accounts. The Irish journalist claimed that he had gone to Spain 'perfectly unbiassed' and through his close observations of local political life had concluded that the Spanish constitution was 'impracticable' and that it should be reformed following the English model.[58] This opinion was shared by many European liberals.

Regardless of their different sympathies, the various authors all agreed that the hostilities between these parties had weakened the revolutionary cause. Blaquiere, worried by the internecine struggles within Spanish liberalism, announced the existence of 'tremendous external perils that threaten the asylum of European freedom' and called for a 'coalition of the Spanish liberals' that with 'unanimity, in sentiment and in action' could face their enemies, 'foreign and domestic'. He even advocated an alliance between Spain and Portugal.[59] By 'domestic enemies' Blaquiere meant the vigorous popular counterrevolution that, under the direction of influential sectors of the Church and the nobility, had formed in the north. The failure to fully understand the needs and impulses of the popular masses they had wanted to liberate proved especially disappointing for Southern European liberals and epitomized the darker side of liberal optimism. Spanish, Italian and Portuguese liberals had hoped to regenerate their respective peoples, composed mainly of illiterate and rural populations, through educational programmes that would swiftly rectify centuries of despotism and ignorance. Those Spanish and Italian liberals who had lauded the Spanish people for their legendarily brave resistance to the Napoleonic invasion were bewildered when the French invaders of 1823 did not meet with a like response.[60] A similar disappointment was experienced by the philhellenes when they encountered a Greek people that had little to do with the idealized versions of them modelled upon accounts from classical Antiquity. Finally, Europeans who believed in the inevitability of the establishment of prosperous republics in Spanish America were bitterly disappointed with their political instability in the years following independence. This succession of failures left their mark upon the subsequent evolution of international liberalism. Indeed, European liberalism suffered ever more fragmentation and was increasingly contested from the margins of republicanism and conservatism, while at the same time facing a tenacious counterrevolution that had also internationalized its connections, discourse and practices.

Conclusion

In the early 1820s, Europeans turned their eyes towards the Mediterranean, especially Spain, revealing the importance that ideas and events coming from the South had for Northern European audiences and for the development of domestic liberalisms. Exile and volunteering represented key moments of reflection and action for liberals from the Mediterranean, as well as for their supporters in the rest of the continent. An increasingly pan-European liberal debate was fostered by trans-continental displacements. Southern liberals migrated across the Mediterranean region. French and English liberals travelled south, attracted by the revolution. Italians, Spaniards and Portuguese liberals emigrated to the north and developed intense literary and political activities centred in the London publishing industry. All these experiences were swiftly available to European readers, who could learn about the politics of a liberal international shaped by conflicting views and an intense transnational debate.

Transnational exchanges were facilitated by a shared European literary culture, which found in the epistolary genre a powerful mode of expression. Books and literature were a fundamental part of the construction and expansion of liberalism and international solidarity, a free press being one of the main liberties claimed by the constitutionalists. The authors of the letters analysed above, mostly exiles, contributed through their epistolary books to the construction of a powerful romantic liberal narrative, of which they became the heroes and protagonists. Readers throughout Europe and across the Atlantic empathized with their adventures and misfortunes as they presented them, thus finding it easier to identify with their values and projects. A liberal epic had been born in the Mediterranean.

Notes

1 Archives Diplomatiques, Paris, France, Mémoires et Documents, Espagne, 308, Espagne 1820. Correspondance interceptée, ff. 8–13, Comte Brunetti to Prince Metternich, no. 70, Madrid, 23 February 1820.

2 AD, Mémoires et Documents, Espagne, 309, Espagne 1820–1. Correspondance interceptée, ff. 54–59, Mr Dernath to Mr de Rosenkrantz in Copenhagen, no. 119, Madrid, 9 October 1820.

3 Maurizio Isabella, *Risorgimento in Exile. Italian Émigrés and the Liberal International in the Post-Napoleonic Era* (Oxford: Oxford University Press, 2009); Agostino Bistarelli, *Gli esuli del Risorgimento* (Bologna: Il Mulino, 2011).

4 Emilio La Parra, *Los Cien Mil Hijos de San Luis. El ocaso del primer impulso liberal en España* (Madrid: Síntesis, 2007); Juan Luis Simal, *Emigrados. España y el exilio internacional, 1814–1834* (Madrid: CEPC, 2012).

5 Edward Clarke, *Letters concerning the Spanish Nation. Written at Madrid during the Years 1760 and 1761* (London: Becket and De Hondt, 1763); Henry Swinburne, *Travels through Spain in the Years 1775 and 1776* (London: P. Elmsly, 1787), 2 vols; Alexander Jardine, *Letters from Barbary, France, Spain, Portugal, &c.* (London: T. Cadell, 1788); Robert Southey, *Letters written during a short residence in Spain and Portugal. With some account of Spanish and Portugueze Poetry* (Bristol: Bulgin and Rosser, 1797). Scholarly accounts include Elena Fernández Herr, *Les origines de l'Espagne romantique. Les récits de voyage 1755–1823* (Paris: Didier, 1973); Ana Clara Guerrero Latorre, *Viajeros británicos en la España del siglo XVIII* (Madrid: Aguilar, 1990); Consol Freixa Lobera, *La imagen de España en los viajeros del siglo XVIII* (Barcelona: Universidad de Barcelona, 1992).

6 Southey, *Letters*, p. v.

7 Diego Saglia, *Poetic Castles in Spain: British Romanticism and Figurations of Iberia* (Amsterdam and Atlanta: Rodopi, 2000); David Howarth, *The Invention of Spain. Cultural Relations between Britain and Spain (1770–1870)* (Manchester: Manchester University Press, 2007); Léon F. Hoffmann, *Romantique Espagne. L'image de l'Espagne en France entre 1800 et 1850* (Princeton-Paris: Princeton University Press-PUF, 1961); Pere Gifra-Adroher, *Between History and Romance: Travel Writing on Spain in the Early-Nineteenth Century United States* (Illinois: Associated University Press, 2000).

8 Elías Durán de Porras, 'John Allen, la otra mirada de Holland House. Apuntaciones sobre *Journal of a Tour of Spain and Portugal*, 30 de octubre de 1808 – 13 de enero de 1809', in *Cuadernos de Ilustración y Romanticismo* 18 (2012), pp. 55–106.

9 Simal, *Emigrados*.

10 Michael Joseph Quin, *A Visit to Spain; detailing the transactions which occurred during a residence in that country, in the latter part of 1822, and the first four months of 1823. With general notices of the manners, customs, costume, and music of the country* (London: Hurst, Robinson and Co., 1824, second edition).

11 Charles Laumier, *Histoire de la révolution d'Espagne en 1820, précédé d'un aperçu du règne de Ferdinand VII, depuis 1814, et d'un précis de la révolution*

de l'Amérique du Sud (Paris: Plancher/Lemonnier, 1820); Dominique de Pradt, *De la révolution actuelle de l'Espagne, et de ses suites* (Paris: Béchet, 1820).

12   Edward Blaquiere Esq., *Letters from the Mediterranean; containing a civil and political account of Sicily, Tripoly, Tunis, and Malta . . .* (London: Henry Colburn, 1813); idem, *An Historical Review of the Spanish Revolution, including some account of religion, manners and literature in Spain* (London: Whittaker, 1822); Giuseppe Pecchio, *Anecdotes of Spanish and Portuguese Revolutions, with an introduction and notes by Edward Blaquiere* (London: Whittaker, 1823); idem, *Journal of Military and Political Events in Spain during the Last Twelve Months, with some introductory remarks on the present crisis by Edward Blaquiere* (London: Whittaker, 1824).

13   Pecchio, *Anecdotes*, pp. 5–6.

14   Guillaume de Vaudoncourt, *Letters on the internal political state of Spain, during the years 1821, 22, & 23; extracted from the private correspondence of the author, and founded upon authentic documents* (London: Ibotson & Palmer, 1825, third edition), pp. 3–4.

15   Florencio Galli, *Memorias sobre la guerra de Cataluña, en los años 1822 y 1823* (Barcelona: Bergnes, 1835); Pecchio, *Journal of Military and Political Events.*

16   *Memorie del Generale Guglielmo Pepe intorno alla sua vita e ai recenti casi d'Italia* (Paris, 1844) (soon translated into French and English); *Memorias del General don Francisco Espoz y Mina* (Madrid: Rivadeneyra, 1851).

17   Eugenia Roldán Vera, *The British Book Trade and Spanish American Independence: Education and Knowledge Transmission in Transcontinental Perspective* (Aldershot: Ashgate, 2003).

18   *Letters from Spain, by Leucadio Doblado* (London: Colburn, 1822), pp. v–vi. The letters had already appeared in a different form in the *New Monthly Magazine*. They were soon translated into German, *Briefe aus Spanien* (Hamburg: Campe, 1824); Martin Murphy, *Blanco White: Self-banished Spaniard* (New Haven: Yale University Press, 1989); Fernando Durán López, *José María Blanco White, o la conciencia errante* (Seville: Fundación José M. Lara, 2005).

19   See, for instance, *Ocios de Españoles Emigrados*, vol. I, 1824, 'Extracto de dos cartas de España . . .', dated 28 February 1824, pp. 175–9.

20   *Ocios* . . . p. 181 . . .; *Vida literaria de don Joaquín Lorenzo Villanueva . . .*, Vol. II (London: Macintosh, 1825), pp. 384–5.

21   *Resumen histórico de la Revolución de los Estados Unidos Mejicanos; sacado del 'Cuadro Histórico' que en forma de cartas escribió el Lic. D. Carlos María Bustamante, i ordenado en cuatro libros, por D. Pablo de Mendíbil* (London: Ackermann, 1828), p. x.

22   Pecchio, *Anecdotes*, p. 39.

23   *Sei mesi in Spagna nel 1821. Lettere di Giuseppe Pecchio a Ledi G.O.* (Madrid: Michele di Burgos, 1821); *Tre mesi in Portogallo nel 1822. Lettere di Giuseppe Pecchio a Ledi G.O.* (Madrid: Michele di Burgos, 1822).

24   *Six mois en Espagne. Lettres de M. Joseph Pecchio à Lady J. O. Traduites de l'italien par Léonard Gallois, et augmentées de notes par M. Corradi, chef du Bureau de la Rédaction des Procès-Verbaux des Cortes* (Paris: Corréard, 1822);

Alberto Gil Novales (ed.), *Diccionario Biográfico de España (1808–1833). De los orígenes del liberalismo a la reacción absolutista* (Madrid: Fundación Mapfre, 2010).

25 *Six mois en Espagne. Lettres de M. Joseph Pecchio à Lady J.O. Traduites de l'italien par Léonard Gallois, et augmentées de notes par M. Corradi, chef du Bureau de la Rédaction des Procès-Verbaux des Cortes, précèdes de l'aperçu des révolutions survenues dans le Gouvernement d'Espagne de 1808 à 1814, par le Comte de Torreno, membre des Cortès; Traduit par M. Dunoyer, rédacteur du Censeur, 1822* (Paris: Corréard, 1822). The first German edition of the Spanish letters appeared in Leipzig in 1822: *Neueste Schilderung von Spanien, in Briefen an Lady J.O. von Mai bis November 1821, nach seiner Flucht aus Italien geschrieben* (Leipzig: Magazin für Industrie und Literatur, 1822).

26 *Anekdoten zur Geschichte der spanischen und portugiesischen Revolution von Grafen Pecchio nach der englischen Ausgabe übersetz* (Dresden: Hilscher 1824). However, the book does not seem to have been published in Spanish or Portuguese.

27 *Cartas a Lord Holland sobre los sucesos políticos de España en la segunda época constitucional* (Madrid: Rivadeneyra, 1852); on Holland see Manuel Moreno Alonso, *La forja del liberalismo en España. Los amigos españoles de Lord Holland, 1793–1840* (Madrid: Congreso de los Diputados, 1997).

28 They were included in *Three Tracts relative to Spanish and Portugueze Affairs; with a continual eye to English Ones;* for details and the text: *The Collected Works of Jeremy Bentham. On the liberty of the Press, and Public Discussion and other Legal and Political Writings for Spain and Portugal*, edited by Catherine Pease-Watkin and Philip Schofield (New York: Oxford University Press, 2012). José Joaquín de Mora translated Bentham's letter as *Consejos que dirige a las Cortes y al pueblo español Jeremías Bentham* (Madrid, 1820). Read in a Madrid political club, it won Bentham an honorary membership for his 'work, addressed . . . to all liberal Spaniards'; Watkin and Schofield (eds), *Collected Works*, p. xxiii.

29 *Letters to Count Toreno on the proposed Penal Code, delivered in by the legislation committee of the Spanish Cortes, April 25th, 1821: written at the count's request by Jeremy Bentham, Esq.* (London: Taylor, 1822). They also appeared in Spanish: *Cartas de Jeremías Bentham al señor Conde de Toreno, sobre el proyecto del código penal presentado á las Cortes* (Madrid: García y Campoy, 1821–1822), 2 vols.

30 Simal, *Emigrados*, p. 344.

31 *The Works of Jeremy Bentham, now first collected under the superintendence of his executor, John Bowring* (Edinburgh: William Tait, 1838); F. Rosen, *Bentham, Byron and Greece. Constitutionalism, Nationalism and Early Liberal Political Thought* (Oxford: Clarendon Press, 1992).

32 *Cartas sobre la educación del bello sexo, por una señora americana* (London: Ackermann, n.d., probably 1824); Roldán Vera, *The British Book Trade*; Iona Macintyre, *Women and Print Culture in Post-Independence Buenos Aires* (Woodbridge: Tamesis, 2010), pp. 113–38.

33 Pecchio, *Anecdotes*, p. 68.

34 Juan Ferrando Badía, *La constitución española de 1812 en los comienzos del 'Risorgimento'* (Rome-Madrid: CSIC, 1959); Vittorio Scotti Douglas, 'La Constitución de Cádiz y las revoluciones italianas en Turín y Nápoles de 1820 y 1821', in Alberto Gil Novales (ed.), *La revolución liberal* (Madrid: Ediciones del Orto, 2001), pp. 257–62; Gonzalo Butrón Prida, *Nuestra Sagrada Causa. El modelo gaditano en la revolución piamontesa de 1821* (Cadiz: Ayuntamiento de Cádiz, 2006); Jens Späth, *Revolution in Europa 1820–23. Verfassung und Verfassungskultur in den Königreichen Spanien, beider Sizilien und Sardinien-Piemont* (Koln: shVerlag, 2012); Gabriel Paquette, *Imperial Portugal in the Age of Atlantic Revolutions: The Luso-Brazilian World, c. 1770–1850* (New York: Cambridge University Press, 2013).

35 N. Cosores, 'England and the Spanish Revolution of 1820–1823', *Trienio* 9 (1987), pp. 39–131; 'El impacto de la Constitución de Cádiz en Europa', special issue of *Historia Constitucional* 13 (2012); Jörg Ludwig, *Deutschland und die spanische Revolution 1820–1823* (Leipzig: Leipziger Universitätsverlag, 2013); Richard Stites, *The Four Horsemen: Riding to Liberty in Post-Napoleonic Europe* (New York: Oxford University Press, 2014).

36 Pecchio, *Anecdotes*, p. 3.

37 Vaudoncourt, *Letters*, pp. 7, 18.

38 Pecchio, *Anecdotes*, p. 18.

39 Simal, *Emigrados*, pp. 151–8.

40 Simal, *Emigrados*, pp. 159–78; Emmanuel Larroche, *L'expédition d'Espagne. 1823. De la guerre selon la Charte* (Rennes: Presses Universitaires de Rennes, 2013).

41 Introduction to Pecchio, *Anecdotes*, pp. xxi–xxii.

42 Vaudoncourt, *Letters*, p. 254.

43 Walter Bruyère-Ostells, *La Grande armée de la liberté* (Paris: Tallandier, 2009).

44 Manuel Morán Ortí, 'La cuestión de los refugiados extranjeros. Política española en el Trienio Liberal', *Hispania* XLIX/173 (1989), pp. 985–1016.

45 Introduction to Pecchio, *Anecdotes of Spanish and Portuguese Revolutions*, p. v.

46 William St Clair, *That Greece Might Still Be Free. The Philhellenes in the War of Independence* (Cambridge: Open Book, 2008); Denys Barau, *La Cause des Grecs. Une histoire du mouvement philhellène (1821–1829)* (Paris: Honoré Champion, 2009).

47 Isabella, *Risorgimento in exile*; Simal, *Emigrados*; Maurizio Isabella, 'Entangled Patriotisms. Italian Liberals and Spanish America in the 1820s', in Mathew Brown and Gabriel Paquette (eds), *Connections after Colonialism: Europe and Latin America in the 1820s* (Tuscaloosa: University of Alabama Press, 2013), pp. 87–107.

48 *Cartas de un americano sobre las ventajas de los gobiernos republicanos federativos* (London: Imprenta Española de M. Calero, 1826), p. 2; Vicente Llorens, *Liberales y románticos. Una emigración española en Inglaterra (1823–1834)* (Valencia: Castalia, 2006 [1954]), pp. 318–19; J.E. Rodríguez O., *The Emergence of Spanish America. Vicente Rocafuerte and Spanish*

Americanism, 1808–1832 (Berkeley: University of California Press, 1975), pp. 180, 185.

49 Pecchio, *Anecdotes*, p. 34.

50 Blaquiere, Introduction to Pecchio, *Anecdotes*, p. x.

51 Isabella, *Risorgimento in exile*, p. 37.

52 Pecchio, *Anecdotes*, pp. 21, 86, 52.

53 Vaudoncourt, *Letters on the internal political state of Spain*, p. 22.

54 *The Greek Revolution. Its Origin and Progress* (London: Whittaker, 1824).

55 Blaquiere, Introduction to Pecchio, *Anecdotes*, pp. xx, xxi; he was probably referring to Britain.

56 Vaudoncourt, *Letters*, pp. 8–9.

57 Pecchio, *Anecdotes*, p. 22.

58 Quin, *A Visit to Spain*, p. 359.

59 Introduction to Pecchio, *Anecdotes*, pp. xviii, xix.

60 Pecchio trusted in 1821 that 'should the Holy Alliance invade Spain, its invasion will have precisely the same results as that of Napoleon', *Anecdotes*, p. 8.

CHAPTER TWO

An Itinerant Liberal:

Almeida Garrett's Exilic Itineraries and Political Ideas in the Age of Southern European Revolutions (1820–34)

Gabriel Paquette[1]

João Baptista da Silva Leitão de Almeida Garrett (1799–1854) was a Portuguese poet, man of letters, political writer and politician. In this latter capacity, in the mid-1830s and 1840s, he served as Portugal's emissary to Belgium before he was elected to the lower chamber of parliament (*Camara dos Deputados*) for several constituencies – Braga, Lisbon, Angra (Azores) and Beira, successively – in 1837, 1839, 1840, 1841, and then again between 1846 and 1852. At the end of his life, he was a viscount (and *Par do Reino*, a member of the upper legislative chamber), and also briefly served as minister of foreign affairs and as a member of the governmental council responsible for colonial (ultramarine) affairs during the initial stages of the decade-long reform of the Portuguese government, known as the *Regeneração*, of the 1850s.

Almeida Garrett had just finished his training in law at the University of Coimbra when the Portuguese Revolution of 1820 broke out, part of the sequence of European revolutions that reverberated throughout the Mediterranean. As in Spain, there was an imperial dimension to the revolutionary upheaval in Portugal. Economic stagnation was complemented by the refusal of the royal family to return the seat of the monarchy to Portugal at the conclusion of the French Revolutionary Wars. Instead the Braganzas opted to remain in Brazil, where they had sought refuge when French armies swept across the Iberian peninsula and occupied Portugal in late 1807. Their intention to remain on the western shore of the Atlantic was signalled when Brazil was raised to the status of a kingdom, co-equal with Portugal, in 1815. Adding insult to injury, Portugal was governed by a British army of occupation, under the command of William Carr Beresford, in consultation with a small committee of unpopular, impotent, crown-appointed Portuguese administrators. Discontent bubbled beneath the surface until it exploded in the form of a barracks revolt in Porto, rapidly spreading to the rest of the country. The leaders of the revolt proclaimed the 1812 Spanish Constitution in effect until the Portuguese king, Dom João, returned and a constitutional assembly could be convened to frame a new constitution. That Spanish constitution, together with its attendant decrees, outstripped most contemporary charters in several respects, heralding the abolition of the Inquisition, Indian tribute (in America), forced labour and seigneurial jurisdiction. In lieu of overlapping jurisdictions, it declared a universal state, with equality before the law. The 1812 Spanish Constitution had been restored in neighbouring Spain, and it remained in effect throughout the period of constitutional rule (1820–3), known as the *Trienio Liberal* in Spanish. The Portuguese Revolution of 1820 was thus a hybrid of several species of revolt: a transatlantic revolution that had inverted the statuses of colony and metropole; a loosely pan-Mediterranean revolution united by certain liberal political precepts and constitutional formations; and a national revolt against an occupying, extractive foreign military force.

The Mediterranean and the Atlantic dimensions were quite pronounced. Portuguese liberals were keenly aware of contemporaneous Spanish and Neapolitan events, as those revolts radiated outward and became a rallying cry for other European peoples struggling against analogous instantiations of external occupation or revanchist restored neo-absolutist regimes. Portugal's 1820 revolution thus formed part of the wave of Mediterranean revolutions. It was connected to the Atlantic revolutions as well and, like Spain, formed a bridge linking the Mediterranean constitutionalist upheavals with the escalating conflict over the future relationhip between Europe and America. The long-absent king, Dom João, returned to Portugal and, in 1822, a new constitution was proclaimed, which declared Portugal a constitutional monarchy and bore a striking resemblance to the 1812 Spanish constitution. These achievements aside, the radical liberals who forged this new political order, known as *Vintistas* ('1820-ers'), soon alienated the Brazilians, who denounced their revolutionary activity as part of a broader effort to 'recolonize' Brazil. The *Vintistas* demanded that the seat of government revert to Lisbon, and the abolition of the myriad institutions created in Brazil when the monarchy relocated there – courts, administrative offices, and so forth. Brazil eventually declared its independence from

Portugal in 1822, unifying behind crown-prince Dom Pedro. Portugal's efforts to return Brazil to the imperial fold by military means failed miserably and the short-lived constitutionalist regime was overthrown in 1823, the same year that the *Trienio Liberal* in Spain collapsed.[2] Portugal formally recognized Brazil's independence in 1825.

In the nineteenth century, Almeida Garrett was best known for his varied and prolific literary production. He is often considered as the person who introduced Romanticism into Portugal (though he was critical of Romanticism and rejected the appellation of both Classicism and Romanticism to his own work consistently throughout his career). Historical plays, poems, and fictional travel accounts secured his reputation and did much to shape the Portuguese language and Lusitanian literary taste in the nineteenth century. But Almeida Garrett did not confine himself to literary pursuits. Reflecting back on his youth, in the 1820s, he exclaimed that 'due to the times in which we lived, everything was jumbled together, to the extent that the history of literature and poetry is mixed together with political events and matters'.[3] Between 1820 and 1834, Almeida Garrett founded, edited and published multiple political newspapers and played an active role in the political life of Portugal, both from within Portuguese territory and in exile. During the Portuguese Revolution of 1820–3, then during exile in Britain and France following the restoration of neo-absolutism in 1823, and finally throughout the Portuguese Civil War (ended 1833–4), Almeida Garrett was a steadfast advocate of the constitutionalist cause.[4] While best known for his early celebrations, which he later repudiated, of *Vintismo* (that is, early, radical 1820s Portuguese liberalism) and for his tract *Portugal na Balança da Europa* (*Portugal in the Balance of Europe*) (1830), Almeida Garrett's most long-lasting political contribution was perhaps the assistance he lent to the framing and redaction of several new legal codes for Portugal, codes generally associated with arch-reformer José Xavier Mouzinho da Silveira, written when the renegade government loyal to Dona Maria II captured the Azorean island of Terceira and were preparing to invade mainland Portugal, then ruled by the usurping, absolutist King Miguel. The legal codes would be applied to Portugal, with disruptive effects, following the final victory of the constitutionalist cause in 1834.

This chapter traces Almeida Garrett's intellectual trajectory from the Portuguese Revolution of 1820 until the aftermath of the Portuguese Civil War. These years were marked for Almeida Garrett by several sustained periods of exile that prompted his exposure to, and engagement with, different national-linguistic-cultural-political traditions. Between 1823 and 1834, Almeida Garrett spent a mere four years in Portugal itself and two of these (1832 until 1834) were spent in active service in the Civil War, first in the Azores and then in Oporto (and its environs).

These years afforded him an opportunity to reflect on the failure of the revolution he had supported, an experience he shared with countless other exiles from elsewhere in Southern Europe in the same years. In London and

Paris, Almeida Garrett encountered other Southern European exiles and these interactions surely influenced his understanding of Portugal's place in Europe and the impossibility of 'liberalism in one country'.[5] While he did not use the concept of the 'Mediterranean' explicitly, he did use the concept of the 'South' and 'Southern Europe', by which means he connected Portugal's situation to that of those countries bordering the Mediterranean, grouped them together, and viewed them under the same analytical lens. Paradoxically, while those experiences deepened his commitment to international cooperation in the political sphere, his periods of exile also coincided with a turn away from cosmopolitanism and toward autarky in the cultural sphere.

In particular, the chapter will focus on several important texts which reflect Almeida Garrett's emergent, and increasingly divergent, political and cultural sensibilities. In the political sphere, it focuses attention on his extended tract *Portugal na Balança da Europa* (1830), in which he broached and described a 'system of Southern liberty', not simply Portuguese liberty, for the first time. Some attention is given to his role in the major reform legislation of the early 1830s. In the cultural sphere, this essay addresses Almeida Garrett's turn away from cosmopolitanism and promotion of what might be described as cultural nationalism. In general terms, then, this chapter seeks to demonstrate that Almeida Garrett came to understand Portuguese liberalism's prospects in pan-European terms (and how he distinguished between a Southern liberalism and a Northern variant) while he simultaneously came to reject cultural hybridity and common values and instead urged a celebration of 'traditional', unadulterated and unalloyed Portuguese culture and language, disconnected from other traditions, both from the North and from the South.

Almeida Garrett played a largely peripheral role in these political events of the early 1820s, serving as a mid-ranking official in the revolutionary government's department responsible for public education, but he emerged as one of the chief publicists of the *Vintistas*. His best-known work of this period, *O Dia Vinte e Quatro de Agosto* (*The Twenty-Fourth of August*),[6] published in 1821, was a paean to the recovery of long-lost political rights and a denunciation of absolutism in all of its forms. This tract was a celebration of political equality and freedom, which are inextricable and mutually-sustaining ('men are equal because they are free; and they are free because they are equal') in Almeida Garrett's thought. But it was also a tract that displayed a post-French revolutionary sensibility, for it disparaged the idea that abstract principles alone were a sufficient basis for the establishment of a political system. He denounced previous experiments of this sort as having produced 'the most horrible anarchy'. Constitutional monarchy, or mixed government, he contended, offered the best hope of conjugating, or at least harmonizing, liberty and order, for it effectively modernized long-standing institutions and traditions of governance. But the monarch in such a system, Almeida Garrett argued, must recognize that he was merely the 'executor of the nation's will': any other right he sought to arrogate to himself was purely a 'fantasy'. As such, any monarch who 'infringed, forgot, abused or preferred any other system' of government was a tyrant, and thus illegitimate.[7] These political principles would remain fairly constant in Almeida Garrett's thought over the next fifteen years, though he would come to repudiate some of the radical flavour of his denunciation of tyranny and arbitrary government of the early 1820s. Like many of his fellow travellers of the early 1820s, he gravitated increasingly toward constitutions modelled on the French *Charte* in the late 1820s.

The overthrow of the constitutional regime in Portugal in 1823 forced Almeida Garrett into exile. He first travelled to Birmingham, England, in November 1823, where he jotted some notes on liberal constitutionalism's future in Portugal, which reflect his growing disillusionment with its prospects:

> Can the present constitution of Portugal and Spain ever survive in the future? I think not. Just as it would be absurd for there to exist an absolutist government in one of Europe's enlightened nations, it would be equally so to establish a lasting democratic government, or [hybrid] democratic-monarchical government, in the circumstances in which the population [of Spain and Portugal] is found.[8]

Such despondency perhaps led Almeida Garrett away from explicitly political pursuits momentarily and towards literature. After some time in London, he relocated to France, and lived in Paris and Le Havre, where he wrote and published several influential works of epic poetry, including *Camões* (1825) and *Dona Branca* (1826), now considered classics of Portuguese literature. With the death of Dom João and the promulgation of Dom Pedro's *Carta Constitucional* in 1826, which appeared to signal a political thaw, Almeida Garrett and many other exiles returned to Portugal.[9] Dom Pedro, it must be recalled, was the emperor of independent Brazil yet had remained heir to the Portuguese throne. When his father Dom João died in 1826, he succeeded to the throne as Dom Pedro IV, but only long enough to promulgate the *Carta Constitucional* and abdicate in favour of Dona Maria II, his daughter. He never set foot in Portugal in 1826, as the Brazilian Assembly forbade his departure from Brazil. Taking advantage of the removal of the strict censorship ushered in by the *Carta*, Almeida Garrett immersed himself once more in political journalism, publishing several leading newspapers, including *O Cronista*. Almeida Garrett was forced to flee Portugal for a second time in 1828, again for France and Britain, when Dom Miguel's coup d'état prematurely ended the new constitutionalist experiment. While he turned increasingly to literary pursuits, he continued to engage in political journalism while in exile, helping to publish a major liberal mouthpiece, *O Chaveco Liberal*, as well as the influential tract *Portugal na Balança da Europa* in 1830, which diagnosed the reasons for liberalism's fickle fortunes in Portugal and sought to situate them against the panorama of European politics.

Before turning to his *Portugal na Balança da Europa*, Almeida Garrett's experience as an exile deserves mention. He actually said very little about his period of exile in England and France, and still less about the impact of that interval of his life on his politics and literature. Certainly, the range of his reading enlarged,[10] but, in general, it may be affirmed that Almeida Garrett was much less effusive than his fellow exiles, of whom there were several thousand in the 1828–32 period.[11] One of them, Antonio Bernardino Pereira do Lago, published a book of his impressions. Paris was for him 'the asylum of the belles-arts, the temple of science, the home of good taste, the fount of pleasure and the centre of civilization'. He lauded England for its 'sciences, philanthropy, charity, arts, machines, manufacturing, roads, comforts, security, greatness and liberty'.[12]

It is impossible to know, from his published writings, whether Almeida Garrett shared such a fulsome appreciation of Paris and London. He said little, too, in his public utterances, concerning the hardship and perpetual penury about which other exiles complained incessantly. His unpublished work suggests that he was both puzzled by and enamoured of England. In an unpublished article from the 1830s, for example, he mused that 'in European theatre, the English characters are [always] eminently comic ones, extremely popular and guaranteed to draw a laugh, from the orchestra seats to the boxes, from all classes of society, without exception'. He went on to extol the qualities evoked by the mention of the word 'Englishman': 'brave and loyal, entrepreneurial, frank and generous, well-educated, noble . . . and comical!'.[13] Almeida Garrett was more loquacious about the suffering he endured in his private correspondence than in his published writing. As he explained in a letter to the acting minister for foreign affairs in 1834, protesting his assignment to the Portuguese legation in Belgium, Almeida Garrett lamented that he had spent 'twelve years in exile for the cause of liberty', enduring incarceration, confiscation of property and declining health along the way.[14]

Whether in spite of these hardships or because of them, Almeida Garrett put his pen at the service of the constitutionalist cause in exile. His awareness of Portugal's utter dependence on the vagaries of Great Power politics – whether Anglo-French rivalry, Austrian diplomacy or the fate of constitutionalist government in neighbouring Spain – informed his *Portugal na Balança da Europa*.[15] This long pamphlet was published as the fate of the constitutionalist cause in Portugal hung in the balance. Better put, it was published when the moribund Portuguese constitutionalist cause, increasingly divided against itself and seemingly soundly defeated by the pretender Dom Miguel, received an unexpected (and unearned) reprieve as a result of the French July Revolution. The pamphlet was published, in London, just after the July Days in Paris.

Yet, as Almeida Garrett indicated in the preface to the pamphlet, its composition had been begun in 1825 and most of an earlier version of the first section was published in several instalments in a variety of *emigrado* (exile) newspapers and journals. The mid-1820s were a fertile moment for international solidarity. Italian exiles had flocked to Spain and Portugal in the early 1820s, after their revolutions had been crushed, and Southern Europeans retained a sense of their common plight during exile after the failure of the Iberian revolutions in 1823. Various schemes percolated, including for an Iberian union, broached in 1824 and 1825 by the London-based exile periodicals O *Portuguez* and *El Español Constitucional*.[16] By the early 1830s, a polarized vision of international politics united some of the Southern European exiles, who planned for the imminent 'war of kings against nations, of liberty against slavery'.[17] In other words, while much of the success of Almeida Garrett's *Portugal na Balança* may be explained by its author's beautiful prose and the impeccable timing of its publication, many of its central ideas had been available to, and were percolating in, exiled Portuguese liberal circles for some time, predating the July Revolution, which provided an impetus for its publication but not its drafting.

In *Portugal na Balança da Europa*, Almeida Garrett argued that liberty, and the exercise of that liberty, form part of the natural, original condition of humankind. This natural condition had been degraded as a result of, chiefly, monarchical despotism (exacerbated in the Iberian case by pernicious customs engendered by overseas empire-building), but also of what he denigrated as 'oligarchy'. A mark of civilization is the capacity to recover lost liberty (through the removal of despotism) in a form consistent with public order and international peace. These principles guide the first part of the work, which is essentially a philosophy of history, an account of Europe's preceding fifty years in which this dynamic – of despotism's encroachment on liberty and the recovery of that liberty – serves as the main narrative thread.

For Almeida Garrett, and many other liberals of the late 1820s, the American Revolution of the 1770s represented the first stage in the recovery of liberty. The French Revolution might have brought about an equivalent process in Europe, but it was subverted, chiefly by Napoleon's machinations. However, Bonapartist rule awakened long-dormant clamourings for lost liberties among several peoples, chiefly in Southern Europe, liberties he claimed had been enjoyed, albeit in a form largely useless (or inapplicable) to the contemporary nineteenth-century moment, in their medieval and early modern pasts. But such past experience, however distant, was an important inspiration for contemporary politics. The 1812 Spanish Constitution, the Constitution of Cadiz, adopted in various forms and slight differences throughout Southern Europe in 1820–1, was praised by Almeida Garrett as an essential step in the recovery of liberty. He referred to it as the foundation of a 'sistema da liberdade meridional' (or 'system of Southern liberty').[18]

The geographical adjective, of course, is in certain ways unsurprising. The purported distinction (and tension) between Southern vs Northern was standard fare in European Romanticism due to Madame de Staël, though the contrast was more often applied to literature and music, not political culture or varieties of political liberty.[19] In Almeida Garrett's hands, such *liberdade meridional* became associated with a particularly self-consciously 'moderate' form of revolution, a 'serene', 'magnetic force', standing in stark contrast to the 'destructive' and 'abrasive' 'detonation' of late eighteenth-century revolutions, particularly the French Revolution.[20] For Almeida Garrett, nations subscribing to these principles formed a natural bloc aligned against the congress system. Only as a bloc could political liberty survive in each of the individual states.[21] The chief example he held up was the *Trienio Liberal* (to invoke the Spanish term for the 1820–3 revolutionary period), when governments espousing such principles throughout the Mediterranean might have provided mutual succor before they were overrun by endogenous and exogenous forces of reaction. This misfortune and lost opportunity, Almeida Garrett opined, was attributable less to any intrinsic defect in this system of 'Southern liberty' (though he later enumerated what its shortcomings were) than what he considers the misconduct of the men who guided the respective revolutions, the 'new revolutionary aristocracy', who left the '*povo* [people] neither more happy nor more free' than they had been prior to the 1820 revolutionary conflagration. The all-too-human errors and failures of the leadership, he argued, paved the way, in Portugal, for Dom Miguel's 1828 usurpation, the overthrow of the 1826 *Carta Constitucional*, and the jettisoning of the figure Almeida Garrett maintained was the legitimate monarch, Queen Dona Maria II, daughter of Brazilian Emperor Pedro I (the framer of that *Carta Constitucional*, who retained the Brazilian crown until his 1831 abdication).[22]

The frailties and foibles of the *Vintistas* and their fellow travellers elsewhere aside, Almeida Garrett asserted, political liberty in a single state could only be preserved through solidarity with, or mutual support for, other states possessing similar political systems. He therefore urged the creation of an alliance in support of the July Revolution then unfolding in France. Only through international cooperation could the counterrevolutionary tide be turned in each country, an idea prefiguring the Quadruple Alliance of the mid-1830s, which ultimately included Spain, Portugal, Britain and France. Almeida Garrett's *Portugal na Balança da Europe*, then, is less of a policy or legal tract than an exhortation and abbreviated philosophical history. Chiefly, it conveys his hopelessness for change in the political system of a single state without the existence of a robust alliance of similarly-oriented polities. He thus casts national political issues in international terms. Composite monarchies, empires and federations were less stable than loosely allied and aligned congeries of independent states working cooperatively to maintain the liberty of their allies. Almeida Garrett thus argued that strength was gained paradoxically through multiplicity and heterogeneity. A diverse political ecosystem was, in his view, the most propitious environment in which to protect the tree of liberty.

But Almeida Garrett's emphasis on international cooperation should not be overstated. There were two types of liberty of concern to Almeida Garrett. They jostle for primacy and his advocacy of both of them is not entirely consistent, for these two conceptions are in tension with each other. The first has been mentioned already: domestic liberty, the establishment of a constitutional system in a state and the concomitant destruction of despotism, such as Dom Miguel's tyrannical regime. The second type of liberty was that exercised by an individual state in the international system: national independence, or freedom from the rule of others. Preservation of this condition, which might be referred to as 'sovereignty', but for which Almeida Garrett employed the words '*liberdade*' and '*ser livre*', vis-à-vis other states, was of paramount importance to him. In particular, the prospect of Portugal becoming a province of Spain in a reprise of the 1580–1640 period alarmed him. Even if Portugal were absorbed into a Spain governed by liberal institutions, the enjoyment of free institutions without national independence would be catastrophic. Opting for political liberty on the model of the 1812 Spanish Constitution in domestic politics without national independence was a bad bet for Portugal, Almeida Garrett reasoned. Better, then, to inhabit a stable, autonomous constitutional monarchy under a more conservative constitution than to become a province of a larger polity in which an ample liberty were gained at the cost of national sovereignty.[23]

Almeida Garrett was thus preoccupied with the potential incompatibility of the two types of liberty outlined in the preceding paragraphs. It is clear that national sovereignty was prioritized over domestic political liberty (i.e. constitutional government) should the two conflict. But national sovereignty itself could only be maintained if Portugal found a new niche in the international system, and the best such system for the maintenance of each nation's sovereignty was one in which constitutionalist principles predominated: perhaps a league of small, independent states with constitutionalist regimes. Almeida Garrett wrote his tract in the immediate aftermath of Brazil's independence from Portugal, and a post-imperial bafflement infuses his meditations. As he stated unequivocally, in the old pre-1808 political order, the relative stability of which he described as a 'balance', Portugal served as a 'counterweight' in Western Europe, indispensable for the maintenance of an equilibrium among France, Britain and Spain. Such a position had guaranteed Portugal's national independence and prevented its absorption into Spain or its permanent subjugation as a British satellite. The pre-1808 equilibrium had been obliterated by the Napoleonic occupation of the Iberian peninsula and the relocation of the Braganza dynasts to Brazil. Further turmoil resulted from Brazil's independence, which deprived Portugal of its captive markets, of course, but also its leverage with the great powers, which had derived advantages from access to Portuguese America and had proven inclined to reciprocate by protecting Portugal against the machinations of other states, particularly Spain. In the new state of affairs, shorn of Brazil, Almeida Garrett argued,

Portugal's sovereignty was imperilled and its internal stability would remain jeopardized until it occupied a new, stable position in a revamped international order.

But what new geopolitical position would be possible? Brazil's mineral wealth had vanished forever and further colonial ventures seemed improbable around 1830. Almeida Garrett's answer to Portugal's external relations conundrum therefore entailed an inward turn toward domestic politics, economy and political culture. The consolidation of free institutions within Portugal itself was the key to the maintenance of its national sovereignty and national sovereignty was indispensable to the preservation of those free institutions. Thus, the mutually reinforcing interplay of domestic and international politics was the central axis around which Almeida Garrett's argument in *Portugal na Balança da Europa* turned. He was not so naïve as to assert that the adoption of a certain constitutional system would guarantee, as if by magic, national independence. That illusion had been shattered twice, in 1823 and 1826. Rather, whatever political institutions were enshrined must be embraced and entrenched by all political factions, which must prioritize national sovereignty above all other considerations. Above all, these institutions must promote stability and shield Portugal from further chaos, protecting it from the shocks it might receive from the reverberation of disruptions elsewhere in the international system. For Almeida Garrett, Britain was the crucial example to emulate in this regard. He claimed that it had remained unscathed by the violence and chaos unleashed by the French Revolution because '*já era liberal*' (it was already liberal). As he elaborated,

> in continental Europe, thousands of men killed one another out of love for a constitution; no one was killed in Britain because it already possessed a constitution. Britain was content with its strong, free and monarchical institutions, and cared nothing for dangerous innovations, and saw no need to try to improve upon what it already possessed; in all other countries, however, which remained despotic, [people there] did not hesitate to risk everything.[24]

To be sure, Almeida Garrett did not abandon his earlier commitment to constitutional government. But he now privileged domestic stability as a precondition of liberty, within the context of national independence. He embraced monarchy tempered with aristocratic institutions and the incorporation of the 'democratic element' of the 'growing middle class' as the combination most likely to produce a felicitous result.[25]

Portugal na Balança da Europa was undoubtedly the most influential tract written by a Portuguese political exile in the 1820s and 1830s. Still, Portugal's *emigrados* remained riven by factions. Finally, in 1829, a small group was able to overthrow the local government of the island of Terceira, in the Azores. With this beachhead in Portuguese territory, albeit thrust hundreds of miles from continental Europe in the North Atlantic, erstwhile faction-riven exiles gathered and put themselves under the command of a regency in favour of Dona Maria II and the restoration of the *Carta Constitucional*. In February 1832, Almeida Garrett left France for Terceira, where the regency awaited sufficient international support (or at least benign neglect) to launch an invasion of Dom Miguel's Portugal. Almeida Garrett joined a military unit, then coalescing, as a soldier. Given his enormous reputation as a writer, he was spared the normal miseries endured by enlisted men, and served as the secretary to Mouzinho da Silveira, an arch-reformer who was tasked by the regency with responsibility for devising new legal and administrative codes for Portugal and directing the reforms which would, presumably, transform that country after the constitutionalist cause triumphed. The Terceira regency's reforms were wide-ranging, ambitious and radical. They eventually proved to be a Lusitanian 'Great Leap Forward'.

Almeida Garrett was charged with the responsibility of writing, together with Mouzinho da Silveira, a preliminary report on the new Administrative Code, a landmark piece of legislation.[26] Deeply influenced by Charles-Jean Baptiste Bonnin's early nineteenth-century *Abrégé des Principes d'Administration*,[27] Mouzinho da Silveira's subsequent fiscal reforms essentially dismantled the *ancien régime*'s property system, including the abolition of the *forais* (town charters), *morgadios* (entail), tithes and personal duties, all in an effort to undermine ecclesiastical and seigneurial land-holding and the related systems of privileges, exceptions, and exemptions.[28] Given their intellectual inspiration, it is not surprising that Mouzinho's reforms bore a strong resemblance to Napoleonic reforms. The Terceira reforms would become among the most controversial of all Portuguese legislation of the nineteenth century. Almeida Garrett, who eventually became a harsh critic of the legislative programme he had helped to design, nevertheless recognized it as 'a great moment, the juncture where the Old Portugal ended and the New began'.[29]

In the preliminary report, or *relatório*, Almeida Garrett commenced with the observation that the great conundrum for Europe c. 1835, convulsed by revolution and war, was to secure liberty without forfeiting the rule of law and general security, a theme he had sounded in his early *Vintista* writings as well as in *Portugal na Balança da Europa*. It was with this general precept that he addressed Portugal's situation. He denounced the 'ancient constitution' of Portugal, with its jumble of authorities and overlapping jurisdictions, as 'absurd' and 'chaotic', tending toward 'confusion' and 'disorder'.[30] Only by transforming the legal basis of Portuguese society, economy and politics would it be possible to rescue Portugal from its current predicament. By replacing the accretions of the ages with a rational code of new laws, the authors of the preliminary report contended, Portugal's miseries would be alleviated and the long-festering sources of its plight demolished. After completing this report, Almeida Garrett participated in the successful invasion of northern Portugal, landing as a common soldier on the beaches of Mindelo in July 1832. He reached the city of Porto, but left before the siege of that city by absolutist forces began, as he was assigned as secretary to several legations for the victorious constitutionalist regency to Britain and France until the conclusion of the civil war in 1834, when he was dispatched as an emissary to Belgium.

If Almeida Garrett had displayed a notable cosmopolitanism throughout the 1820s and 1830s, embracing constitutional models from abroad, imbibing French administrative science and stressing international cooperation as indispensable to Portugal's very survival as a sovereign state, he rejected syncretism and cross-cultural pollination in important respects. His literary theories, especially as they evolved after the Portuguese Civil War, suggest movement in the opposite direction, and the limitation of the cosmopolitanism characteristic of the liberal international. For example, in 1827, he lamented the glut of translations of French literature into Portuguese, which had the effect of 'making [French] the model and exemplar of everything; depreciating that of the Portuguese, whose own style, spirit, and genius (everything that is national) has disappeared'. He argued that it was necessary to study other languages, but 'without following any school, learning from all of them, without deluding or confusing them with our own, national language'.[31] Almeida Garrett's previous rejection of Portugal's political past was counterbalanced in the cultural sphere by an effort to revive fossilized literary forms, believing that they could enrich modern Portuguese letters. Medieval and early modern political forms should be entombed, he reckoned, but long-extinct literary forms from those epochs should be resurrected.

In the 1828 preface to the romance *Adosinda*, Almeida Garrett described his ambition to revive 'our primitive and eminently national poetry'. In that poetry, he contended, one encountered 'a different style, a different mode of seeing, perceiving, and representing, [one which is] freer, more eccentric, more fantastical, more irregular and, for this reason, more natural in many respects'.[32] While it might be possible to argue that Almeida Garrett's more nationalistic cultural views clashed irreconcilably with his ostensibly cosmopolitan political views, it is more probable that they were complementary as opposed to mutually exclusive views: political cooperation might erode the boundaries of the nation, which could be buttressed by the countervailing force of cultural separateness and celebration of difference.

After the conclusion of the Portuguese Civil War in 1834 and amidst an active political career, Almeida Garrett pursued the cultural autarky theme further in the 'Introduction' to his second volume of the *Romanceiro* (published in 1845–6), a collection (and reworking in many cases) of popular songs, narratives in verse (*xácaras*), romances and ballads (*solaús*), primarily drawn from the late medieval and early modern periods. He began his 'Introduction' with the stark declaration of intent to 'launch a literary revolution in the country'.[33] Of what would this 'revolution' consist? The literary revolt he envisaged would free Portugal from the 'oppressive, anti-national dominion' and encourage Portugal's 'talented youth' to desist from 'imitating foreigners' and, instead, to 'study our primitive poetical sources, both *romances* in verse and *legendas* in prose, fables, and old beliefs, customs and old superstitions'. It was here, Almeida Garrett argued, that one would encounter 'the true Portuguese spirit', which he defined unambiguously as 'the people and its traditions, its virtues and vices, its beliefs and its erroneous judgments'.[34] Thus Almeida Garrett had come to embrace an inwardly-directed cultural autarky, or even cultural nationalism, jostling uneasily with his professed political ideas and even his earlier literary proclivities (for example, his engagement with Shakespeare left a lasting impression on his work).

Exile, resulting from the fickle fortunes of Portugal's intermittent liberal revolution, shaped the trajectory of Almeida Garrett's ideas concerning both politics and culture. The exact ways it shaped his views in precise instances may be difficult to discern, but conceived in the aggregate it is clear that the exposure of exile facilitated and shaped his literary preferences, political thought and grasp of the dynamics of international relations. The 'system of Southern Liberty' he espoused in the late 1820s and early 1830s is scarcely imaginable without his participation in the exilic networks of London and Paris. It was this 'Southern Liberty' that connected Portugal and its ultramarine territories to the Mediterranean world that is the focus of this volume. Almeida Garrett's later retreat, in the late 1830s and early 1840s, to cultural autarky and a more parochial cultural nationalism may represent a belated recoiling from the cosmopolitanism engendered by exile. In both cases, his exilic itineraries of the 1820s loom large in any explanation of his intellectual development.

Notes

1   An earlier, shorter version of this essay was given as a paper at the Workshop 'Re-imagining Political Communities in the Mediterranean: Peoples, Nations and Empires in the Age of Democratic Revolutions', held at Columbia University in September 2013.

2   On these events and processes, see Gabriel Paquette, *Imperial Portugal in the Age of Atlantic Revolutions: The Luso-Brazilian World, c. 1770–1850* (Cambridge: Cambridge University Press, 2013), Ch. 2.

3   Almeida Garrett, 'Prefácio' to the second edition of *Romanceiro I* (dated 12 August 1843), in *Obras Completas: Romanceiro* (Lisbon, 1983), I, pp. 65–6.

4   This constitutionalist cause is sometimes conflated with 'liberalism' but, at least in the Portuguese case, is better understood as intersecting and infusing it.

5   On the 'Liberal International' between 1815 and 1848, see Maurizio Isabella, *Risorgimento in Exile: Italian Émigrés and the Liberal International in the Post-Napoleonic Era* (Oxford: Oxford University Press, 2009); on the Spanish

exile communities, see Juan Luís Simal, *Emigrados: España y el Exilio Internacional (1814–1834)* (Madrid: Centro de Estudios Políticos y Constitucionales, 2012)

6   The day on which the Portuguese Revolution commenced in 1820.

7   Almeida Garrett, 'O Dia Vinte e Quatro de Agosto' (1821), in *Obras Completas de Almeida Garrett. Obra Política, 1820–23. Escritos do Vintismo* (Lisbon: Estampa, 1985), pp. 193–201 *passim*.

8   Almeida Garrett, 'Apontamentos "Constituição"' (24 November 1823), in ibid., p. 297. He contemplated seeking refuge in Brazil but finally decided against that option in January 1824, noting in his diary 'he would go to Brazil if he did not fear that [Brazilians] lacked the judgment to maintain' their newly-won political liberty. See Almeida Garrett, 'Extractos Políticos do Diário do Primeiro Exílio', in ibid., p. 306.

9   Gabriel Paquette, 'The Brazilian Origins of the 1826 Portuguese Constitution', *European History Quarterly* 41/3 (2011), pp. 444–71.

10 Lia Noemia Rodrigues Correia Raitt, *Garrett and the English Muse* (London: Tamesis, 1983).

11 The precise number of Portuguese exiles has been notoriously difficult to pin down. The largest cohort of exiles fleeing Portugal after Dom Miguel's coup first landed in Plymouth in 1828, numbering 2,383. Paris police records suggest that there were slightly more than 1,000 Portuguese resident in Paris in 1830. For the Plymouth figures, see Isabel Nobre Vargues and Luis Reis Torgal, 'Da Revolução à Contra-Revolução: Vintismo, Cartismo, Absolutism. O Exílio Político', in José Mattoso (ed.), *História de Portugal* (Lisbon: Editorial Estampa, 1993), Vol. V, p. 80; for the Paris figure, see Lloyd S. Kramer, *Threshold of a New World: Intellectuals and the Exile Experience in Paris, 1830–1848* (Ithaca: Cornell University Press, 1988), p. 26. The quotidian experience of the Portuguese exiles, as well as the quantitative dimensions of the *emigração* as a whole, still awaits its historian.

12 Antonio Bernardino Pereira do Lago, *Cinco Annos D'Emigração na Inglaterra, na Belgica e na França* (Lisbon: Imprensa Nacional, 1834), Vol. I, p. 244; Vol. II, p. 540.

13 Biblioteca Geral [University of Coimbra], Espólio Literario de Almeida Garrett, doc. 106, fo. 3.

14 Biblioteca Geral [University of Coimbra], Espólio Literario de Almeida Garrett, doc. 128-b, Almeida Garrett to Agostinho José Freire, 8 August, 1834, fo. 1.

15 Almeida Garrett, *Portugal na Balança da Europa* [1830] (Lisbon: Livros Horizontes, 2005).

16 Vicente Llorens, *Liberales y Románticos. Una Emigración Española en Inglaterra (1823–1834)* (Valencia: Editorial Castalia, 1979, third edition), pp. 147–8.

17 Hispanic Society of America [New York], Colección Torrijos, [?] Hernandez (in Brussels) to Ignacio Lopes Pinto (in London), 10 January, 1831.

18 Almeida Garrett, *Portugal*, p. 41.

19 Madame de Staël distinguished between Romanticism as poetry of northern Europe, of Ossian, and Southern Europe synonymous with Homer and classicism more generally, in her 1813 *De L'Allemagne*, a distinction that entered soon after into the mainstream.

20 Almeida Garrett, *Portugal*, p. 40.

21 It is unclear whether other, non-Southern European states, can form part of the coalition/bloc against the congress system, in Almeida Garrett's view. One presumes they might act as patrons or protectors, but Almeida Garrett is vague on the details.

22 Almeida Garrett, *Portugal*, p. 44.

23 Ibid., pp. 120–2.

24 Ibid., p. 97.

25 Ibid., p. 124; the term 'democratic element' refers to the involvement, in some capacity, of a popular sector of society not previously represented under the terms of the unwritten, 'ancient' constitution.

26 The official title is 'Relatório do Código Administrativo de 1832'.

27 José-Augusto França, *O Romantismo em Portugal: Estudo de Factos Socio-Culturais* (Lisbon: Livros Horizonte, 1974), I, pp. 129–30.

28 José Luís Cardoso and Pedro Lains, 'Public Finance in Portugal, 1796–1910', in Cardoso and Lains (eds), *Paying for the Liberal State: The Rise of Public Finance in Nineteenth-century Europe* (Cambridge: Cambridge University Press, 2010), pp. 259–60.

29 Almeida Garrett, quoted in Theophilo Braga, *Garrett e o Romantismo* (Porto: Livraria Chardron, 1903); for Almeida Garrett's subsequent criticism, in 1854, see the 'Relatório e Bases para Reforma Administrativa' (1854), in *Obras de Almeida Garrett* (Porto: Lello & Irmão Editores, 1966), I, pp. 1331–5.

30 'Relatório do Código Administrativo de 1832', in ibid., I, p. 1097

31 Almeida Garrett, *O Cronista* 1/4 (March 1827), pp. 15–17, quoted in Álvaro Manuel Machado, 'Almeida Garrett e o Paradigma Romântico Europeu: Modelos e Modas', in Ofélia Paiva Monteira and Maria Helena Santana (eds), *Almeida Garrett. Um Romântico, um Moderno* (Lisbon, 2003), I, pp. 44–5; in the introduction to the *Lírica de João Mínimo*, he bluntly stated that 'to imitate foreign works and reject those of one's own nation is ignorant and stupid', in *Obras* (1966), I, p. 1497.

32 Preface ['Ao Sr. Duarte Lessa'] (1828) to *Adosinda*, in *Obras* [1966], I, pp. 1748–9, 1751.

33 Almeida Garrett, 'Introducão', *Romanceiro*, II, p. 49 (n.b. originally published, as serial of five articles, in the *Revista Universal Lisbonense* [1845–6]).

34 Ibid., pp. 50, 54–5.

CHAPTER THREE

Learning Lessons from the Iberian Peninsula:

Italian Exiles and the Making of a Risorgimento Without People, 1820–48

Grégoire Bron

In 1820 and 1831 the impact of two Europe-wide international revolutionary movements was felt in the Italian peninsula. The first, inaugurated by a military *pronunciamiento* in Spain, led to the promulgation of the Cadiz Constitution, which soon after spread across Southern Europe. Portugal, like Spain, experienced a constitutional regime between 1820 and 1823; by the same token the absolute monarchies were temporarily overthrown, in Naples in 1820, and in Piedmont in 1821, the year in which the War of Independence broke out in Greece. Ten years later, the July Revolution in Paris brought down Charles X and precipitated a second international revolutionary wave: liberal and national insurrections flared up in Belgium, Poland, Switzerland, Germany and, in the Italian peninsula, in Modena, Bologna and Parma, in February 1831, before ideological civil wars between liberals and reactionaries broke out in Portugal in 1832 and in Spain in 1833.[1]

Led by former Napoleonic officers and civil servants and by the liberal nobility, these Italian uprisings, swiftly suppressed by the Austrian army, have traditionally been interpreted as the final product of an archaic liberalism conceived and disseminated by secret societies, lacking any broader social support and characterized by a constitutionalist and pre-national political thought inherited from the French period (1796–1814) by an entire generation of patriots.[2] Yet, as a new cohort of historians has recently demonstrated, the early decades of the Risorgimento, despite the residual impact of an old-fashioned political culture, were also original and innovatory. To begin with, the political culture of the Italian revolutionaries of the Restoration was the product of the transnational context in which it had evolved.[3] The intertwining of the Italian revolutions with the other European liberal episodes is borne out by the multiple ties between them – ties which were in turn reinforced by the political emigration precipitated by the failure of the insurrections of 1820–1 and 1831. Convinced as they were that the cause of liberty was common to all patriots across the globe, the Italian exiles, like countless liberal militants from a wide range of different countries, mobilized to support foreign struggles and enrolled as military volunteers in ideological wars abroad.[4] Conspiracies with international ramifications were organized; they linked revolutionaries of different origins who sought the victory of the ideals of liberty and nation wherever possible – ideals that were furthermore promoted internationally by active propaganda campaigns through the press and the widespread distribution of other printed material. The international revolutionaries fostered closely knit international networks and prided themselves upon being a 'Holy Alliance of the Peoples', combating the Holy Alliance of the Kings established at the Congress of Vienna. They represented a transnational Republic of Letters and civil society which historiography has dubbed a 'Liberal International'.[5] The Italian liberalism of the Restoration was therefore no anachronism, but rather an integral part of a globalizing process of revolutionary and liberal ideas carried by a political and intellectual debate that crossed national borders. It evolved through the proliferation of contacts with foreign patriots, not least thanks to the efforts of the Italian political exiles.

Furthermore, recent studies of Italian nationalism have shown the importance of these same years in the affirmation of a new cultural definition of the nation through literary representations drawn from such authors as Vittorio Alfieri and Ugo Foscolo.[6] This cultural definition of the nation was typical of the political culture of the generation of patriots associated with the second wave of revolutions of the Restoration, the Italian insurrections of Modena, Bologna and Parma in 1831. Born at the turn of the century, these younger patriots grew up with the heroic memory of the Napoleonic period, and after the failure of the 1831 uprising became followers of *Giovine Italia* (Young Italy), the republican association founded by Giuseppe Mazzini.[7] Their political engagement was more sentimental, emotional and Romantic in tone than that of the liberals involved in the revolutions of the 1820s, who had been born in the previous century.

During the first half of the nineteenth century, the Iberian peninsula was one of the main destinations for Italian liberals choosing the path of exile, after both the 1820 and the 1831 revolutionary waves.[8] In 1820 Spain enjoyed an extraordinary prestige in Italy due to the 1808 national uprising against the Napoleonic armies.[9] The Constitution of Cadiz, which proclaimed the sovereignty of the nation as represented in a unicameral parliament, became the watchword of the Italian revolutionaries, who adopted it as the fundamental law in Naples and Piedmont.[10] Representing a shared political reference and being widely admired by Italian, Spanish, Portuguese and Latin American patriots also, the Constitution of Cadiz was to make Spain, where it was in force until 1823, the destination of choice for the Italian exiles of 1821.[11] In the Iberian peninsula, they fomented international plots, sometimes even in Portugal; they were active in the Spanish political arena and fought alongside the Spanish liberals against the national counterrevolution in 1822 and against the French invasion which restored King Ferdinand VII as an absolute ruler in 1823, the year in which the Portuguese constitutional regime collapsed, even without foreign intervention.[12] The civil wars between liberals and supporters of absolutism, which raged in the 1830s, made the Iberian peninsula once again a natural destination for the Italian exiles of 1831. In order to promote the cause of liberty through action, around 100 Italian exiles belonging to the younger generation of Risorgimento liberalism enrolled in the Portuguese liberal army as volunteers between 1832 and 1834 to fight the Miguelites, who supported the counterrevolutionary rule of Prince Dom Miguel.[13] After their victory in Portugal, they joined the Spanish army and, starting in 1835, fought the Carlists, i.e. the supporters of Don Carlos, the counterrevolutionary pretender to the Spanish throne.[14]

This chapter examines the impact that the revolution in the Iberian peninsula had on the political culture of these two different and successive generations of Italian exiles. An analysis and close observation of Spanish and Portuguese society led them to reformulate the political and intellectual principles informing their revolutionary engagement in Italy. As I will argue, the failure of the constitutional regimes in Spain and Portugal witnessed by the Italian exiles between 1821 and 1823 prompted them to review their constitutional ideas; likewise, the victory of liberalism through civil war in Portugal in 1834, and in Spain in 1840 – with the active participation of the exiles of 1831 – caused them to formulate a new definition of the Italian nation and Risorgimento. In either case, however, the exiles' reaction to the social realities of the Iberian civil wars was one of pessimism regarding the possibility of building the political institutions of modernity on the basis of a broad popular participation. This pessimism affected their political projects for Italy.

The Italian exiles of 1821 in the Iberian peninsula

In the spring of 1821, the suppression of the Italian revolutions by the Austrian army left about 2,000 liberals with no choice but to flee into exile, the majority of them – probably around 1,000 – taking refuge in Spain. More than 75 per cent of them were already adults at the end of the Napoleonic period. They came mainly from the defeated constitutional armies of Naples and Piedmont, but many civilians, for the most part students, professional men and a handful of aristocrats, also emigrated to Spain.[15] Their involvement in Spanish and Portuguese political life reinforced their commitment to international political solidarity, which underpinned and stimulated military volunteering.[16] In addition, they adopted the new revolutionary models in evidence in Spain, such as the military *pronunciamiento* and guerrilla warfare.[17]

On the eve of the insurrections in Italy, the Italian revolutionaries had supported the Constitution of Cadiz, welcoming its defence of the Catholic religion and reckoning that the principles of administrative decentralization and provincial autonomy featuring in it would help establish a far more harmonious relationship between institutions and society than that achieved during the constitutional experiments of the French period.[18]

This admiration for the Constitution of Cadiz led the Italian liberals to move to the country that had drafted and enacted it. Direct experience of revolution in the Iberian peninsula convinced them, however, of the shortcomings of the Cadiz Constitution, which seemed to them to have lost some of its lustre. The Constitution proclaimed the sovereignty of the nation represented in a unicameral parliament elected by universal (albeit indirect) suffrage, and reduced the role of the king to that of the head of the executive branch in a system of government by assembly.[19] However, once in Spain the Italian liberals discovered that the constitutional regime did not function well, not least because of the tensions between parliament, the government and the king.[20] More importantly, Spanish and Portuguese society appeared to the Italian exiles to be horrifyingly backward, and the majority of the population unsuited to the exercise of political rights. The Piedmontese aristocrat Giacinto Provana di Collegno thought the Iberian countries were 'half-African';[21] according to the democrat Carlo Bianco di Saint-Jorioz, who was likewise from Turin, Portuguese and Spanish peasants were 'barbarians' and had 'African manners'.[22] 'In Portugal', the Neapolitan general Guglielmo Pepe observed, 'civilisation was less advanced than in Spain, and in Spain, far less advanced than in Italy'.[23] For the Milanese Count Giuseppe Pecchio, 'the Portuguese people enter[ed] the realm of Liberty as if they were suddenly emerging from darkness: the light dazzle[d] them and they [could not] yet see any object'.[24] In such backward Iberian societies, the Constitution of Cadiz paved the way to counterrevolution: it did not completely neutralize the king, it had too much respect for religion and granted too much power to the clergy; consequently, it allowed the enemies of liberty to exert a strong influence on passive and superstitious populations and to incite them to rise up against the constitutional regime. All the Italian exiles were mindful of this point, and swift to condemn the role of priests in the counterrevolutionary mobilization.[25] As a consequence, they came to the conclusion, after 1823, that the Constitution of Cadiz had contributed to the failure of the Spanish revolution and they started to look for alternative ways to establish a regime of popular sovereignty able to guarantee human rights.[26] They did so with the problem of introducing freedom to the Italian peninsula in mind, and took stock of the Spanish experience in order to rethink the foundations of the Italian Risorgimento.

After 1823, some of the exiles continued to draw inspiration from the Jacobin revolutionary tradition, concerned as they were to ensure the triumph of the sovereignty of the people, in line with Rousseau's definition of the latter. This was the case with Count Bianco di Saint-Jorioz. A revolutionary aristocrat who had distinguished himself during the Piedmontese revolution of 1821, Bianco not only judged that the Spanish constitution gave enemies of freedom too much room for manoeuvre, but also believed that the cause of the people had been betrayed by the revolutionary leaders. After 1823, the count became the advocate of a kind of republicanism inspired by the French Revolution, because he now reckoned that only a republican regime of that kind could guarantee the natural rights and the equality of the citizens that the Spanish constitution had failed to safeguard. In order to establish the regime he aspired to in Italy, Count Bianco developed a terrorist conception of the revolution with a view to unifying the peninsula. A dictatorial government, inspired by the *Comité de Salut Public* of the French Revolution, had to wage guerrilla warfare along the lines of the Spanish anti-Napoleonic uprisings of 1808 and of the 1822 counterrevolutionary insurrection in Catalonia, against which Bianco himself had fought. Although the count admitted that the popular uprising in Spain had been facilitated by 'the power and influence of the ecclesiastical estate on the souls of ignorant peasants' and 'by the use of the confessional [. . .] as the most secret, powerful and effective way of conspiring for the mother country', he was still convinced, under the influence of Rousseau, that, through terror, the people would be the most solid foundation upon which to build future freedom. Spain taught Bianco the technique of the people's revolutionary war.[27] Its goal was to exterminate ruthlessly all the enemies of liberty so that they could not subvert the regime of republican equality to be established after the victory.[28]

Like Bianco, a number of other exiles, while revising their political thought after Spain, neither wholly relinquished their trust in the capacity of the people to rule themselves, nor reneged upon the revolutionary radical tradition. The evolution of General Pepe's political thought is a case in point. After the defeat of the Iberian revolution, Pepe, a former Napoleonic officer and commander-in-chief of the Neapolitan constitutional army, actively promoting international revolutionary plots during his Spanish exile, became disillusioned with the Constitution of Cadiz, which he subsequently judged to be 'complex and inconsistent'. He denounced the attribution of the military authority to the king and recommended the abolition of the monarchy and the aristocracy alike, labelling them 'unnatural, unjust and absurd' institutions. Pepe did not air any new constitutional theory but remained loyal to the democratic and republican revolutionary tradition, adopting a political stance similar to that of his friend General Lafayette.[29] He sought a firmer foundation for a national representation based on a direct, and not on a three-degree, electoral system, and he recommended fighting the Spanish clergy tooth and nail, even going so far as to call for the deportation of a good three-quarters of their number, the more elderly contingent, to America, and for marrying off the last quarter – the only 'true method of interesting a priesthood in the cause of liberty'.[30]

Nevertheless, Pepe's sojourn in the Iberian peninsula between 1820 and 1823 also led him to become more pessimistic about the revolutionary potential of the masses. While he had admired the Spanish people's patriotism displayed in the anti-Napoleonic insurrection of 1808, he also noted that this patriotic war led by the people had a pronounced counterrevolutionary dimension. For it had been led by 'the men of the lowest classes of the people' influenced by 'a wealthy clergy [which] urged them to defend religion and Castilian independence'. 'The princes of the deposed dynasty had a thousand ways of inciting the Spaniards to rise.'[31] The repetition of such uprisings against the constitution during the revolution of 1820–3 led the Neapolitan general to posit a relationship between this sort of popular mobilization and the backwardness of the Iberian peninsula: in 1823, 'the conduct of the lowest class of people, who, against all expectation, seconded the French in re-establishing the Bourbon despotism, show[ed] . . . that the Spaniards were not entirely ripe for freedom'.[32] Because the Spaniards were still none too civilized, they could sustain such a fierce and stubborn war against the French in 1808 and against the liberals in 1822–3.

These reflections on Spain raised a number of comparative questions about the feasibility of such Spanish-inspired guerrilla warfare in Italy. Pepe's conclusions were that such a technique could not be applied in Italy. Here the masses were at the same time more educated and less influenced by the reactionary clergy than in Spain, but nonetheless not ready to support a liberal revolution either. Thanks to Napoleon and his religious policy, the clergy had lost in the Italian peninsula the influence it had in Spain and Portugal. Evidence of this could be found in the fact that nobody had welcomed the Austrian troops in Naples in 1821.[33] Far more civilized than the Iberian peninsula, Italy was not inhabited by the simple and natural men who could engage in guerrilla warfare:

> Would it be perhaps among the Venetians or the Lombards, in Piedmont, in Central Italy or in Tuscany that we could find those Spaniards who would walk forty or fifty miles in one day, barefoot or only with *spardillos*, wearing light trousers and shirts of rough cloth, without property in this world and fed with but a few olives and dark bread?[34]

At the same time, however, they had not been uniformly converted to the principles of liberalism, and were therefore not likely to support a revolutionary effort. In Italy, 'the wealthy classes set the example. The popular classes follow. . . . But perhaps not everyone is going to fight, and perhaps not immediately, especially the peasants', because the influence of the liberals was not as strong as that of the clergy over the Spaniards.[35] Consequently, Italians should not contemplate making their revolution a people's guerrilla war. Since they had to face the Austrian army, they needed to fight it with another regular army. Irregular partisans might well play a part, but Italian military leaders ought not to take their inspiration from the Spanish precedent: 'From the Spaniards, we should only take the example of tenacity.'[36]

Other exiles, however, who were intellectually more sophisticated than Pepe, did not confine themselves to reflections on military strategy but entirely recast their political thought in the light of the Spanish experience, and, in view of the backwardness they had witnessed on the Iberian peninsula were still more inclined to doubt the ability of the people to rule themselves, since the Italians too were backward. So far as these exiles were concerned, the triumph of liberty was to be found less in the existence of universal and rational principles applicable to all societies, than in a history of civilization, whose degree of development determined revolutionary strategies and political institutions. This was the case with Giuseppe Pecchio, among others.

In 1822, the Milanese aristocrat, a former member of the Napoleonic Senate of the Kingdom of Italy, remained critical of the Constitution of Cadiz, while lavishing praise upon the 1822 Portuguese constitution. He saw the Portuguese code, which was closer to the French republican constitutions, as a future model for all Europe.[37] But in Portugal he also discerned a very backward society, one that had not been regenerated simply through the introduction of a constitution: '. . . I traversed the whole of this Kingdom without seeing a single sign of regeneration. The ancient building still stands. It was announced that the constitutional edifice would be erected; to this day, however, only the façade exists: I mean the constitution'.[38] He began to think that the goal of the liberal revolutionary struggle was more to spread civilization than to introduce political rights based on an abstract conception of natural equality, for the benefit of exceedingly passive and backward populations unable to appreciate their meaning.

In England, where he resided from 1823 onwards, Giuseppe Pecchio discovered the advanced civilization that was lacking in the Iberian peninsula. There, even an ordinary worker was a thoroughgoing citizen who participated in public life on election days, even if the right to vote was denied him.[39] Pecchio attributed this feature to the economic wealth procured by industry and trade. Thus, in order to bring civilization to societies like Spain and Portugal, and also Italy, it was necessary to develop these two sources of prosperity according to the principles of Adam Smith's classical political economy, which Pecchio studied thanks to his Whig friends in London, and to the principles of Italian economic thought. Unlike the Scottish theorist, however, Pecchio held that the economy could prosper only within a constitutional framework – which allowed him to justify the revolution anyway.[40] But the introduction of a constitution through revolution was only one of the necessary preconditions for the development of civilization, which, through the advance of trade and industry, would emancipate the people from the sway of superstition and the deleterious influence of the clergy. This being the case, the sovereignty of the people ought not to be expressed, Pecchio argued, through universal suffrage, but through the political participation of the people in the extra-parliamentary public sphere, as in the patriotic societies he observed in Spain, or at the British hustings.[41] This perspective implied deep changes in the significance and nature of the constitution. Pecchio now believed that its goal was primarily to guarantee rights, and, more particularly, those serving 'to safeguard the person and property, which are the two most precious and inalienable rights of every citizen'.[42] The right to vote had to be granted only to capable citizens. Pecchio's liberalism was now based on an admiration for the British bicameral parliamentary system, the expression as he saw it of the 'sovereignty of the people'.[43]

The end of the Iberian revolutionary experience rendered most exiles pessimistic about the capacity of the people to govern themselves. As a result, by the late 1820s, very few Italian revolutionaries continued, as did Bianco di Saint-Jorioz or Filippo Buonarroti, a Tuscan Jacobin exile from the revolutionary period, to favour a Jacobin conception of the people and a unicameral parliamentary system. Like Pecchio, the overwhelming majority of Italian liberals scattered across Europe and beyond rallied to a monarchical and bicameral constitutionalism, an arrangement better suited in their view to the requirements of contemporary civilization. The failure of the Iberian revolution, due in large measure to the strong popular counterrevolution, contributed largely to this evolution which, however, did not lead the Italian liberals to relinquish the principle of the sovereignty of the people.

Italian liberal exiles of 1831 in the Iberian peninsula: searching for a new definition of the nation

After 1820, the exiles believed civilization to be a necessary process that would lead in due course to the establishment of constitutional governments across Europe and would by the same token unify the continent. The promotion of civilization in Portugal through the introduction of constitutional institutions, as Pecchio observed in 1822, would enable this country to join the 'great European family'.[44] The Italian revolutionaries of 1831 inherited this same commitment to supporting the cause of freedom abroad as a means of advancing civilization. To quote one such militant,

Enrico Cialdini, exiled in Paris after the failure of the uprisings of 1831: 'It seems to me that the cause of liberty is universal and that every man is obliged to serve this holy cause with devotion wherever he may be on the globe.'[45] Such beliefs led Cialdini to enrol as a volunteer on the liberal side in the Iberian civil wars of the 1830s, as did more than 100 other Italian exiles of 1831 and several thousand international liberals from other countries. They wanted to fight the supporters of absolutism and to 'ensure the triumph of the common interests of civilization', as wrote one of their number the Piedmontese volunteer Giacomo Durando, exiled from Turin after the failure of a liberal conspiracy.[46]

Most of the Italian volunteers stayed in the Iberian peninsula until 1848, when they returned to Italy to fight against Austria. They were mostly young and represented a new generation of Italian middle-class liberals.[47] It was during their exile in Iberia that they became politically moderate. In actual fact, during the second half of the 1830s most of them had still been very close to the republican democrats Giuseppe Mazzini and Nicola Fabrizi, the latter having fought with them in Spain for a few months.[48] But after 1848 they rallied behind the banner of the Savoy monarchy in Italy and fought for it in the military and political battles of the Risorgimento. Several veterans of Iberian campaigns, former volunteers such as the Durando brothers, Enrico Cialdini, Domenico Cucchiari and Manfredo Fanti, achieved prestigious positions within Piedmont's and, subsequently, Italy's political and military elites. By the time of the unification of Italy, they were in the upper echelons of the regular army.[49] Their readiness to rally to the Piedmontese constitutional monarchy had been determined by a new conception of the nation, one forged through their political experiences in Portugal and Spain. This is best demonstrated by the writings of Giacomo Durando, who was the one to produce the most sophisticated analysis.

When they rallied to the Italian revolutions in 1831 and fought afterwards as volunteers in the Iberian civil wars, these young militants had a markedly romantic conception of the nation derived from their patriotic reading and their families' memories of the Napoleonic period. While they were still drawing on the revolutionary tradition when identifying the nation with the people, their engagement with the national cause, as influenced by Romanticism, was deeply emotional. They considered their military endeavours to promote this cause in Italy and abroad as the fulfilment of a quest for individual glory that could only be achieved through sacrifice and martyrdom in the name of higher, profoundly noble, political ideals. The search for adventure and action that resulted from this political engagement also represented an escape from the gloomy and prosaic reality of life in Restoration Italy.[50]

But the Iberian civil wars in which the Italian exiles fought lent the struggle for the nation a far less chivalric character than the one they had dreamt of for so long. Their Portuguese and Spanish experiences did not measure up to their romantic political enthusiasm. 'We lost Poetry in the

[Spanish] mountains', Manfredo Fanti wrote in a letter to his democrat friend Fabrizi in 1842.[51] During this same period, Giacomo Durando's assessment of his experience in Portugal and Spain was bitter indeed: 'Let us confess it, the Spanish revolution has been poor. It created neither great ideas, nor great deeds. . . . I found neither great virtues, nor great talents, nor the energy of great crimes. Everything has been marked by mediocrity.'[52]

Disappointment among Italian liberals resulted certainly from endemic infighting between their Iberian counterparts, but above all from the political behaviour of the people, whose extensive counterrevolutionary mobilization did not match the liberal ideal of a nation that rose as one to regain its liberty. Like the exiles of 1821, they attributed the extent and intensity of the popular backlash against liberalism to the low cultural level of populations that had been in the grip of monarchical and clerical despotism for centuries.[53] Consequently, just as ten years earlier, the people could not be perceived as the main agent of national resurrection. Yet the liberal victory in Portugal and Spain had taught the Italian exiles two lessons.

First, the introduction of parliamentary institutions was not sufficient to ensure the existence of the nation, which also needed to be sustained by a high degree of civilization to survive. This reinforced the internationalist persuasion of the Italian exiles: international liberal solidarity, which had contributed to the military victory, had to be complemented by civilization, without which the Iberian nations could not be regenerated. This was demonstrated by the unbalanced relationship between Portugal and Spain and the most civilized European nations, such as France and England. While the former had to derive their inspiration from the more advanced nations, the latter, for their part, had to offer a helping hand to their more backward counterparts, and to show them the path towards civilization. In Portugal, Durando went so far as to propose the colonization of the country by the former international volunteers who, according to him, represented a 'powerful source of regeneration'.[54] Secondly, the Iberian experiences led to a national reevaluation of the monarchy and the regular army as institutions. As Durando wrote, 'the political Risorgimento of Portugal and Spain' could only be explained in terms of 'the political fever' that the kings ruling them had managed to transmit to the populace.[55] The regular army, which had shown great courage in repulsing the guerrillas, was well-placed to achieve victory. Indeed, both the army and the monarchy might prove to be agents of national regeneration.

Convinced as the Italian exiles were that Italy presented a very strong 'analogy of customs, character and tendencies' with Portugal and Spain, the political conclusion which they drew from the introduction of liberalism into the Iberian peninsula was also applicable to the Italian.[56] This same conclusion led the former volunteers to rally to the Piedmontese crown, which they served in the regular army from 1848 onwards. This, however, did not mean jettisoning the national ideal which had characterized their political engagement in the early 1830s. According to Durando, the king must be chosen 'by a solemn act of national will, which is tantamount to saying that the nation must make itself the master of the dynasty, by neutralizing the old principle of *divine right* by means of the *elective principle*'. And gravely disappointing though the Iberian revolutions had been, Durando still considered them to be a success because, by virtue of the introduction of a constitution, they permitted the nation to be 'sovereign by law and in practice'.[57] In the same way, in 1848, Fanti was prepared to rally to the Piedmontese monarchy, on condition that it 'nationalized the war' against Austria.[58]

Yet, once their youthful romantic enthusiasm had been quenched, the exiles ceased to associate the sovereignty of the nation they fought for with the principle of popular sovereignty, which had been discredited by the anti-liberal popular mobilization in Portugal and Spain: the sovereignty of the nation was now sufficient in itself. As most of them were soldiers rather than thinkers, they rallied very pragmatically to the dynasty of Savoy because they thought that it was genuinely achieving the national Risorgimento by entering into a war against Austria and by granting a constitutional charter. But Durando tried to supply this position with an intellectual foundation by developing a theory that would engender a definition of the nation devoid of any reference to the principles of either monarchical or popular sovereignty. In order to achieve his purpose, he addressed geographical considerations drawn from his observation of the Iberian nations.

In Durando's view, Portugal contradicted the common idea of a geographical and natural definition of a nation. As he noted in 1834, 'nature refused a properly national situation to the Portuguese', but nonetheless 'Portugal set herself up as a nation, eminent by her tongue, her habits and her tastes, which sustained her independence with a noble courage and a tenacity that make her worthy of holding a distinguished place in the European family'.[59] So Portugal became an example of an entirely artificial nation, a term he used himself to describe a nation devoid of natural borders and whose very existence was due to historical, political and cultural factors. This led him to define the nation in terms of 'geo-strategy', a concept he had himself invented in order to develop the theory of the nation he would subsequently apply to Italy.[60]

According to Durando, a nation is the result of the occupation of a territory by a tribe able to defend it. It begins by taking advantage of topographical obstacles; the national borders are then natural. But thanks to advances in civilization, technology is able to prevail over natural borders. A more civilized nation can therefore overcome its backward neighbours and absorb them harmoniously into a new nation. Conversely, an unnatural nation with a higher level of civilization than its neighbours and with a strong military defence can maintain its existence in spite of geography. He therefore proposed the following definition: 'I understand the Nation to be the political union of various populations, associated naturally by their geographical situation and artificially by language, customs, traditions, legislation, material and moral interests.'[61]

This led Durando to posit a gradual unification of the Italian peninsula. A fragmented territory where civilization had by that date brought together only a tiny part of the population who shared 'the common feeling of Italian nationality', the peninsula still had too many regions which were too different from each other, and where the spread of civilization among the people was still too weak to allow for an immediate and successful unification.[62] He recommended consequently the establishment of a Kingdom of Upper Italy under the Savoy dynasty and of a Kingdom of Lower Italy under the Bourbons of Naples. These two kingdoms would be located in two geographical sub-regions of the peninsula, the plain of the Po and the Apennines respectively. At some point in the distant future they might merge to form one nation thanks to the slow action of a civilization whose precise nature was not specified by Durando.

Taking into consideration geographical-natural and cultural-political factors simultaneously to explain the formation of nations, Durando gave a very flexible and pragmatic, if very arbitrary, definition of the nation: any successful military enterprise might lead to the creation of a nation. This allowed him to welcome with enthusiasm the unification of the whole peninsula in 1861. Thus the interest of Durando's intellectual approach lies less in its intrinsic aspects than in his efforts to achieve a rational, and not emotional, definition of the nation in order to dissociate it from any particular political regime. Durando's revolutionary and national engagement was certainly still liberal. He even hoped that a republican and democratic regime might at some unspecified point in the future, through the advance of civilization, rule a unified Italy.[63] The introduction of parliamentary and constitutional institutions, although required by civilized opinion in the Europe of the nineteenth century, was not, however, a necessary condition for the life of a nation, as nations existed beyond the temporary political arrangements that governed them:

> The political forms of every people are determined by current opinion, as clothes are by fashion. One could maintain that the obsession for representative government is a pure whim of the peoples, a quirk or a caprice . . .; but it is a fact, and it is also a fact that today or tomorrow, this whim will need to be satisfied, like any other endorsed by one and all.[64]

Durando had lost his romantic faith in the revolutionary potential of the people, and his disappointment with his Iberian experience led him to rally to the royal flag. Nevertheless, he developed a theory to make such a political evolution intelligible. Discarding the principle of popular sovereignty, discredited by the backing the Iberian populations had given to the counterrevolution, Durando's decision to side with the monarchy was intellectually coherent, because his programme was national in scope and sustained by a belief in the inexorable advance of progress. He refused, however, to submit himself unconditionally to the king (even if he frequently behaved as a courtier during his political career in Italy). He devised a new and more flexible notion of sovereignty that could be embodied either in the people or in the king, depending upon local circumstances and the degree of civilization attained by each nation.

As a matter of fact, what Durando did was simply to theorize the pragmatic political choice made by all the Italian exiles of 1831, who had supported the Savoy dynasty after their fight as volunteers in Portugal and Spain. In the social and political circumstances prevailing in Italy, which they imagined to be very similar to those of the Iberian peninsula, they thought that the Italian Risorgimento led by the monarchy and by a small political elite had more chance of succeeding than if it were led by the people. Nevertheless, they would rally behind the monarchy only if it were to adopt the cause of the nation, which the Savoy dynasty ruling over Piedmont could lead through a war against Austria, and the granting of a constitutional charter. This shows how nationalism became the predominant feature of their political culture born of their Iberian experience. Certainly they did not envision their engagement outside the general framework of the progress of civilization in Europe as characterized by constitutional liberty.[65] Thus Durando and the other exiles did not abandon the liberal dimension of their engagement. But since they considered the emancipation of the nation their primary and overarching political objective, and one that had to take precedence over any other preoccupation, they took a stance that could potentially lead to the justification of an authoritarian regime in the name of national liberation and the independence of the nation.

Conclusions

The study of the political and intellectual evolution of Italian liberals during and after their Iberian exile in 1821 and 1831 shows that this experience led not only to transnational exchanges of ideas, but was also crucial in allowing them to draw lessons and to produce representations that had a direct impact on the transformation of Italian liberalism prior to the actual unification of the country. The Iberian experience provided the exiles with novel representations of the people, of the nation and of the revolution. As these images determined their political conduct in Italy, the exiles of 1821 and 1831 are emblematic of the transnational aspects of the liberal and patriotic culture of the Risorgimento – aspects which have so far been studied mainly from a national point of view. But if the Iberian experience, with very few exceptions (for example, Bianco), led them to lose faith in the revolutionary capabilities of the people and to temper their liberalism, the evolution of their political culture and their disappointment with the political experiences of their exile are symptomatic of the profound differences which characterize these two generations of patriots.

In 1820, Italian exiles, by dint of reflecting upon the nature of the popular backing for the liberal cause and upon the counterrevolutionary mobilization in Portugal and Spain, began to consider alternative ways of establishing a regime of liberty. Their commitment to the nation was first and foremost a commitment against despotism, for they were the heirs of the intellectual and political culture of the Enlightenment. If forced to choose, all the exiles would have given priority to freedom over the nation. Even when they were obsessed, as Bianco assuredly was, by the national unification of Italy, they reckoned that only through liberty could a people become a nation.[66] While their Iberian experience instilled in the majority of them a new admiration for a bicameral parliamentary system, all the exiles of 1820 retained their faith in the revolutionary and democratic principle of the sovereignty of the people.

Conversely, the young exiles of 1831, although still construing their fight as a struggle for liberty, began to consider the possibility of separating the idea of the nation as sovereign and that of the nation as a cultural and natural entity. As early as 1837, Durando had asked which of the two was to be given priority in the Italian struggle for the Risorgimento, if it proved to be impossible to achieve both nationality and freedom at one and the same time.[67] This gave rise to the emergence of a more purely nationalist culture.

Risorgimento historiography has highlighted the extent to which this belief in the role the Piedmontese monarchy should play in leading the struggle for national liberation after 1848 was shared by the overwhelming majority of moderate liberals. During the 1850s, many democratic patriots likewise rallied behind the same royal banner and decided to dissociate the aims of national liberation from the establishment of democratic or republican institutions.[68] As Daniele Manin, the republican and democratic leader of the Venetian revolution of 1848, wrote in 1855: 'The Republican party tells the Savoy monarchy: Make Italy, and I am with you, if you do not, I am not.'[69] By that date the nation had become a more important ideal than the institutions that were supposed to rule it. Historians have ascribed this shift to the failure of the 1848 revolutions and of later democratic uprisings, to the liberal policy of the government of Camillo Cavour in Piedmont and to the impact and circulation of cultural representations of the nation through literature and visual material. But, as this chapter has sought to demonstrate, such an evolution can be understood only when placed in the transnational framework from which it emerged, and in particular when viewed in the light of the Iberian experience shared by successive waves of Italian patriots. And if the naturalized idea of the nation endorsed by the exiles could potentially acquire an authoritarian overtone, the Italian liberals nonetheless continued to associate it with an ideal of international civilization which would ultimately lead to the Europe of the Congress of Vienna being replaced by a Europe of liberal nations, a change ensuring the reign of peace and the development of progress in the continent.

Notes

1   Marion S. Miller, 'A "Liberal International"? Perspectives on Comparative
    Approaches to the Revolutions in Spain, Italy, and Greece in the 1820s', in
    Richard W. Clement, Benjamin F. Taggie and Robert G.Schwartz (eds), *Greece
    and the Mediterranean* (Kirksville: Sixteenth Century Journal Publishers,
    1990), pp. 61–7; Sylvie Aprile, Jean-Claude Caron and Emmanuel Fureix
    (eds), *La Liberté guidant les peuples. Les révolutions de 1830 en Europe*
    (Seyssel: Champ Vallon, 2013).

2   Giorgio Candeloro, *Storia dell'Italia moderna* (Milan: Feltrinelli, 1958–78),
    vol. II.

3   Maurizio Isabella, *Risorgimento in Exile. Italian Émigrés and the Liberal
    International in the Post-Napoleonic Era* (Oxford: Oxford University Press,
    2009).

4   Gilles Pécout (ed.), *International Volunteers and the Risorgimento*, *Journal of
    Modern Italian Studies* 14/4 (2009).

5   Isabella, *Risorgimento in Exile*; Aprile, Caron and Fureix (eds), *La liberté
    guidant les peuples*.

6   Alberto M. Banti, *La nazione del Risorgimento. Parentela, santità e onore alle
    origini dell'Italia unita* (Turin: Einaudi, 2000).

7   Arianna Arisi Rota, *I piccoli cospiratori. Politica ed emozioni nei primi
    mazziniani* (Bologna: Il Mulino, 2010); idem and Roberto Balzani,
    'Discovering politics. Action and Recollection in the First Mazzinian
    Generation', in Silvana Patriarca and Lucy Riall (eds), *The Risorgimento
    Revisited. Nationalism and Culture in Nineteenth-Century Italy* (New York:
    Palgrave Macmillan, 2012), pp. 77–96.

8   Marco Mugnaini, *Italia e Spagna nell'età contemporanea. Cultura,
    politica e diplomazia (1814–1870)* (Alexandria: Edizioni dell'Orso,
    1994); Isabel Pascual Sastre, 'La circolazione di miti politici tra Spagna
    e Italia (1820–1869)', in Alberto M. Banti and Paul Ginsbord (eds),
    Storia d'Italia. Annali 22, Il Risorgimento (Turin: Einaudi, 2007),
    pp. 797–824.

9   Giorgio Spini, *Mito e realtà della Spagna nelle rivoluzioni italiane del 1820–21*
    (Rome: Perella, 1950).

10 Antonino De Francesco, *Rivoluzione costituzioni. Saggi sul democratismo
    politico nell'Italia napoleonica, 1796–1821* (Naples: ESI, 1996); Gonzalo
    Butrón Prida, *Nuestra sagrada causa. El modelo gaditano en la revolución
    piamontesa de 1821* (Cadiz: Fundación Municipal de Cádiz, 2006).

11 Agostino Bistarelli, *Gli esuli del Risorgimento* (Bologna: Il Mulino, 2011).

12 Ibid.

13 Grégoire Bron, 'The exiles of the Risorgimento: Italian volunteers in the
    Portuguese Civil War (1832–34)', *Journal of Modern Italian Studies* 14/4
    (2009), pp. 427–44.

14 Mugnaini, *Italia e Spagna*; Pascual Sastre, 'La circolazione di miti politici'.

15 Bistarelli, *Gli esuli del Risorgimento*, pp. 77–84.

16   Gilles Pécout, 'Le rotte internazionali del volontariato', in Mario Isnenghi and Eva Cecchinato (eds), *Gli Italiani in guerra. Conflitti, identità, memorie dal Risorgimento ai nostri giorni*, vol. I, *Fare l'Italia: unità e disunità nel Risorgimento* (Turin: UTET, 2008), pp. 120–8.

17   Vittorio Scotti Douglas, 'La guerriglia negli scrittori risorgimentali italiani prima e dopo il 1848–1849', *Il Risorgimento* XXVII (October 1975), pp. 93–122; Pascual Sastre, 'La circolazione dei miti politici'; Isabella, *Risorgimento in Exile*.

18   De Francesco, *Rivoluzione costituzioni*.

19   Ibid.

20   Alberto Gil Novales, *El trienio liberal* (Madrid: Siglo XXI Editores, 1989).

21   Giacinto Provana di Collegno, 'Diario d'un viaggio in Ispagna nel 1823 (trovato fra le carte di un Emigrato del 1821)', *Il Cronista* 8 (24 August 1856), p. 43.

22   Isabella, *Risorgimento in Exile*, p. 39.

23   Guglielmo Pepe, *Memorie del Generale Guglielmo Pepe intorno alla sua vita e ai recenti casi d'Italia* (Paris: Baudry, 1847), vol. 2, p. 103.

24   Giuseppe Pecchio, *Trois mois en Portugal en 1822* (Paris: chez les marchands de nouveautés, 1822), p. 17.

25   Ibid., p. 49; Guglielmo Pepe, 'The non-establishment of Liberty in Spain, Naples, Portugal and Piedmont', in *The Pamphleteer* XLVII (July 1824), pp. 226–9; Carlo Bianco di Saint-Jorioz, *Della guerra d'insurrezione per bande, applicata all'Italia* ([Marseilles], 1830), vol. II, p. 256.

26   Pepe, 'The non-establishment', p. 230.

27   Bianco di Saint-Jorioz, *Della guerra*, vol. I, p. 53

28   Ibid.; Giuseppe Rizzo Schettino, *'Terrorista per sistema, non per cuore'. Vita e pensiero di Carlo Bianco* (Rome: Carocci, 2007).

29   Aldo Romano, 'Lafayette, Guglielmo Pepe e l'Italia (Un carteggio inedito)', *Rassegna storica del Risorgimento* XX/4 (1933), pp. 585–614.

30   Pepe, 'The non-establishment', pp. 228–30.

31   Idem, *Mémoire sur les moyens qui peuvent conduire à l'indépendance italienne* (Paris: Paulin, 1833), p. 17–18.

32   Idem, 'The non-establishment', p. 226.

33   Ibid., p. 229; idem, *Mémoire sur les moyens*, p. 21.

34   Ibid., p. 17.

35   Ibid.

36   Ibid., p. 19.

37   Pecchio, *Trois mois*, p. 62.

38   Ibid., p. 16.

39   Maurizio Isabella, '"Una scienza dell'amor patrio": public economy, freedom and civilization in Giuseppe Pecchio's work (1827–1830)', *Journal of Modern Italian Studies* 4/2 (1999), pp. 157–83.

40   Ibid.

41   Ibid.; Giuseppe Pecchio, *Six mois en Espagne* (Paris: Alexandre Corréard, 1822), p. 85.

42   Giuseppe Pecchio, *Scritti politici*, ed. by Paolo Bernardelli (Rome: Istituto per la Storia del Risorgimento, 1978), p. 561.

43   Giuseppe Pecchio, *Un'elezione di membri del parlamento in Inghilterra* (Lugano: Vanelli, 1826), pp. 7–8.

44   Pecchio, *Trois mois*, p. 53.

45   Giovanni Canevazzi, 'Nella giovinezza di Enrico Cialdini', *Rassegna storica del Risorgimento* 10/1 (1923), p. 28.

46   Grégoire Bron, 'Un manuscrit inconnu de Giacomo Durando. *De la colonisation des troupes étrangères en Portugal* (1834)', *Mélanges de l'Ecole française de Rome. Italie et Méditerranée* 122/1 (2010), pp. 207–30.

47   Grégoire Bron, *Révolution et nation entre le Portugal et l'Italie. Les relations politiques luso-italiennes des Lumières à l'Internationale libérale de 1830*, unpublished PhD thesis (Paris and Lisbon: EPHE and ISCTE, 2013).

48   Franco Della Peruta, *Mazzini e i rivoluzionari italiani. Il 'partito d'azione', 1830–1845* (Milan: Feltrinelli, 1974).

49   Mugnaini, *Italia e Spagna*; Sastre, 'La circolazioni di miti politici'.

50   Arisi Rota, *I piccoli cospiratori*.

51   T. Palamenghi-Crispi, 'Gli Italiani nelle guerre di Spagna', *Il Risorgimento italiano* 7 (1914), p. 174.

52   Ibid., p. 61.

53   Bron, 'Un manuscrit inconnu'.

54   Ibid., p. 224.

55   Giacomo Durando, *Della nazionalità italiana. Saggio politico-militare* (Lausanne: S. Bonamici, 1846), p. 226.

56   Ibid.

57   Museo Nazionale del Risorgimento di Torino (MNRT), cart. 102, no 10, fol. 12–13.

58   MNRT, cart. 107, no 19.

59   MNRT, cart. 102, no 5.

60   Ferruccio Botti, *Il pensiero militare e navale italiano dalla Rivoluzione francese alla Prima Guerra mondiale (1789–1915)* (Rome: Stato Maggiore dell'Esercito, 1995), vol. I, pp. 717–69.

61   Durando, *Della nazionalità*, p. 58.

62   Ibid., pp. 243–4.

63   Ibid., p. 159.

64   Ibid., p. 51.

65   MNRT, cart. 145, no 21, after 1846.

66   Bianco di Saint-Jorioz, *Della guerra*, vol. I, p. 132.

67 Palamenghi-Crispi, 'Gli Italiani nelle guerre', p. 61.

68 Candeloro, *Storia dell'Italia moderna*, vol. IV; Lucio Villari, *Bella e perduta. L'Italia del Risorgimento* (Rome: Laterza, 2009); Banti, *La nazione del Risorgimento*.

69 Bistrarelli, *Gli esuli del Risorgimento*, p. 267.

CHAPTER FOUR

Mediterranean Liberals?

Italian Revolutionaries and the Making of a Colonial Sea, ca. 1800–30

Maurizio Isabella[*]

One of the key features of the geopolitical transformations of the early nineteenth century was the strengthening of the British imperial presence in the Mediterranean, which by the 1840s had become a 'British lake'.[1] The formation of Britain's Mediterranean empire was originally precipitated by the wars against Napoleon, and then facilitated by the temporary crisis of the Ottoman Empire. It included Malta, which became British in 1800, involved the temporary occupation of Sicily and, after 1815, the possession of the Ionian Islands. By 1840 Britain was the uncontested political and economic power in the region. This phase of imperial expansion, as Christopher Bayly has argued, coincided with a British imperial meridian, a phase of military rule appropriately described as one of 'vice-regal' or 'proconsular despotism' on account of its authoritarian nature.[2] The period was first marked by the defeat and withdrawal of France, expelled from the

[*] An earlier, shorter version of this essay was published as 'Patriottismo mediterraneo, civiltà europea ed imperi: gli scritti di Alfio Grassi, Giorgio Libri e Gianbattista Marochetti, 1825–1830', in S. Levati and M. Meriggi (eds), *Con la ragione e col cuore. Studi dedicati a Carlo Capra* (Milan: Franco Angeli, 2008), and given as a paper at the workshop 'Rethinking the Early Nineteenth Century' organized by Glenda Sluga at the University of Sydney in July 2012.

Mediterranean, but also by a revival of its colonial ambitions. This revival, which built on memories of Napoleon's expedition in Egypt, culminated in the seizure of Algiers in 1830. Without resulting in any form of direct colonial rule, the Greek war of independence likewise not only provided ample opportunities for the European powers to intervene in Ottoman politics and shape the outcome of events that led to the formation of the new Greek state, but put this latter under their tutelage and increased their influence over the Porte.[3]

It is with the intellectual consequences of this formal and informal imperial expansion that I am concerned in this chapter. As the work of Linda Colley, Maya Jasanoff and Ian Coller, among others, has shown, between the eighteenth and nineteenth century, at a time when war, military expansion and occupation, as well as revolution, were forcing people to move in new and unpredicted ways, individual trajectories connected imperial peripheries and metropolitan centres in both directions. The new mobilities produced by imperial expansion provided opportunities for cultural exchanges, or transculturation, between Europeans and the local populations, exchanges that had an impact on colonized and colonizers alike.[4]

This chapter discusses a set of early nineteenth-century Italian intellectuals whose 'liberal ideals' were shaped by displacement, exile and travel, moving as they did between the continental or insular regions of the Mediterranean affected by the presence of the French and British Empires and by revolutionary circumstances, and their metropolitan centres. The network of trans-Mediterranean patriots whose writings I am discussing here was made up of individuals directly or indirectly in contact with each other, and at the same time acquainted with prominent intellectuals and with debates taking place in London and Paris. Their peculiar position as intermediaries between the new imperial peripheries they came from, and their political and intellectual capitals, enabled them to engage with, discuss, reject or reshape imperial ideologies, adjusting them to suit their political purposes, and tailoring the political languages and aspirations of the age of revolution to fit the realities and intellectual justifications of the new empires. This more or less loosely connected community of Mediterranean liberals who came from different states within the Italian peninsula included Vittorio Barzoni (1767–1843), a Lombard writer whose passionate anti-democratic and anti-revolutionary beliefs made him an enthusiastic advocate of the British presence in the Mediterranean and an imperial ideologue; Filippo Pananti (1766–1857), a Tuscan democrat and supporter of the French Revolution who went into exile in London, where he became a poet at the Royal Italian Theatre, returning subsequently to the Mediterranean in order to travel widely in the region; Ugo Foscolo (1778–1827), arguably the most famous Italian writer and poet of the nineteenth century, a national icon, but also an Ionian patriot exiled in London from 1816 and concerned with the political regeneration of his islands; Alfio Grassi (1766–1827), a Sicilian revolutionary, an officer of the *Grande Armée* exiled in Paris, who never managed to return to his homeland, but in the 1820s travelled across the Mediterranean, from Malta to Constantinople, and wrote about Mediterranean politics; Giorgio Libri-Carucci Della Sommaia, Conte di Bagnano (1782–1836), a Tuscan radical and Bonapartist who left Italy in 1801, for France first and then for Brussels, only to die in Amsterdam; and Gianbattista Marochetti (1772–1851), a Piedmontese revolutionary involved in the 1821 revolution and later exiled in France, for whom the solution to the Italian national problem lay in the reorganization of the Mediterranean and the Balkans.

These case studies cast some light on the political dilemmas patriots faced during decades marked by uncertain political circumstances, not to mention sudden changes in borders and governments, and also point to the sheer variety of solutions that could be advanced to accommodate demands for autonomy, freedom and self-government in a period of great flux. This era of expanding empires seemed to provide unforeseen opportunities and challenges to rethink creatively political problems, and led the subjects of the present study to envisage projects in the face of political decisions that were beyond their own control. The writings of these early liberals – who were culturally Italian or Italo-Greek – manifest a preoccupation with the geopolitical transformations taking place in the region, that is to say, the Mediterranean sea, a space where small fatherlands, empires and national projects had to be reconciled. Their concern for the Mediterranean regional dimension of freedom thus forced them to engage with contemporary debates about the legitimacy of Europe's expansion southward and eastward. As I shall demonstrate, their views can be understood in terms of a dialogue with those developed at the time by British and French political or intellectual circles either directly involved or interested in the European presence in the region at a time when liberal imperialism was being forged and debated.[5]

Retrieving the voices of these somewhat neglected figures is important at two levels. First, an analysis of their intervention in disputes regarding the legitimacy of new and old systems of power and hegemony adds to our understanding of the contentious (and contested) nature of imperial liberalism and liberalism *tout court*, and offers perspectives and viewpoints that have generally been ignored by historians of political thought, who have studied imperialism from the viewpoint of intellectuals in France or Britain, and have tended to overlook the reactions of intellectuals in imperial peripheries. Second, recovering the Mediterranean framework of their political imagination forces us to set aside or substantially revise traditional historiographic frameworks of analysis that locate these early liberals within the Italian or Greek *Risorgimento* – that is to say, the Greek and Italian national movements aspiring to the creation of nation-states. Yet these figures, as I shall argue, were neither primarily nor exclusively Italian or Greek nationalists. Rather, they were Mediterranean liberals, and often also imperial subjects, engaged in transnational disputes related to the political reorganization of the Mediterranean Sea, in which national questions were part of a broader set of issues, whereby freedom might sometimes be compatible with imperial rule and colonial expansion. Although occasionally, as in the case of Foscolo's writings on the Ionian Islands, their work remained unpublished or had a limited circulation, their writings, published in Paris, Brussels or London in French and English, addressed European liberal audiences as well as the community of Italian expatriates.

The British Empire and Mediterranean liberty: from Vittorio Barzoni's liberal imperialism to Ugo Foscolo's disappointment

What first defined the debate about the benefits or drawbacks of the British presence in the region for the regeneration of the Mediterranean was Great Britain's clash with revolutionary France. The military confrontation between the two powers resulted also in an ideological struggle soon to be associated with competing visions of the Mediterranean. England or France could each describe themselves as championing the liberation of the peoples of the region, both in its continental and insular territories, from despotism. In the language of the ideologues of the British or French Empires, a belief in the duty to defend or export freedoms was ambiguously associated with the language of civilization, with projects of colonization, and with a condemnation of the slaving activities and piratical conduct of the Barbary states. In continuity with earlier debates, French revolutionary, Napoleonic and early Restoration visions of the Mediterranean shared a condemnation of Oriental despotism as incompatible by turns with revolutionary notions of popular sovereignty and/or with Christian ideas of civilization and freedom.[6] Italian supporters of the French Revolution were quick to use some of these arguments to reframe their own plans for the regeneration of the peninsula. The earliest and most sophisticated of these Mediterranean revolutionary and anti-British projects produced in conjunction with French southward expansion are probably those devised by Matteo Galdi (1765–1821), a Neapolitan enlightened writer who, as early as 1796, foresaw in the establishment of the sister republics in northern Italy the first step towards the creation of an alliance between France and Italy, and wished to establish the Mediterranean islands as independent but confederated states or annex them directly to one of the two southern Italian states. In Galdi's view, the opening up of Suez to trade, and the colonization of North Africa, would create opportunities for the development of Southern Europe. Natural rights would underpin this new Mediterranean based on the expansion of free trade, and the introduction of an international congress recognizing the rights of the people. Galdi considered England to be the foremost enemy of freedom in the region, shielding despotism in southern Italy and prone to monopolistic tendencies where the control of trade was concerned.[7]

The expansion of Britain in the region during the Napoleonic wars was likewise accompanied by a reformulation of imperial ideology, reflecting its sudden expansion into broad swathes of the Mediterranean, and in its firm control over Malta and Sicily. Two British officers in particular, Gould Francis Leckie and Charles Pasley, contributed to rethinking a British Mediterranean empire, once Lord Bentinck had assumed responsibility for the British occupation of Sicily, becoming as they did his advisors. Leckie and Pasley's imperial visions were somewhat different: the former imagined a maritime empire based exclusively on islands and control over the seas, of which the Mediterranean could become the centre, as opposed to the French continental empire; while Pasley argued in favour of British expansion not only in the Mediterranean, but also on the continent. However both of them were imperial patriots who, in spite of being indebted to earlier imperial ideologies, conceived the empire not only in terms of conquest, grandeur, and national pride, but were concerned also with 'the rule of law', benevolence and improvement. For them these features made Britain the polar opposite of France, for, 'while France conquers to devastate, Britain conquers to do good'. They both framed this sharp contrast in terms of the differences between an authoritarian, imperial Rome, and a maritime, commercial Carthage, according to a long-standing tradition in European political thought very much revived at this time.[8] Leckie was an imperial reformer who, in the wake of Burke, criticized British policy in India, and argued for the need to exert a benign influence over the Mediterranean and over the populations of Sicily and Malta in particular. For him, these islanders deserved a reforming government, and should be spared a purely military exploitation. Both writers recommended the annexation of Sicily by Britain, 'so as to form an integral part of our territory', a project that found further justification in the despotic, corrupt nature of Bourbon rule over the island, and in the moral responsibility of Britain to impose liberal reforms.[9] Both Pasley and Leckie were also advocates of Italian independence, favouring the creation of a single unified, or else two unified, states in the peninsula, which would, in their view, 'become our natural ally'.[10] Their ideas would seem to have been influenced by those of Lord Bentinck, who ruled over Sicily between 1811 and 1815 and, after granting a constitution to the island, became so disillusioned by the incapacity of the Sicilian elites to embrace representative institutions that, notoriously enough, he contemplated annexing Sicily to the empire.[11]

Leckie and Pasley's vision of a benign empire defending European liberties against Napoleonic despotism was shared by Italian anti-French writers like Vittorio Barzoni, who was well acquainted with the British military leadership in the Mediterranean, from Leckie to Bentinck. Barzoni became one of the Italian ideologues of the British imperial presence in the region, using as his mouthpiece a number of periodicals subsidized directly by the British. Thus, in his *Il Cartaginese*, published in Malta, Barzoni, like Leckie, compared the clash between France and Britain to that between Rome and

Carthage. Unlike modern Britain, however, Carthage had only been defeated, Barzoni argued, because it had abandoned its mixed constitution. Indeed, it was only by preserving its perfect constitution, Barzoni maintained, that Britain would defeat Napoleon.[12] As in the case of Bentinck or Leckie, so too Barzoni saw in the imperial presence of Britain around Italy the precondition for its political emancipation. It was from the pages of *Il Cartaginese* that in October 1805 he launched an appeal for the insurrection of the Italians against the French oppressor as a first step towards the establishment of an independent state with a constitution modelled upon the English example.

Other contemporary English observers, however, were not necessarily directly associated or aligned with British governmental policies in the region, but might nonetheless believe in the potentially liberal nature of the British imperial presence in the Mediterranean.[13] As is well known, in the 1820s Jeremy Bentham and his circle developed a keen interest in the regeneration of the Mediterranean space, with the Benthamite milieu becoming involved in the revolutions across the region, from Portugal to Greece. Bentham himself was keen on helping liberals, from Tripoli to Greece, drafting a number of constitutional charters. Although his views on this theme had not always been consistent, Bentham had been by and large critical of colonial settlements and empires. Some of his followers involved in Mediterranean projects, however, saw the British presence in the Sea as a guarantee of the emancipation of its people, a role that entailed a combination of direct rule, benevolent protectorates and support for full emancipation.

Among Bentham's followers, Edward Blaquiere is remembered mainly as the most enthusiastic supporter of the revolutionary wave that broke over Southern Europe, and the closest of all the Benthamites to the Southern revolutionaries involved in the Greek war of liberation. Against the more lukewarm philhellenes like Leicester Stanhope, who were unconvinced of the Greeks' readiness to enjoy full political rights, he advocated full emancipation of the country without any reservations. Yet, as early as 1813, when Blaquiere had just started a correspondence with Bentham, his *Letters from the Mediterranean* bear witness to an interest in the regeneration of the whole Mediterranean basin, with the British Empire playing a leading role. In his own words, 'the state of Europe and the world require that England should be the first power in the Mediterranean'.[14] To comply with its liberal duties, argued Blaquiere, Britain had to fight Christian slavery and defend Southern Europe and the Mediterranean islands from the attacks of the pirates from the Barbary states, against whom the use of military force was legitimate and in relation to whom, given the uncivilized nature of their governments, the constraints imposed by international treaties did not apply. Whereas Malta had to remain a British dependency, albeit one in which Britain had the duty to reform the civil codes and the judicial system, Blaquiere, unlike Pasley or Leckie, was against the transformation of Sicily into a colony. Rather, the island should be emancipated from Bourbon despotism, and gain full independence. Meanwhile, Blaquiere supported Lord Bentinck's introduction of a constitution along British lines, while criticizing excessive interference in the day-to-day running of the island's affairs. The promotion of reform, and the respect due to a sovereign country and ally were the principles Britain should follow in its dealings with Sicily.

Blaquiere's liberal imperialism and loose affinities with Benthamite utilitarian philosophy converged with the ideas of some Italian revolutionaries, themselves close to Bentham, who had left the peninsula during or after the collapse of Napoleonic rule, and had come to admire Britain's political system. Among them, the one displaying the closest affinities was perhaps the Tuscan poet Filippo Pananti, whose *Narrative of a Residence in Algiers*, an account of his captivity in Algeria, Blaquiere himself edited and annotated in 1818.[15] For Pananti too, the naval presence of Britain was crucial for the security of the Mediterranean against pirates and slavery, and Britain was the only country that could guarantee the regeneration of the entire region. Under the influence of liberals like Blaquiere, the former revolutionary, by now settled in London, Pananti considered that after 1815 the British Empire, and not France, represented the hegemonic power that would guarantee peace, freedom and the protection of human rights across the sea. In espousing an anglophile liberal imperialism, the Tuscan poet was not necessarily reneging upon his earlier revolutionary and democratic ideals. But in the new political circumstances of a post-Napoleonic Europe and Mediterranean, Pananti, like many other exiled revolutionaries, viewed Britain's influence in the area as offering the best opportunities for guaranteeing peace, stability, and gradual political reform.

Blaquiere and Pananti's writings reveal the importance of another element of imperial ideology shared by yet other contemporary British politicians interested in the Mediterranean, namely, the idea that the British Empire had a major role to play in the protection of the smaller, weaker states. As Richard Whatmore has recently demonstrated, there existed a tradition, dating back to the middle of the eighteenth century, that associated the British commercial empire with the defence of the European balance of power, and the protection of small republics against conquest and military expansion. Since the late eighteenth century, moreover, and after the French Revolution in particular, an increasing number of republican patriots recognized in their turn that Britain was a precious ally whose protection might well prove vital to the survival of their countries.[16]

It was on the basis of this idea of empire that in 1817 Ugo Foscolo supported the British protectorate of the Ionian Islands, when diplomatic agreements transferred them to British rule. Like Filippo Pananti, Ugo Foscolo had been directly involved in the political events of Napoleonic Italy. Born in the Ionian Islands and educated in Venice, his political trajectory transformed him from a Venetian citizen and a product of the Adriatic intellectual world into an Italian patriot, enthusiastic about French revolutionary principles and hopeful that Napoleon would facilitate the creation of an independent and democratic Italian republic. He had participated in this project both as an army officer and as a celebrated intellectual. In fact, like many other Italian revolutionaries of his generation, Foscolo came to be disillusioned with Napoleon's despotic rule, and less and less certain about the capacity of Italians to thrive under conditions of freedom.[17] With the end of Napoleonic rule, Foscolo left the Italian peninsula and settled in London. While in London, the acquisition of the Ionian Islands by Britain made him hopeful that a further round of reforms could be implemented, and that he might even be able to return there and take up a teaching post in a newly-established university. Thus his English exile offered him the opportunity to become once again an Ionian patriot, and turned him also into a liberal imperialist. Foscolo voiced his opinions regarding the political circumstances prevailing on the Ionian Islands under British rule in a document written in 1817, just as Parliament was debating the constitution to be granted to them by the British government, entitled *Stato politico delle isole Jonie* (*Political State of the Ionian Islands*), a text destined never to be published during his lifetime.

Three reasons, in Foscolo's judgement, made the choice of an English protectorate the best possible solution for the Islands, and one that could reconcile empire and liberalism. First, in the post-revolutionary world, one in which the balance of power had been destroyed, imperial protection was the only feasible solution available for small states like the Ionian Islands. Second, England, owing to its promotion of free trade, was the only imperial power that could safeguard civil liberties and the economic development of the Islands, in marked contrast to the military Austrian and French Empires, which exploited financially and economically the territories they conquered. Finally, while not denying the Ionian Islands' right to aspire to independence, Foscolo believed that their citizens were not ready for it, as centuries of Venetian rule had corrupted their character, fomented divisions and dissension, and increased the diversity of their customs. It was Foscolo's firm belief that unity among citizens should be reached through the gradual adoption of common values and beliefs as a precondition to independence. Public education and a free press, through which the Ionians could communicate their grievances to the British Parliament, would play a vital role in this process.[18] Yet what Foscolo foresaw was not the outright transfer of English political institutions to the Ionian state. As Eugenio Biagini has argued, Foscolo's political thought in these constitutional writings revealed how his newly adopted Whiggism coincided with 'a return to his own ancestral republicanism in the Venetian and Adriatic tradition'.[19] His admiration for Britain was based on a conviction that no constitution, including that of the Islands, could survive if it ignored the local conditions and history and avoided abstract principles. Foscolo believed that the protectorate required a federal constitution, in order to reflect the relative autonomy of each island, and a political system based on a single parliamentary assembly, with political rights being restricted to landowners.[20] Unfortunately, he was soon to be bitterly disappointed: in 1820 he acknowledged that the constitution granted to the Ionian Islands was little more than a formal recognition of Lord Maitland's despotic power, as 'the Lord High Commissioner is virtually responsible to nobody'.[21] There was no division of powers, and no real possibility for the assembly of landowners to exert any influence whatsoever on government, as Lord Maitland had an iron grip upon the legislature and the judiciary. The high commissioner was accountable neither to the assembly, nor to the monarch, nor to the parliament. In short, he held in his hands 'an absolute, arbitrary and monstrous authority'.[22] Foscolo's bitter disillusionment with the British Empire, its liberal pretensions having proved to be spurious, reflected an increasing distrust among Italian patriots for the British presence in the Mediterranean. If after 1815 the earlier supporters of revolutionary France like Pananti or Foscolo had also believed in Britain's liberal credentials, in the 1820s the stark reality of British support for the new European system in Southern Europe and the harshness of its colonial rule in the Ionian Islands and in Malta turned admiration and hope into condemnation. Combining imperial protectorates over small countries like the Mediterranean islands with the emancipation of large nations like Italy and the presence of European empires was perhaps more difficult a balancing trick than it had seemed in the transition from the Napoleonic era to the new international order.

Opposing colonial rule in the name of universal rights for freedom

A particularly harsh condemnation of all empires in the Mediterranean, and of the British Empire in particular, came from the Sicilian revolutionary Alfio Grassi. Unlike Pananti or Foscolo, Grassi had lived in Paris since the fall of the Neapolitan republic of 1799, in whose defence he had fought against the Bourbon troops. Alfio Grassi had participated as an officer in several Napoleonic campaigns, during which he obtained the *Légion d'Honneur* in recognition of his services.[23] While he never went back to Sicily and died in France, Grassi made a last tour of the Mediterranean which took him to Istanbul at the time of the Greek revolution. Grassi's *Charte Turque* (1825) and his *La Sainte-Alliance, Les Anglais et Les Jésuites; Leur systéme politique à l'égard de la Gréce* (1827) provided an original comparative assessment of all the empires involved in the control of the Mediterranean Sea.[24] What made Grassi's argument provocative and peculiar was his conviction that the Ottoman Empire was more tolerant, or even 'more liberal', than any other European empire, and the British one in particular. In addition, his works demonstrate that in the 1820s philhellenism and pro-Ottoman attitudes could in fact coexist.

Grassi's critique echoed French contemporary liberal views that condemned the British Empire for its protectionism, which advanced exclusively the economic interests of a corrupt and warmongering oligarchy of aristocrats. For Grassi, England's aim was to dominate the whole of the Mediterranean and to monopolize world trade.[25] He contrasted French ability to spread individual rights through their rule over Europe during the revolutionary period, which had enabled France to be so successful in its European conquests, with Britain's colonial government which '*augmente ses protégés, et non ses citoyens*' ('increases her subjects, not her citizens').[26] Lord Maitland's governorship had been notoriously despotic, and the Ionian Islands were now in a deplorable economic state, because the British had replaced local tradesmen, foodstuffs had doubled in price with the arrival of British troops, and English consumer goods now dominated the local market. Grassi lamented the fact that the British colonial government in Malta was even more despotic than the one in the Ionian Islands, since there the division between executive, legislative and judiciary powers was not respected. High taxation, protection of British commercial interests at the expense of the local ones, a brutal administration and a backward criminal justice system were the main features of British rule there.[27] Grassi's conclusion was that British government was more tyrannical than that of any pasha.[28]

While a critique of British despotism in Malta may not have been uncommon, and people like Foscolo may have come to similar conclusions by the early 1820s, Grassi's originality lay in combining them with lavish praise for the Ottoman Empire and a fervent philhellenism. His pro-Ottoman stance was developed as a consequence of a visit to Constantinople and Greece in 1825, but owed much also to a breathtakingly broad knowledge of the seventeenth- and eighteenth-century European and French, in particular, literature on the Ottoman Empire.[29] In short, Grassi admired the Ottoman Empire because it allowed a high degree of religious and cultural tolerance, and because it lacked an aristocracy. Grassi's overall analysis of the interaction between the different agencies within the empire led to a single conclusion, namely, that the body of Ottoman legislation, based upon the Koran, represented nothing less than a genuine constitution, a *charte*, since even the sultan was forced to comply with it. The emperor was constantly controlled by the muphtis and ulemas, as well as by the military, civil and religious classes, who could even take it upon themselves to strangle him, if he was found to have gone against the principles of the laws of the Prophet.[30] While eighteenth-century observers had made reference to such institutions to argue that the Ottoman Empire contained a genuinely democratic element, Grassi went much further, even suggesting that the Ottoman Empire could to some extent be seen as a 'liberal' polity *ante litteram*: 'Well before civilized nations had constitutions, chambers and an opposition party, Ottomans had already established one and the other, and relied on these three foundations as the pillars which were intended to sustain their Empire ...'.[31] The implication was that Russia and Austria might well be European, but they were not therefore civilized. Even British rule might not measure up to the standards of this model of civilization, because it denied constitutional rights to the populations under its sway.

Grassi's originality thus did not lie in the arguments themselves, based on the manipulation of eighteenth-century ideas, but rather in the fact that support for them in the age of philhellenism was rare. His provocative preference for Ottoman rule over the other empires, and his dismissal of the stereotypical description of the Turkish population was instrumental in exposing Russian, British and Austrian rule to a particularly damning comparison and highlighting the inadequacies of imperial rule in general. In fact, Grassi fully endorsed the grievances of the Greek revolutionaries, and unconditionally supported their claims for emancipation.[32] Grassi identified constitutionalism with the very notion of liberalism and self-determination as universally applicable principles.[33] By so doing, he was also questioning a central feature of philhellenic discourse, the superiority of Christian and European civilization over eastern Islamic culture, a feature endorsed by a majority of exiled Italian and Greek liberals. For this reason, his works were attacked by many European writers, among them a prominent Greek intellectual, Jacovaky Rizo Néroulos, a historian, Phanariot, and man of the Orthodox enlightenment who in a long and unpublished *Analyse raisonnée de l'ouvrage intitulé Charte Turque* stated that the Ottoman polity was a theocratic despotism, and that Grassi's work was nothing less than a 'hideous absurdity'.[34]

Grassi's peculiar Mediterranean vision was, however, shared by other exiles who, like him, were keen to expose the contradictions implicit in the European policies in the region, questioning the dominant terms of philhellenic discourse. Giorgio Libri-Bagnano's writings include an attack upon Chateaubriand's *Note sur la Grèce* (Paris, 1825), in which he denounced the ambiguity of European philhellenic discourse and the notion that the Greek war of independence could merely be defined as a clash of civilizations. More generally, it criticized the Holy Alliance, French foreign policy in Southern Europe and Chateaubriand's decision to intervene militarily in Spain in 1823 to put an end to the constitutional regime.[35] Inspired by the ideas of toleration and universal justice contained in the works of Voltaire and Montesquieu, Libri adopted the literary model and comparative approach of Montesquieu's *Lettres Persanes* to take an extra-European, and Ottoman in particular, point of view, in order to criticize France's contemporary foreign policy.[36] Describing himself as the son of Muslim immigrants living first in Livorno and later in Marseilles, where he had studied European institutions and manners without abandoning his ancestral faith, Libri declared himself to be an enthusiastic supporter of the emancipation of Greece, to him a quintessentially anti-despotic cause.[37] 'Muslim as I am, I am strongly inclined to believe that no king, whatever his title, has the slightest right to rule by force over people who do not want him . . .'.[38] Adopting a viewpoint similar to that of Grassi, Libri argued that the European powers had not been more respectful of national and individual rights in the Mediterranean (where the British had disregarded the aspirations of the local populations) and in Southern Europe alike. What was striking in his view was the constant inconsistency in their conduct and the manifest incoherence of their political stances. Chateaubriand had decided to intervene in Spain in order to defend the principle of legitimacy and Bourbon despotism. However, Libri argued, the principle of the legitimacy of Christian ruler was not superior to that of the Ottoman sultans. Chateaubriand's rallying to the Greek cause had not been matched by a similar stand against slavery worldwide. Yet human rights had to be defended regardless of skin colour and geographical area. Thus Libri's own brand of philhellenism was in sharp contrast to that upheld by Chateaubriand: 'Fight for the Greeks, not because they are Christians, but because they are oppressed! Attack the Turks not because they are Turks, but because they are oppressors!'[39]

Grassi's and Libri-Bagnano's Mediterranean vision thus condemned the hypocrisy of the notion that the European powers had a civilizing role to play, regardless of their actual conduct, and advanced the belief that constitutional rights and full independence had to be equally distributed among small and large nations alike, both in Europe and in the Mediterranean, in the West as well as in the East. Their faith in the universal ability of individuals to exercise political rights and self-rule led them to reject any kind of paternalistic government in the region, whether in the form of direct colonial administration, or protectorates, or in the form of foreign interventions that clashed with the people's political aspirations. For Grassi and Libri, all peoples around the Mediterranean had to enjoy the same rights to self-determination, with no exclusion or exception whatsoever. Thus their adoption of a pro-Ottoman, anti-British and anti-French stance helped them unveil the double standards of European liberalism, and represented also an indirect attack on, or a distancing from, the liberal imperialism other fellow exiles had been espousing when reframing their hopes for the regeneration of the Mediterranean.

Gianbattista Marochetti and European expansion eastward

At the time of the publication of Grassi's and Libri-Bagnano's works, however, an increasing number of intellectuals viewed the civilizing mission of France as the key to promoting progress in the Mediterranean in particular. This idea, often resting on a nostalgia for the Napoleonic adventures in the Middle East, fostered a number of different visions of a French Mediterranean. French liberals could support at one and the same time Greek independence, colonial expansion eastward and the conquest of Algeria on the grounds that it would advance Europe's and France's commercial and industrial development as well as the principles of civilization. For some this could be achieved through the expansion of free trade, and the dissemination of republican principles under French rule. For others, like Chateaubriand, it was in the name of Catholicism that France had a duty to civilize and conquer the Middle East. But it was first and foremost the Saint-Simonians who in the 1820s committed themselves to imagining the Sea as the new frontier of industrial modernity, and to reinventing the Mediterranean as the space where Western and Oriental civilization would merge, where European progress would surrender its excessive individualism in favour of the Oriental vision of society as an organic whole. These civilizing projects were always accompanied by an assessment of their geopolitical consequences, and the drawing of newly imagined political maps of the Balkans and the Mediterranean that combined the creation of new nation-states with the proliferation of French and European colonial settlements.[40]

It is a telling fact that this civilizing discourse was endorsed by some Italian exiled revolutionaries who framed the solution to the Italian and Greek national questions in like terms so as to produce visions of the Mediterranean radically different from those entertained by Grassi. Thus France could expose Mediterranean exiles to a variety of ideological tools with which to reimagine the Mediterranean geopolitical space. This is the case with the Piedmontese revolutionary Gianbattista Marochetti's *Partage de la Turquie* (1826), republished in 1830 as *Independence de l'Italie*. A republican since Bonaparte's descent into Italy, and a sub-prefect in Napoleonic Piedmont, he had been one of the leaders of the uprising there in 1821, after which he fled to Switzerland and then to France.[41] Marochetti's work appears to be first and foremost a reply to the proposal to take seriously the diplomatic implications of the Greek revolution in the Balkans and the Mediterranean put forward by the influential liberal writer Dominique De Pradt, whose writings on international affairs were widely commented on at the time. Marochetti agreed with the latter that the solution to Europe's geopolitical problems lay in the East. For him there was no doubt that the Ottoman Empire was incapable of sustaining itself. For Marochetti, Turkey represented the opposite of Western civilization, a country whose life he associated with ideas of degeneration and decay, and which he crudely compared to 'a paralysed and gangrenous limb whose severance and separation from the rest of the body could not come soon enough'.[42] Arguing against De Pradt's proposed revival of the ancient Greek Empire, he welcomed instead the expansion of Austria eastwards, and the birth of a Turkish independent state under the rule of an Austrian prince. For the Piedmontese exile, letting the Austrian Empire expand eastward and abandon the Italian peninsula would enable Italy to attain the status of an independent country, as the qualities and merits of its inhabitants deserved.[43] Marochetti regretted the fact that De Pradt, in neglecting to solve the 'Italian question', had denied Italy a role in the European balance of power, thus reducing it to being merely Europe's museum, 'a curio to be used by artists and amateurs'.[44]

However Marochetti's reaction against De Pradt's condescending attitude did not result, as had been the case with Grassi, in an outright condemnation of European imperialism. To the contrary, Marochetti was convinced that European expansion both southwards and eastwards was compatible with Italian and Greek emancipation, and would advance civilization both in Europe and in Asia. Marochetti proposed to integrate the Mediterranean into the civilizing process by calling for the colonization of islands like Sardinia, Cyprus, Malta and Crete, which in his view did not deserve self-government, by France and Great Britain, powers blessed with an undoubted economic and political superiority.[45] In particular, for Marochetti, Sardinia's agricultural production could help stimulate southern France's trade, and its possession would counterbalance England's hegemony in the Mediterranean. Italy was not a sufficiently strong nation to govern Sardinia, whose character in Marochetti's view was closer to the Spanish than to the Italian. In addition, he proposed that France should colonize Cyprus, and England take Crete. Significantly enough, Marochetti contrasted modern colonialism, based exclusively on commercial exploitation, which in his opinion was doomed to disappear, with the colonies of classical Antiquity. Contemporary French administrators were advised to do as the ancient Romans had done and to introduce the principles of modern economy and administration. Marochetti was convinced that the new settlements would enlarge the space of civil rights.[46] This distinction is telling, because it shows that for him a Mediterranean colonialism entailed the expansion of civil and political rights to the islands. Beyond the Mediterranean islands, he saw in the conquest of North Africa and the Middle East an extension of the same programme.[47] In particular, he called for a modern Crusade in the Middle East, which, unlike its medieval predecessors, would bring civilization and tolerance to the Holy Land: 'Europe will take revenge upon Asia through its good deeds, whose benefits will be mutual; and does the essence of our sublime religion not lie in these good deeds?'[48]

Although Marochetti's words were reminiscent of Voltaire's condemnation of the medieval Crusades, here he endorsed Chateaubriand's equation, as expounded in his *Itinéraire*, between the spirit of the Crusades and the moral, religious and civil task of advancing civilization in the Holy Land, whose current destitution he contrasted with its thriving commercial life in classical Antiquity.[49] In the case of the Mediterranean islands, Marochetti had been adamant that colonization would go hand in hand with rights; when discussing the Middle East, however, he remained ambiguously silent on this issue. Adumbrated in the context of the preparations for the French expedition to Algiers, a venture precipitated by commercial tensions with the Bey and by the concern to put an end to the pirates' disruption of Mediterranean trade, Marochetti's belief in France's civilizing mission built on the self-fashioning of Charles X as '*Roi trés Chretien*' and legitimate heir of Saint-Louis.[50]

Employing the industrialist language of *Le Globe* and the *Revue Encyclopédique*, Marochetti considered his political and moral project to be consistent with Europe's current commercial needs. Reshaping the political boundaries of Europe and the Balkans had to go hand in hand with the facilitation of international trade, and the abolition of monopolies and commercial protectionism, in order to foster European 'arts, industry and commerce'.[51] In addition he viewed the expansion of European trade eastward as the ideal antidote to any future commercial crisis caused by there being insufficient outlets for the increasing production of European industry.[52] An Italian adaptation of French liberal geography, Marochetti's redrawing of European and Asian borders served to place the Italian question within the framework of French liberalism's preoccupation with the political and economic primacy of France in the Mediterranean. This is why his own vision could seem plausible to contemporary liberal audiences in France, and perhaps even win their backing.

Conclusions

The liberals I have discussed here were equally preoccupied with making their liberal claims for the protection of civil liberties and with advocating a degree of self-determination compatible with the European colonial presence in the Mediterranean and in the empires bordering on it. At a time when, as Jennifer Pitts has demonstrated, liberalism and empire were increasingly being associated in the minds of Northern European intellectuals, patriots from the margins of Europe and from smaller states on the peripheries of expanding empires were faced with the intellectual and political challenge to make their claims heard and their arguments feasible and justifiable within the existing geopolitical and intellectual context. The attraction of Mediterranean intellectuals and revolutionaries toward the metropolitan centres of Europe gave them the opportunity to absorb, engage with and revise new political languages and adapt them to their aspirations. The story I have told is therefore one of the attempts made to formulate liberal demands in the context of imperial hegemony, a context that in fact seemed, in the eyes of many, to provide new ideological and practical opportunities, and of others, to represent a threat and a challenge to the principle of self-determination and the universal rights of freedom. It is also a story of resistance and reaction to dominant intellectual stances, or of manipulation of them. Intellectuals at the margins like Alfio Grassi and Giorgio Libri still managed to develop and advance arguments that, while common in the previous century, had become exceptions and oddities by the 1820s. Their views show how liberalism could also develop against the existing geopolitical status quo, with the adoption of liberal arguments serving to unmask the hypocrisy of certain European arguments based on notions of superior civilization. One could see these early debates as precursors of an intellectual tradition in Italian nationalism, which was divided over the liberal nature of the European colonial empires in the Mediterranean, and produced arguments either asserting or denying their compatibility with Italian national aspirations.[53]

The debates I have explored here do, however, belong to what Christopher Bayly has defined as the constitutional moment of early global liberalism, one which held that constitutional rights, and civil liberties, like the freedom of the press, were the precondition for any quest for autonomy, but which envisaged that these latter could be guaranteed within a variety of political systems, not necessarily confined to nation-states but including empires old and new. In this respect, the views of the Italian patriots I have discussed could be associated with those of other contemporary colonial intellectuals on both the southern and the northern shores of the Mediterranean, and in other imperial peripheries, who were grappling with the very same problems. The Indian Rammohan Roy, for instance, like Foscolo or Pananti, had believed in the compatibility of British imperial rule and forms of local autonomy, while the Algerian Othman Khodja, like Grassi and Libri, made coherent attacks upon French colonial rule on the basis of the same universal values and principles as had been advocated by the French Enlightenment.[54] Thus recovering the Mediterranean horizon of these Italian exiles' political imagination, and resituating their ideas within a broader transnational context, serves to demonstrate the extent to which these intellectuals belonged to a global colonial South where aspirations for self-determination were everywhere faced with similar constraints, and shows the benefit of reinscribing colonial rule and imperial history within the history of Europe in its southernmost peripheries.

Notes

1　　Robert Holland, *Blue-Water Empire. The British and the Mediterranean since 1800* (London: Allen Lane, 2013).

2　　C.A. Bayly, *Imperial Meridian, The British Empire and the World 1780–1830* (London: Routledge,1989), p. 196.

3　　Davide Rodogno, *Against Massacre. Humanitarian Interventions in the Ottoman Empire 1815–1914* (Princeton: Princeton University Press, 2011), pp. 36–90; Christine M. Philliou, *Biography of an Empire: Governing Ottomans in an Age of Revolution* (Berkeley: University of California Press, 2011).

4　　Linda Colley, *Captives: Britain, Empire and the World, 1600–1850* (London: Jonathan Cape, 2002); Maya Jasanoff, *Edge of Empire: Lives, Culture, and Conquest in the East, 1750–1850* (New York: Knopf, 2005); Ian Coller, *Arab France. Islam and the Making of Modern Europe, 1798–1831* (Berkeley: University of California Press, 2011).

5　　On these see Jennifer Pitts, *A Turn to Empire. The Rise of Imperial Liberalism in Britain and France* (Princeton: Princeton University Press, 2006).

6   Yves Benot and Marcel Dorigny (eds), *Grégoire et la cause des noirs (1789–1831), Combats et projets* (Paris: Publications de la Société française d'histoire d'Outre-mer et de l'Association pour l'étude de la colonisation européenne, 2005).

7   Anna Maria Rao, 'L'espace méditerranéen dans la pensée et les projets politiques des patrioties italiens. Matteo Galdi et la "république du genre humain" ', in Marcel Dorigny and Rachida Tlili Sellauti (eds), *Droit des gens et relations entre les peuples dans l'espace méditerranéen autour de la Révolution française* (Paris: SER, 2006), pp. 115–37.

8   David Armitage, 'The elephant and the whale: empires and oceans in world history', in *Foundations of Modern International Thought* (Cambridge: Cambridge University Press, 2013), p. 54.

9   Charles Pasley, *Essay on the Military Policy and Institutions of the British Empire* (London: Edmund Lloyd, 1810), p. 68.

10 Gould Francis Leckie, *An Historical Survey of the Foreign Affairs of Great Britain, with a View to Explain the Causes of the Disaster of the Late and Present Wars* (London: J. Bell, 1808), p. 47.

11 John Rosselli, *Lord William Bentinck and the British Occupation of Sicily* (Cambridge: Cambridge University Press, 1956).

12 'Cose della Gran Brettagna', *Il Cartaginese* (1804), p. 7.

13 Frederick Rosen, *Bentham, Byron and Greece. Constitutionalism, Nationalism, and Early Liberal Political Thought* (Oxford: Clarendon Press, 1992).

14 Edward Blaquiere, *Letters from the Mediterranean: Containing a Civil and Political Account of Sicily, Tripoli, Tunis and Malta* (London: Henry Colburn, 1813), vol. II, p. 225.

15 Filippo Pananti, *Narrative of a Residence in Algiers*, with notes and illustrations by Edward Blaquiere (London: Colburn, 1818).

16 Richard Whatmore, 'Neither masters nor slaves: small states and empire in the long eighteenth century', in Duncan Kelly (ed.), *Lineages of Empire. The Historical Roots of British Imperial Thought* (Oxford: Oxford University Press, 2009), pp. 53–81. See also idem, *Against War and Empire: Geneva, Britain and France in the Eighteenth Century* (New Haven: Yale University Press, 2012).

17 Christian del Vento, *'Un allievo della Rivoluzione'. U. Foscolo dal 'noviziato' letterario al 'nuovo classicismo' (1795–1806)* (Bologna: Clueb, 2003).

18 Ugo Foscolo, *Stato Politico delle Isole Jonie, Edizione Nazionale delle opere di Ugo Foscolo* 13/I (Florence: Le Monnier, 1964), pp. 8–9, 11–13.

19 Eugenio Biagini, 'Liberty, Class, and Nation-Building. Ugo Foscolo's English Constitutional Thought 1816–1827', *European Journal of Political Theory* 5 (2006), pp. 34–49; Maurizio Isabella, *Risorgimento in Exile. Italian Emigres and the Liberal International in the Post-Napoleonic Era* (Oxford: Oxford University Press, 2009), pp.70–5.

20 Foscolo, *Stato Politico*, p. 32.

21 Foscolo, *Narrative of Events Illustrating the Vicissitudes and the Cession of Parga* [1820], *Edizione Nazionale* 13/I, p. 285.

22   Quotation from Foscolo, 'Come ottenere modifiche alla costituzione delle isole
     ionie', *Edizione Nazionale* 13/II, p. 45; see also Foscolo's 'Mémoire relative
     aux affaires des isles Ioniennes', in *Edizione Nazionale* 13/II, pp. 56–61.

23   M. Calì, *Merito e patriottismo. Profili biografici e critici* (Acireale, 1884),
     pp. 63–142; Anna Maria Rao, *Esuli. L'emigrazione politica italiana in Francia
     1792–1802* (Naples: Guida, 1992).

24   Full titles are: Alfio Grassi, *Charte Turque, ou Organisation Religieuse, civile et
     militare del'Empire Ottoman: suivie de quelques réflexions sur la guerre des grecs
     contre les turcs* (Paris: Mongie, 1825) [a second edition was published in 1826], 2
     vols; and *La Sainte Alliance, Les Anglais et Les Jésuites; Leur systéme politique à
     l'égard de la Grèce, des gouvernemens constitutionels et des événemens actuels*
     (Paris: Dupont, 1827). The *Charte Turque* was republished in 1833 in Swedish as
     *Turkiska Kartan Eler Ottomanniska Rikets Religiösa, Civila och Militära
     organisation* (Örebro: Lindth, 1833), translation by Gustaf Montgomery.

25   Grassi, *La Sainte Alliance*, p. 175–6.

26   Ibid., p. 125.

27   Ibid., pp. 138–40.

28   Ibid., pp. 141–60.

29   Grassi's sources included: Giovanni Sagredo, *Histoire de l'Empire Ottoman*,
     (Paris, 1724), 7 vols; Paul Rycaut, *Histoire de l'état présent de l'Empire
     Ottoman* (Amsterdam, 1670); Vincent Mignot, *The History of the Turkish or
     Ottoman Empire* (Exeter, 1787), 4 vols; Comte de Marsigli, *Stato militare
     dell'imperio ottomano* (La Haye-Amsterdam, 1728); Achille Syllostri, *Précis
     Historique sur l'Empire ottoman* (Venice, 1757); Lady Mary Wortley
     Montagu, *Letters . . . Written, During her Travels in Europe, Asia and Africa
     . . . which contain Accounts of the Policy and Manners of the Turks* [1762]
     (Paris, 1799); Claude Charles de Peyssonel, *Examen du Livre entitulé
     Considérations sur la Guerre actuelle des Turcs, par M. De Volney*
     (Amsterdam, 1788); Ignatius Mouradgea D'Ohsson, *Tableau Général de
     L'Empire Othoman* (Paris, 1788–1824).

30   Grassi, *Charte*, vol. I, p. 35.

31   Ibid. On the Ottoman Empire as having a 'democratic' aspect see Voltaire,
     Essai sur les Moeurs et l'esprit des Nations [1756], René Pomeau (ed.),
     (Paris: Garnier, 1963), vol. II, pp. 753, 755–6.

32   Grassi, *La Sainte Alliance*, p. 70.

33   Grassi, *Charte Turque*, vol. II, p. 380; idem, *La Sainte Alliance*, pp. 43–4.

34   Jacovaky Rizo Néroulos, *Analyse raisonnée de l'ouvrage intitulé Charte
     Turque* [1827], Bertrand Bouvier (ed.) (Athens: MIET, 2013), p. 61. See the
     introduction for the international reception granted to Grassi's work, and for
     discussion of Rizo's manuscript, pp. 13–43.

35   The pamphlet was published under the peseudomyn of Linny Babagor,
     Réponse d'un Turc à la Note De M. le Vte de Chateaubriand (Bruxelles, 1825).
     A rare copy of this pamphlet is held in the Biblioteque Albertine, Bruxelles.

36   T. Todorov, 'Réflexions sur les Lettres persanes', *Romanic Review* 74 (1983),
     pp. 306–15.

37 Babagor, *Réponse d'un Turc*, p. 10.

38 Ibid., p. 33.

39 Ibid., pp. 15–18.

40 Antoine Picon, 'L'Orient saint-simonien: un imaginaire géopolitique, anthropologique et technique', in Marie-Noëlle Bourguet, Daniel Nordman, Vassilis Panayotopoulos and Maroula Sinarellis (eds), *Enquêtes en Méditerranée. Les expéditions françaises d'Égypte, de Morée et d'Algérie* (Athens: Institut de Recherches Néohelléniques, 1999), pp. 227–38; Magali Morsy, *Les saint-simoniens et l'Orient. Vers la modernité* (Aix en Provence: Edisud, 1989). One example of the discussions surrounding future geopolitical circumstances in the East is to be found in Jean Baptiste Say, 'Notions sur la Grèce, pour l'intelligence des événemens qui se préparent dans cette portion de l'Europe', *Revue Encyclopedique* XXIV (Novembre 1824), pp. 257–74; De Pradt, *L'Europe par rapport à la Grèce et à la Réformation de la Turquie* (Paris, 1826), pp. 150–71.

41 Luigi C. Bollea, 'I rivoluzionari biellesi del 1821', in *La rivoluzione piemontese del 1821* (Turin, 1927), vol. I, pp. 148–76.

42 Marochetti, *Indépendance de l'Italie*, p. 24.

43 Ibid., pp. 32–3, 36.

44 Ibid., p. 37.

45 Ibid., p. 70.

46 Ibid., pp. 68–9. On the difference between ancient and modern colonialism see Anthony Pagden, *Peoples and Empires* (New York: Random House, 2003), pp. 26–34; Guido Abbatista, 'Imperium e libertas: repubblicanesimo e ideologia imperiale all'alba dell'espansione europea in Asia 1650–1780', *Studi Settecenteschi* 20 (2000), pp. 9–49.

47 Marochetti, *Indépendance de l'Italie*, p. 96.

48 Ibid., p. 86.

49 Chateaubriand's references to the Crusades and Napoleonic rule in Egypt are in *Itinéraire de Paris à Jérusalem, et de Jérusalem à Paris* [1810–11], in Maurice Regard (ed.), *Oeuvres romanesques et voyages* (Gallimard, Bibliothèque de la Pléiade, 1969), vol. II, pp. 1052–4, 1137. For Voltaire's critical appraisal of Louis the Saint's Crusades see his *Essai sur les moeurs*, vol. I, p. 594.

50 Marochetti, *Indépendance de l'Italie*, p. 84.

51 Ibid., pp. 80–1.

52 Ibid., pp. 95–6.

53 Maurizio Isabella, 'Liberalism and Empire in the Mediterranean; the view-point of the Risorgimento', in Silvana Patriarca and Lucy Riall (eds), *The Risorgimento Revisited. Nationalism and Culture in Nineteenth-Century Italy* (London-New York: Palgrave Macmillan, 2012), pp. 232–54. Marochetti's ideas were taken on by Charles Didier in his introduction to General Guglielmo Pepe's *L'Italie Politique et ses rapports avec la France et l'Angleterre* (Paris, 1839), pp. 5–20; Léonard de Sismondi, 'L'Avenir', *Revue*

Encyclopédique XLVV (1830), p. 525ff.:, also in Umberto Marcelli (ed.), *Opuscoli Politici* (Bologna: Zuffi, 1954), pp. 125–47.

54   See Jennifer Pitts, 'Liberalism and Empire in an Nineteenth-Century Algerian Mirror', *Modern Intellectual History* 2/6 (2009), pp. 287–313; Christopher Bayly, 'Rammohan Roy and the Advent of Constitutional Liberalism in India, 1800–1830', *Modern Intellectual History* 1/4 (2007), pp. 25–41; and the chapter by Ian Coller in this volume.

CHAPTER FIVE

Ottomans on the Move:

Hassuna D'Ghies and the 'New Ottomanism' of the 1830s

Ian Coller

In January 1836, Hassuna D'Ghies, a North African from Tripoli, was appointed as the editor of *Le Moniteur Ottoman*, the official newspaper of the Ottoman Empire.[1] He held this important post for only a few months, becoming a casualty of the epidemic that raced through Istanbul later that year. In the larger sweep of history this brief tenure might seem insignificant, but it can tell us something about the great changes afoot in the world system at this moment. For the young North African, the journey to Istanbul represented a shift away from the liberal ideas he had advocated in the 1820s, and his associated project of creating a self-governing national state, to the wider embrace of a multinational Muslim empire that had existed for five centuries. This move from nation to empire appears to contrast with the conventional story of European nationalisms. The push to modernize the Ottoman Empire in this period has often been understood as the imposition of Western ideas on a reactionary society clinging to religious conservatism. If we examine D'Ghies' trajectory carefully we can see that this picture is wrong. His embrace of Ottoman modernization was an active and indigenous strategy of resistance to European imperial dominance, rather than a passive imitation of Western 'civilizing' norms. His path, and that of other 'new Ottomans' of the period, suggests a much wider transnational base for Ottoman modernization than has been imagined in nationally-framed studies: a reform agenda that began from a much more plural base, before national, ethnic and religious divisions appeared on the horizon later in the century.

Hassuna D'Ghies came from an important North African family in the Libyan city of Tripoli. The Qaramanli family – descendents of Ottoman Turks and local women – had seized the governorate at the beginning of the eighteenth century and compelled a weakened Ottoman Porte to recognize them as hereditary rulers. The D'Ghies family was also of Anatolian origin, but apparently more legitimate, as Hassuna D'Ghies himself explained, describing himself as 'sixth in lineal descent from an officer who was selected by the Sublime Porte about 150 years ago from a family of Erzurum in Asia to be the Viceroy of Tripoli'.[2] The young Hassuna was given a traditional Islamic education at the Madrasa of Tajura, but in 1813, at the age of twenty-one, he was sent to France, and encouraged by his father 'to travel in Europe in order to unite a knowledge of the civilization of Europe with that peculiar of his own country, foreseeing it probable from the rank and influence of his family that [he] might be summoned to the direction of public affairs'.[3] Speaking French, English and Italian as well as Arabic and Turkish, he was admired by contemporaries as a sophisticated and articulate advocate of liberal reform. His conspicuous Islamic dress marked his continued belonging to Muslim society, as well as his noble lineage as a 'sharif' descended from the family of the Prophet Muhammad. But his impeccable outward appearances and affable manners concealed the profound internal dissonance that he faced as a North African liberal struggling with the onslaught of European empire.

Julia Clancy Smith has written of a 'Mediterranean community of thought' in the middle part of the nineteenth century, created by 'people on the move' who helped to transform both North Africa and the Ottoman Empire, creating new flows between Europe, the Middle East and North Africa, and along the 'older axes of exchange linking the Maghrib to the Ottoman heartlands'.[4] This chapter will explore Hassuna D'Ghies' journeys between Tripoli, Paris, Marseilles, London and Istanbul, and the impact of these 'moves' on his thought, as he drew European ideas, African customs and Islamic principles together in the struggle for a durable constitutional model that could hold at bay both civil war and European aggression.

Mobilities and modernizations in the Ottoman Empire

The first steam boats began to chug along the sea lanes of the Ottoman Empire in the early 1830s: 'Of all economic activities in the Middle East,' Charles Issawi has suggested, 'transport was the one most deeply revolutionized in the course of the 19th century.'[5] After centuries of relative stasis, the speed of travel across the Mediterranean was suddenly accelerated. The travelling time between Ottoman and European capitals was cut by a half or more: it was now possible to travel from Istanbul to Marseilles in just over a week. The new circulation of goods, people and ideas brought new possibilities and new dangers. It brought new connections, contacts and exchanges between the Ottoman world and Europe, whether in commercial, political or military form: but it also made feasible the seizure of further-flung territories by European powers emerging from the arms race of the Napoleonic Wars. This revolution began with mobility of passengers and post, and only later transformed the movement of goods, as steam gradually became cheaper for freight. By the 1850s, European travellers could suggest that the mobility associated with this new ease of transport had rendered the Turks more 'cosmopolite'. European tourists poured into the Ottoman domains for the first time, and their travel accounts flooded the market. These travellers vulgarized what was described in European cabinets as the 'Eastern Question' – the view that the Ottoman Empire was destined either to collapse under the assault of nationalism and religious difference, or to be partitioned among European powers.

The revolution in transport also gave rise to new kinds of movement within the Ottoman domains. Ottoman envoys, merchants, students and travellers increasingly travelled to Europe, and gained a first-hand sense of political developments in European countries, including national struggles in Spain and Italy, military and naval reorganization in Prussia and Britain, and the revolutionary events in France. The new transport also promoted circulation of the Ottoman bureaucracy within the empire, mobilizing travellers and pilgrims, communication and news. It made the new Ottoman newspaper whose helm D'Ghies took in 1836 more than just an almanac for the teeming capital. It brought the capital in new ways into the furthest provinces, and brought the provinces to Istanbul. 'The paper made its way to the coffeehouses', Robert Walsh wrote in 1836, 'and the same Turk that I had noticed before dozing, . . . I now saw actually awake, with the paper in his hand, eagerly spelling out the news.'[6] This vibrant New Ottomanism of the 1830s has been neglected by historians, who have often seen this period only as an uncertain attempt to 'catch-up' with the West, favoured by a handful of elite reformers in the capital, while the rest of the empire remained entrenched in the old ways.

Recent historical work has emphasized the importance of mobility, diaspora and exile in the making of nationalism: what has been called the 'patriotism of the expatriates'. Where exiles were once seen as marginal to the story of national awakenings, they may now be better understood as transnational vectors of the movement of ideas that fostered the emergence of nationalism on a wider scale. Yet at the same time that this 'Liberal International', as Maurizio Isabella has called it, championed self-determination for European nations, it was also moving toward a new embrace of imperialism.[7] While seeking to break away from multi-ethnic empires in Europe, many liberals looked to national expansion in Asia, Africa and the Americas, following the British model. Indeed, many believed that the new imperialism would offer both the stabilizing foundation of prosperity and commerce for national development and civilizing effects that would bring other parts of the world to share their own universal liberal values. This 'liberal turn to Empire' has been studied by a range of recent historians across a variety of European national histories.[8] As the example of D'Ghies demonstrates, North Africans were fully engaged with these developments, and were seeking ways to shape the destiny of their societies. D'Ghies did so, however, in a way that is very different from his European contemporaries, ultimately finding in modernized forms of multinational empire the liberal pluralism he had once sought in constitutional nationalism. A variety of figures from very different backgrounds came to see Ottoman modernization as a potential response to what they viewed as a dangerous imbalance in the world system. It is worth exploring that context before following the particular trajectory of Hassuna D'Ghies from European liberalism through anti-imperialism to the 'Ottoman turn' of the 1830s.

The New Ottomanism of the 1830s

An Englishman, a Turk, a Frenchman and an Arab, had each, in different positions, arrived at almost identical views. They had all, by patient study, and long acquaintance with the East and the West, fitted themselves to become the instruments of counteracting the destructive march of events. They are gone; but they have left behind them a regret, which proves that their labours have not been all in vain; and that the cause they espoused is one which has already established a claim to regard from the sympathies of mankind . . .[9]

In this passage from his book *The Spirit of the East*, David Urquhart, a Scottish writer and diplomat who became the most powerful Western voice in defence of the Ottoman Empire during the second half of the nineteenth century, described an important shift that had taken place in the early 1830s. This phenomenon, which we may call 'New Ottomanism', had a wider dimension parallel to the diasporic dimensions of nationalism recent historians have observed. Şerif Mardin considered the emergence of a self-styled 'Young Ottoman' movement during the 1860s as the point of origin of the modern secular Turkish state.[10] Recent studies of this movement have placed more emphasis on David Urquhart's influence upon this 'pioneering' liberal opposition.[11] Urquhart himself acknowledged that his ideas had emerged alongside and in close connection to those of the generation that preceded him, and in particular this group of individuals whose untimely deaths concealed their influence on an emerging Ottoman model of modernity. This complexity of the flow of ideas – not a great river running from Europe to the rest of the world, but a much broader delta of interconnecting channels and tributaries – becomes evident once we begin to follow the peregrinations of 'people on the move'.

The difference between these 'New Ottomans' of the 1830s and their Young Ottoman successors lay in their national, cultural and religious heterogeneity: Jewish, Christian and Muslim, coming from Europe, Africa and Asia. What each appeared to recognize in the Ottoman system was a structure of plurality very different from the monistic and imperialist nationalisms emerging in Europe: a kind of 'imagined community' quite different from the national model. They sought to modernize the system, not by utopian schemes like those of the Saint-Simonians, for example, but rather through participating in the practical project of Ottoman modernity launched by the Sultan Mahmud II, which culminated in the great reform decree of 1839, known as the Gülhane Rescript.[12]

The four men Urquhart named – along with Urquhart himself – give important context to D'Ghies' 'Ottoman turn'. Their heterogeneity demonstrates a significant shift in understandings of what it meant to be an Ottoman in the early nineteenth century. This was a highly differentiated 'Ottomanity' no longer confined to a single religion or a single ethnicity, but remarkably plural in accommodating diverse origins and belonging. Each of them had been educated in Europe, and had acquired fluency in key European and Ottoman languages. None of them considered their religion a barrier to their Ottomanism. Urquhart's 'Englishman' was Arthur Lumley Davids, an English Orientalist and lawyer of Jewish origin who advocated for Jewish civil rights. His key published work, however, was a book on modern Turkish grammar dedicated to Sultan Mahmud II 'by whose genius and talents the Ottoman Empire has been regenerated'.[13]

The 'Turk' Urquhart named, Osman Noureddin Pasha, was in fact Egyptian, and his 'Ottoman turn' was a turn away from the irredentism of the ambitious governor of Egypt, Muhammad 'Ali. A member of the first group of students sent to Europe in 1818 by the Egyptian governor, Osman Noureddin was later appointed admiral of the Egyptian fleet in its support of the Ottoman defence of Cyprus. After military successes, Muhammad 'Ali declared himself Khedive (viceroy) of Egypt and Sudan, and sent an army to invade and occupy Syria in 1830. Despite the plum position he had been given, Osman defected back to the Ottomans in 1833. His action represented a striking example of the return of provincial notables to the renewed Ottoman model, and away from the Westernizing autocracy represented by the new *khedivial* system in Egypt. This parallels D'Ghies' decision to abandon the tottering Qaramanli state in Tripoli, and to support instead the re-establishment of Ottoman sovereignty in the province.

Urquhart's Frenchman, Alexandre Blacque (Blak Bey in Turkish), preceded D'Ghies in the post he would take up, serving as editor of *Le Moniteur Ottoman* from 1831 to 1835. He was described by the British consul as 'a person of extreme liberal principles'[14] – so extreme indeed, that they brought him into conflict with his own government. In the 1820s he edited a series of French-language newspapers in Smyrna, a town with a large and diverse population. His newspapers, *Le Spectateur Oriental* and *Le Courrier de*

Smyrne, emerged from a line of publications initiated in Istanbul and Izmir during the 1790s. He opposed the French support for irredentist movements within the Ottoman domains, excoriated French compromises with Russian expansionism and considered the imposition of Western forms onto Ottoman society to be a mistake. Blacque's views incurred the wrath of the French consulate, and in 1829 the French government took advantage of the sovereignty over its own subjects accorded by the 'Capitulations' (the code covering subjects of European powers in the Ottoman Empire) to close down the newspaper by force. The sultan then invited Blacque to Istanbul to open the first Ottoman newspaper on the model of his Smyrna gazette, published in French with a concurrent Turkish edition entitled *Takvîm-i Vekâyi* (*The Calendar of Events*). When Blacque was despatched on a diplomatic mission for the sultan, the editorship of the *Moniteur* was taken over by D'Ghies, the last of Urquhart's four exemplary figures. D'Ghies brought with him more than simply a romantic vision of Turkish culture, like Davids, or a political liberalism, like Blacque. He had come from a troubled North African province that had just returned to the Ottoman fold after a century of virtual independence, helping to reinforce its resistance to European colonization, but also serving to strengthen the Ottoman centre in a rare moment of consolidation.

D'Ghies also had a much closer relationship to David Urquhart himself. Urquhart was born in Scotland in 1805, but according to the account of his life printed in his own journal, *The Portfolio*, he was educated in Europe while accompanying his mother on her travels, and began university studies in France before continuing at Oxford. It was in France, at the age of seventeen, that an encounter set him on the path that defined his career:

> A Turk, who had travelled a great deal, and who had met the young Urquhart at Marseilles, called to him the attention of Jeremy Bentham. Bentham was convinced that much useful instruction regarding human Society might be obtained by an unprejudiced Examination of the East, and he moreover foresaw, the great influence these Countries were soon to exercise on the Destinies of Europe.[15]

Most biographers of Urquhart have noted his early and close association with Jeremy Bentham, but have neglected D'Ghies' role in bringing him to Bentham's notice. These five figures, while not constituting a circle, were interconnected in multiple ways through the strategic elements of Ottoman modernization: language, the press, constitutionalism and military reform. Urquhart and D'Ghies maintained the closest connection, however, and their intertwining stories help to illuminate D'Ghies' path toward embracing an Ottoman model of modernization, as well as the legacy of his ideas, which partly found their realization through the friend who outlived him.

Hassuna D'Ghies' liberal trajectory: Marseilles, Paris and London

There is little indication of D'Ghies' activities during his first years in France. Later accounts suggested he made a living importing perfume and shawls from North Africa.[16] It is likely that he mixed with the considerable Arabic-speaking population of Marseilles and Paris, which included both the second generation of Egyptians and Syrians who had arrived in France after the end of the French occupation of Egypt, as well as North Africans, Levantines and Turks attracted to France for study or commerce.[17] Then, in 1822, at thirty years old, he chose a different path, and left Paris for London, the world centre of liberal activity.

D'Ghies' first project in London was the publication of a pamphlet critical of the increasingly interventionist tendency emerging out of the British abolitionist movement. The pamphlet was presented as an open letter to his friend, the MP James Scarlett, from an 'African philanthropist' who challenged the right of this society to speak on his behalf. Nailing his liberal colours to the mast, D'Ghies declared an unconditional commitment to the principle of liberty: 'Nothing is more noble,' he wrote, 'than to contribute all that we can towards the abolition of slavery wherever it exists.'[18] Africans, however, needed real economic development to offset the crisis provoked by abolition, and he called on the members of the society to contribute. Any hopes he may have had for a dialogue with this institution, however, were quickly disappointed. As his pamphlet hinted, this association was devoted more to the furtherance of the evangelizing Protestantism that Linda Colley has seen as a key dimension of British identity, than to any project for improving government in Africa.[19] The African Institution professed for its object 'the welfare of human nature' without clearly declaring its object and purpose, and without consulting Africans.

More important in D'Ghies' evolving political thought was his pamphlet's insistence on the insufficiency of the modes of European knowledge about North Africa:

It is not . . . in ridiculing the customs of the country, – it is not in openly shunning its manners, and its languages, that you can conquer the hearts, and then the minds of the inhabitants; neither is it in filling volumes with frivolous anecdotes and tales; it is by studying circumstances, – it is by respecting the ruling prejudices, even though unreasonable, – it is by preparing innovations at a distance, so that they may no longer appear innovations.[20]

This passage gives some hint of the difference between D'Ghies and the European liberals of his time. He rejected European universalism, and insisted that liberal values in Muslim societies must function in accordance with the 'customs' and the 'circumstances' of Islam to have any chance of success. The notion of 'innovation' so popular in the post-Enlightenment West raised significant obstacles in the Islamic context, because *bid'a*, or innovation in religious matters, was explicitly forbidden.[21] This apparent barrier, D'Ghies believed, could be negotiated by preparing political change at a distance, designing it to suit the commands of Islam, and only then introducing it into North African society.

To accomplish this project, D'Ghies turned to the most influential philosopher of the period, Jeremy Bentham, who had already expressed considerable interest in Africa, and proved very amenable indeed to the kinds of ideas D'Ghies wished to develop. As a disciple of Bentham, D'Ghies served actively to promote British and French liberal connections with the Muslim world, particularly by introducing a number of prominent visitors from Persia, North Africa and the Middle East passing through Paris and London, including the Persian prince Mirzim Mohammed Khan and the Algerian notable, Hamdan ben Othman Khodja. Bentham described the latter as 'another Mahometan disciple . . . who appears a very honest and well-disposed man, and . . . in high trust with his sovereign, the Dey of Algiers'.[22] The young David Urquhart's introduction into this prestigious liberal circle by D'Ghies helped to set him on the path that would make him so closely associated with the Muslim world. Through Bentham, Muslim intellectuals made contact with other circles, including French, Spanish, Italian, Latin American and Indian liberals. Bentham actively promoted these networks as part of his international project of institutional reform and education: 'I need scarce observe' he wrote, 'how truly natural allies Greece and Haiti are of Columbia.'[23]

It is unsurprising, therefore, that Bentham encouraged the youthful David Urquhart to seize the opportunity arising out of the British engagement for the independence of Greece after 1821, one of the great liberal causes uniting British and French liberals, and even many Christian conservatives, in the same camp. Urquhart enrolled in the Anglo-Greek maritime forces in 1827–8 and participated in the Battle of Navarino, a rout of the Ottoman navy that confirmed the grave military weakness of the empire and seemed to portend its imminent disintegration. In the wake of this disaster to which he had contributed, Urquhart was struck by the fortitude of the Turks in defeat rather than the glory of the Greeks in victory:

When I first landed on the shores of Greece, more interested in the nature of the rocks than in the sanguinary contest which was there proceeding, I was soon filled with hatred and aversion for the Turkish name; and, with the enthusiasm of youthful feeling, I became a partisan. But the Ottoman, who had aroused this animosity by the violence of triumph, dispelled it when he appeared in defeat and captivity, – a personification of stoical firmness and of dignified resignation. The sympathy which is the tribute of misfortune, I now transferred to the vanquished; but that sympathy was combined with admiration for a fortitude and respect for a character, the energy and durability of which I never could have known but for the trial to which I had seen it subjected.[24]

Most disturbingly, in place of the Greek flag of independence, Urquhart saw instead the three flags of Britain, Russia and France – the latter not tricoloured, but the white flag of the restored Bourbon monarchy. Where Ottoman rule had 'habitually respected property and local customs', Urquhart began to feel he had been sent 'to plant stakes'.[25] He began to sympathize strongly with the Ottoman system, and to view the Greek insurrection as largely a European imperialist ruse. His views and observations, first despatched as letters to his mother, attracted the attention of other British officials, and travelled as far as the monarch, William IV. During his subsequent residence in Istanbul, Urquhart amplified his views in his pamphlet of 1834, *England, France, Russia and Turkey*, which ran into five editions and did much to convince key members of the British establishment that the disintegration of the Ottoman Empire would undermine British imperial interests.

A constitutional trajectory: securities against misrule

Hassuna D'Ghies, meanwhile, was working closely with Bentham, who had assumed a kind of fatherly mentorship in regard to the younger man. Bentham wrote of his new protégé: 'D'Ghies is a very extraordinary young man: two words will suffice to shew you to what a degree he is so: he is a disciple and an adopted son of mine ... his desire of contributing to the improvement of the state of society in his own country is ardent and indefatigable.'[26] Like Urquhart, Bentham was fascinated by the detail and complexity of Muslim society, having visited Istanbul and Tunis in his youth. He questioned D'Ghies exhaustively about every detail of Tripolitan society. They rapidly conceived a collaborative project to create a constitution for Tripoli, which Bentham later published under the title *Securities against Misrule: Adapted to a Mohammedan State and prepared with particular reference to Tripoli in Barbary*.[27] The prime attraction for Bentham in this project was the long-term development of a universal legal code that would ensure the legal framework for the happiness of all peoples: the application of this code to a Muslim state would be a key test of its effectiveness.

For his young protégé, the stakes were more urgent. The death of the elderly pasha threatened to unleash a civil war, which might come sooner if any of his descendants became impatient and chose to seize power.[28] D'Ghies conceived this as a wider project that would solve some of the problems he had observed in his earlier pamphlet. 'I want to introduce a more liberal system,' he was reported to have said. 'It must be represented to the monarch as a guarantee for his personal safety – to the people it would recommend itself. Adopted in Tripoli, it would spread to Tunis, and so fly along the coast.'[29] His 'African' project had become a 'North African' one, and increasingly centred on the adaptation of an existing sense of Muslim constitutionalism: 'Ruler! act not purely of thy own will. That which is of moment do it not but with wise and honest counsellors.' Thus, where Bentham hoped to develop a universal code that could be applied to Muslim societies, D'Ghies began to view the existing Islamic political structures as a more suitable basis for constitutional change.

A key difference between the developing views of Urquhart and D'Ghies at this time lay in Urquhart's tendency to idealize the 'Turk' in both an ethnic and a religious sense, and to interpret many abuses of the system as degenerations from an earlier and more glorious state – much as his Ottoman interlocutors at the imperial centre tended to do. D'Ghies, coming from the troubled periphery of the empire, was fully aware of the perilous circumstances of contemporary Muslim life, which did not admit of such idealization. Transitions of power in North African societies during this time could be extremely violent: the instability of the laws of inheritance, combined with the questionable legitimacy of the ruling families, could provoke bloody actions on the part of those who wanted to seize power or hold onto it.

D'Ghies' sister was married to the pasha's son: on gaining power, a new ruler might well eliminate members of his family, including women and children. It is unsurprising, then, that D'Ghies became frustrated with gradualist action. In the last months of his residence in Britain, he began to investigate a scheme for military intervention, hoping to gain the backing of John Quincy Adams, the president of the United States. The young republic had already fought a war on the 'shores of Tripoli' in 1801, and Bentham helped D'Ghies to draw up a plan for regime change. In the event, Bentham seems never to have sent these letters to Adams, and the planned military intervention remained a pipe-dream.[30]

Connections between Urquhart and D'Ghies faded during this period. The Scotsman's attraction to the Ottoman system was not shared by his North African friend. Tripoli had broken away decisively from the Ottoman Empire more than a century earlier, and was the most independent of the three 'regencies' of the Maghreb – Algiers, Tunis and Tripoli. The expansion of Algiers during the late eighteenth century, with the withdrawal of Spanish forces, had left it the major power in North Africa, with a powerful influence on its smaller neighbour Tunis. In turn, Tunis played a key role in the power struggles of Tripoli and its tributary cities like Derna and Benghazi. In the West, Morocco had maintained its independence under its own dynasty. D'Ghies saw a similar 'national' path for Tripoli. Moving outside the framework of Bentham's universalizing ideas, he sought to refashion the abstract, highly rational formula to fit the concrete realities of geography, customs and religion. Yet this remained primarily a European model: D'Ghies still viewed the remaining traces of Ottoman suzerainty in North Africa as obsolete. Tripoli's development under European liberal tutelage would transform the local regime into an enlightened constitutional monarchy on the British model.

During this time, as Bentham noted in his letters, D'Ghies received word that his father had died in Tripoli. This news plunged the young man into great turmoil. Although Bentham did not perceive it, this event changed the stakes entirely. Soon afterward, D'Ghies chose to return to Tripoli. To Bentham's dismay, he abandoned the constitutional project and accepted office in the Qaramanli government, stepping into his father's vacant role as minister of foreign affairs. He sought henceforth to reform the regime from within rather than imposing a new constitutional structure from outside. His activity during this period is difficult to gauge: it became notable more in the scandal that brought this brief chapter to an end, than in any clear achievements of reform.

D'Ghies' return to Tripoli in 1825 coincided with the arrival of a highly educated French consul, Joseph Rousseau, a relative of the philosopher Jean-Jacques. Rousseau had been raised in Persia, and had native fluency in a number of oriental languages. At the same time, another accomplished Orientalist, Jacob Gråberg de Hemsö, had been appointed as the Swedish consul. In 1827, the two consuls collaborated to produce a monthly newspaper titled *L'Investigateur africain*.[31] This must be counted among the very first press publications founded in North Africa. No original copies of the journal have been found, despite the researches carried out by Italian scholars, but some summaries of articles were sent to the *Bulletin de la Société Géographique*.[32] It is impossible to determine what role D'Ghies might have played in this publication, which has not survived in printed form. Given his demonstrated links to both consuls, it seems likely that he may have furnished either information or connections: he certainly procured for Gråberg di Hemsö highly sought-after manuscripts of the 'universal history' by the great fourteenth-century North African historian Ibn Khaldun. The Swede described D'Ghies as 'a prodigy of learning, knowledge and civility', noting his proficiency and learning in Arabic and European languages.[33] However, this liberal exchange of ideas was destined to be cut short by the more brutish onslaught of imperial rivalries.

An anti-imperial trajectory: Tripoli and Algiers

The arrival of the French consul Rousseau provoked fierce resentment from the British consul in Tripoli, George Warrington, an irascible figure with the kind of political and financial hold over affairs in Tripoli that has been described elsewhere as 'proconsular despotism'.[34] In 1826 Warrington accused both Rousseau and D'Ghies of involvement in the death of a British explorer, Major Laing.[35] The ensuing scandal – which space precludes me from recounting here – embroiled the whole D'Ghies family, the pasha and the French, British and American consular representatives, and threatened to serve as a trigger for imperial intervention either from France or Britain, or even from other powers such as the Kingdom of the Two Sicilies.[36] D'Ghies was well-placed to observe the disastrous policy being pursued by the pasha under the influence of the British consul.

In 1827, a simple insult to the French ambassador in Algiers by the ruling Dey became the pretext for a French blockade and ultimately a military invasion of Algiers. D'Ghies learned a great deal about the nature of this imperial intervention over the subsequent years. After leaving Tripoli in fear of his life, he worked closely with Algerian notables exiled in Paris to produce an eloquent work protesting the French invasion and conquest of their city. This group did not, however, promote the restoration of Ottoman sovereignty, but rather sought French agreement to the establishment of an independent state.[37] The book they produced, *Le Miroir*, was officially authored by Hamdan Khodja – the same Algerian who had been introduced into Bentham's circle by D'Ghies in the 1820s.[38] The cover page declared that it was translated by 'H.D., Oriental'. No original Arabic manuscript has ever been located, and French commentators of the time claimed that Hamdan could not have written it alone. D'Ghies may well have contributed more extensively to the text he 'translated'. The 'historical and statistical survey' of Algiers it provided appears to reflect D'Ghies' established emphasis on the primacy of indigenous knowledge about Africa. Its title made reference to the long tradition of 'mirrors for princes' that characterized Islamic political writing.[39] In his report to the French Commission of 1833 that set out to determine the future of the French conquest, Hamdan Khodja mentioned D'Ghies' close involvement in the political preparation of the protest deputation. *Le Miroir* drew, like many of D'Ghies' works, upon a wide range of liberal and Enlightenment ideas, and combined a fierce critique of French behaviour in Algiers with a careful study of the terrain, peoples and customs of the region. By using these ideas, D'Ghies and Hamdan Khodja sought to claim a position within the circle of 'civilized' peoples with rights to autonomy and good government. As Hamdan exclaimed in his testimony to the Commission, 'As for me, I do not read French, but I am fully apprised through the faithful translation into Arabic by the Sherif Hassuna D'Ghiez [*sic*] of Vattel's *Droit des Gens* ... Can anyone deny these principles? Are Africans excluded from human society?'[40]

What became clear at the end of this Commission, which revealed so clearly the abuses committed by the French and the absurdity of colonization, was that Africans were indeed excluded from the international 'society' established by Europe after 1815. International law would not protect small states outside Europe against the abrogation of their sovereignty by Europeans. The events of 1830 to 1833 demonstrated that no protection was to be gained even from the most liberal regimes in Europe, and indeed, the turn to imperialism of the liberal opposition demonstrated that the universal values of liberalism had been harnessed into a European expansionist project.[41] The only Muslim state that might still maintain its membership of this new world order was the Ottoman Empire. This helps to explain D'Ghies' Ottoman turn after 1833.

An Ottoman trajectory: from liberal empire to imperial liberalism

Tripoli soon felt the impact of the new imperial climate. After disembarking the army at Sidi Ferruch near Algiers in June 1830, the French fleet sailed east to demand a retraction of the accusations made against the French consul Rousseau by the pasha of Tripoli. The pasha was compelled to sign a humiliating treaty and pay the French an indemnity of 800,000 francs. Tripoli's fate could soon echo that of its neighbour to the west, unless the money was rapidly forthcoming. In 1832, at Warrington's instigation, the British sent their own fleet to demand payment of all sums owing to their merchants, a sum amounting to $180,000: the consul refused to accept anything less than the whole.

To raise these impossibly large sums, the pasha sent his army to squeeze the communities of the interior, who rose in revolt against these extortions. Their cause was adopted by Emhammed, the offspring of the pasha's deceased elder son, who claimed the succession. Reportedly popular with the mass of the population, he was also supported by Warrington, who hoped to foment a situation that would force British imperial intervention.[42] After a siege of the city by the rebel forces in the succeeding months, the pasha abdicated in favour of his son Ali. The rebels insisted that Emhammed must rule instead.

The situation in Tripoli rapidly descended into civil war, with the city supporting Ali while the countryside called for his replacement with Emhammed. Neither candidate had a clear succession according to traditional Islamic principles of legitimacy, which favoured the eldest male member of the family rather than strict primogeniture. Emhammed was supported by a broad alliance of forces, along with the British consul Warrington, who promised them his country's support. Warrington had exceeded his proconsular authority: Tripoli was not an imperial priority, and the activities of D'Ghies, who had travelled to London both to clear his name and to expose Warrington's meddling in local affairs, helped persuade the British to withdraw their ships to Malta, leaving the parties to settle their differences. The rebels then appealed instead to the Ottoman Porte against the rule of Ali, who, they claimed, was brutal and unjust.

In 1835, it appeared that their call had been answered, as an Ottoman fleet sailed into Tripoli. Neither side was sure which claimant would receive the sultan's *firman* recognizing his rule. In the event, a very different project was afoot. When Ali boarded the Ottoman envoy's ship, he was arrested and placed in custody for removal to Istanbul.[43] The envoy himself, Mustafa Effendi, declared himself as the governor appointed by Istanbul. The restoration of Ottoman sovereignty thus served to stabilize Tripoli and the region, and staved off further European intervention for the remainder of the century. It was not until the fracturing of the Ottoman Empire just before the war of 1914 that Italy would seize Libya as a colony.

The D'Ghies family were central to these events leading up to the Ottoman restoration: it is difficult to gauge exactly what part they played, as so many dealings remained secret, and so many accounts were partisan in the extreme. It is clear that Hassuna D'Ghies remained in contact with his friend David Urquhart during this time: the latter was in residence in Istanbul during this period from 1832 to 1837, and this may have provided a line of communication to the Ottoman government. In Paris, it appears that D'Ghies was in contact with the Ottoman ambassador Rechid Pasha, who recommended him for the position in Istanbul. It seems likely that he played some role in the Ottoman decision to support none of the warring parties, but rather to re-establish direct control. Certainly, it demonstrates that he had changed his position on the creation of an autonomous state in Tripoli, and now supported its reintegration into the Ottoman Empire as the only way to resist European imperialism.

It may be the experience D'Ghies brought with him from the short-lived *Investigateur Africain* that recommended him for the position of editor, as he had not otherwise occupied such a role. The *Moniteur Ottoman/Takvîm-i Vakâ'i* was a centrepiece of the new Ottoman model: it was in many ways the response of the sultan, Mahmud II, to the new Arabic language newspaper established in Cairo, and edited by Rifa'a al-Tahtawi, the influential Egyptian liberal thinker. The great challenge to the Ottoman system at this moment came not from Greece or from Europe, but from Egypt, where Muhammad 'Ali threatened to create a rival power base and to take the helm of an Islamic modernity away from Istanbul. Thus we may see in the Ottoman newspaper not so much an imitation of the European press, as the beginning of a powerful rivalry within Islam to take control of the forms of modernization. The defection of Osman Noureddin Pasha, such an important figure in the regime of Muhammad 'Ali, demonstrates the importance of this conflict of loyalties for Muslims in this period.

The choice of Hassuna D'Ghies to edit the newspaper in itself suggests the vitality of Ottoman reform at this moment: certainly in the eyes of Europeans, he was a figure who was able to engage both European and Islamic traditions of thought. Horatio Southgate described him as 'free ... from the narrow prejudices of his religion ... qualified to be an able coadjutor in recommending and defending the great work of reform commenced by his master'.[44] Most of all, he noted, the aim of D'Ghies' work was to introduce reforms by 'show[ing] them to be consonant with the doctrines of Islamism'. One example of such reform was the question of quarantine, which had been opposed by some Islamic scholars as a constraint on the free movement of people and goods, who were under divine protection.[45] But without this practice, trade was obstructed by danger of disease, and epidemics threatened to sweep through Muslim lands, decimating the population and destroying institutional and economic stability. Hamdan Khodja, who had also travelled to Istanbul in exile from Algiers in the 1830s, is known to have written a text in Arabic on the subject.[46] The *Moniteur Ottoman* published a series of articles explaining the practice and its justification in Islamic thought. Tragically, however, D'Ghies himself became a victim of epidemic disease, dying from plague in the winter of 1836–7.

The work to which D'Ghies applied himself was very much an attempt to find a structure *within* Islamic tradition for building a new kind of Ottoman constitutionalism from the ground up, a project that would later be taken up by the 'Young Ottomans'. The newspaper itself

> simultaneously appeared in three languages, Turkish, Greek and French, to these were to have been added Persian, Arabic, Armenian, and Bulgarian, but a watchful power, alarmed at this revelation of the importance of Constantinople, arrested the further prosecution of the design; though she was unable to put an entire stop to a publication, which had awakened the full sympathies of the Turkish empire.[47]

On his death, Hassuna D'Ghies was to be succeeded in his post by his brother Mohammed, but according to a French contemporary, who had been hired to work on the *Moniteur Ottoman*, their North African origin provoked hostility among the Turkish notables: 'Ottoman pride could not bear the idea that two brothers of this origin, whose talents were a reproach to the locals, could succeed one another in a position that might lead to the highest rank.'[48] In this sense, the internal ethnic, linguistic and nationalist strains of the Ottoman system may be seen even at this early moment. The 'Young Ottomans' who would emerge as the successors to this earlier movement would include only Turks, and they would be followed by a movement that called itself quite explicitly the 'Young Turks'.

Of the five men with whom we began, then, Hassuna D'Ghies' ideological shift in this moment of the 1830s is the clearest. Where the others had long maintained pro-Ottoman or neutral views, D'Ghies had actively worked for the independence from Ottoman rule of Tripoli, and North Africa in general, whether autonomously or under European tutelage. His decision to enter Ottoman service was not taken lightly, and it seems to have provoked resentment among those in the capital who viewed the North African provinces as a fractious periphery to be controlled by force. Hassuna D'Ghies' trajectory, taken in the context of a larger movement, suggests that the resistance to European imperialism in its earliest moments could take forms other than those of religious insurrection or territorial proto-nationalism. Nor was this path toward the 'Ottoman turn' a simple one: it took him from his initial attempts to reposition North African polities in the new post-revolutionary world system, to a more authoritarian model of state-based reform in the government of his native city of Tripoli, and finally to the model of a reformed multi-ethnic empire. Like D'Ghies, many of those who have been considered the 'subject peoples' of the Ottoman Empire in fact both drew upon and helped to shape its path to modernity, as an alternative to the advance of European imperialism. D'Ghies read widely in the constitutional thought of Europe, but he applied it in quite different ways, seeking to find ways to adapt it to the requirements of a Muslim society, and then using European ideas to critique European practices. Above all, as Rabindranath Tagore would put it a century later, he learned to distinguish what was 'merely European' from what was substantively modern in the sense of a larger human experience. His path anticipated the increasing mobility of the generation that followed, Ottomans who moved more and more fluidly through the empire, and between Europe, Asia and Africa. Despite his early death, his ideas left a mark in the work of his friend and colleague David Urquhart, who passed it on to the new generation of 'Young Ottomans' in subsequent decades. In this sense, despite his relatively small published output, he may be seen as a significant figure in the development of modern Muslim political thought.

Notes

1   More correctly transliterated in standard Arabic as *al-Daghīs*, Hassuna's name has been transliterated in a bewildering multiplicity of ways, making it difficult to follow his traces. The adoption of an apostrophe – D'Ghies – which reflects the elision of short vowel sounds in Maghrebian dialect, also helped to suggest a noble origin when travelling in Europe.

2   Abdeljalil Temimi, *Recherches et documents d'histoire maghrébine: L'Algérie, la Tunisie et la Tripolitaine (1816–1871)* (Tunis: Revue d'histoire maghrebine, 1980), p. 55.

3   Ibid., p. 159

4   Julia Ann Clancy-Smith, *Mediterraneans: North Africa and Europe in an Age of Migration, c. 1800–1900* (Berkeley: University of California Press, 2011), p. 318.

5   Charles Issawi, *An Economic History of the Middle East and North Africa* (London: Routledge, 2013), p. 44.

6   Robert Walsh, *A Residence at Constantinople During a Period Including the Commencement, Progress and Termination of the Greek and Turkish Revolutions* (London: Westley & Davis, 1836), p. 283.

7   Maurizio Isabella, *Risorgimento in Exile: Italian Émigrés and the Liberal International in the Post-Napoleonic Era* (Oxford: Oxford University Press,

2009); idem, 'Liberalism and Empires in the Mediterranean: The View-Point of the Risorgimento', in Silvana Patriarca and Lucy Riall (eds), *The Risorgimento Revisited: Nationalism and Culture in Nineteenth-Century Italy* (London: Palgrave Macmillan, 2012), pp. 232–54.

8   Jennifer Pitts, *A Turn to Empire: The Rise of Imperial Liberalism in Britain and France* (Princeton: Princeton University Press, 2009); Theodore Koditschek, *Liberalism, Imperialism, and the Historical Imagination: Nineteenth-Century Visions of a Greater Britain* (Cambridge: Cambridge University Press, 2011); Matthew P. Fitzpatrick, *Liberal Imperialism in Germany: Expansionism and Nationalism, 1848–1884* (New York: Berghahn Books, 2008).

9   David Urquhart, *The Spirit of the East* (London: H. Colburn, 1839), vol. 2, p. 264.

10 Şerif Mardin, *The Genesis of Young Ottoman Thought: A Study in the Modernization of Turkish Political Ideas* (Syracuse: Syracuse University Press, 2000), pp. 3–4.

11 Nazan Cicek, *The Young Ottomans: Turkish Critics of the Eastern Question in the Late Nineteenth Century* (London: I.B. Tauris, 2010).

12 Butrus Abu-Manneh, 'The Islamic Roots of the Gülhane Rescript', *Die Welt Des Islams* 34 (1994), pp. 173–203.

13 Arthur Lumley Davids, *A Grammar of the Turkish Language* (London: Parbury & Allen, 1832), dedication page.

14 Christine M. Philliou, *Biography of an Empire: Governing Ottomans in an Age of Revolution* (Berkeley: University of California Press, 2010), p. 128.

15 *The Portfolio: Diplomatic Review* (London: J. Maynard, 1844), vol. 2, p. 216.

16 *London Literary Gazette*, 26 September 1829.

17 See Ian Coller, *Arab France: Islam and the Making of Modern Europe, 1798–1831* (Berkeley: University of California Press, 2010).

18 Hassuna D'Ghies, *A Letter addressed to James Scarlett on the abolition of the slave trade Translated from the French, by Dr Kelly* (London: Printed for the Author, 1822).

19 Linda Colley, *Britons: Forging the Nation, 1707–1837* (New Haven: Yale University Press, 2005). For a fuller discussion of D'Ghies' 'African' critique, see my article, 'African Liberalism in the Age of Empire? Hassuna D'Ghies and Liberal Constitutionalism in North Africa, 1822–1835', *Modern Intellectual History*.

20 D'Ghies, *A Letter addressed to James Scarlett* (Bentham, Paris edition, 1820).

21 See Mehran Kamrava, *Innovation in Islam: Traditions and Contributions* (Berkeley: University of California Press, 2011).

22 Jeremy Bentham, *The Collected Works of Jeremy Bentham: Correspondence*, vol. 11: *January 1822 to June 1824* (Oxford: Oxford University Press, 2000).

23 Ibid.

24 Urquhart, *The Spirit of the East*, p. 22.

25 Ibid., p. 89.

26   Jeremy Bentham, *Collected Works: Correspondence*, vol. 11, p. 181

27   Jeremy Bentham and Philip Schofield, *Securities against Misrule and Other Constitutional Writings for Tripoli and Greece* (Oxford: Clarendon Press, 1990).

28   L.J. Hume, 'Preparations for Civil War in Tripoli in the 1820s: Ali Karamanli, Hassuna D'Ghies and Jeremy Bentham', *The Journal of African History* 21/3 (1980), pp. 311–22.

29   John Bowring and Lewin Bentham Bowring, *Autobiographical Recollections of Sir John Bowring* (London: H.S. King, 1877), p. 323.

30   Hume, 'Preparations for Civil War in Tripoli', p. 320.

31   María José Vilar, 'El nacimiento de la prensa en libia: "L'Investigateur africain" de Trípoli, 1827', *Africa: Rivista trimestrale di studi e documentazione dell'istituto italiano per l'africa e l'oriente* 59/2 (2004), pp. 221–30.

32   Ettore Rossi, 'Una "rassegna africanista" manoscritta a tripoli un secolo fa: I consoli Gråberg e Rousseau', *Oriente Moderno* 12/5 (1932), pp. 256–60.

33   Jakob (Count) Graberg de Hemsö, 'An Account of the Great Historical Work of the African Philosopher Ibn Khaldun', *Transactions of the Royal Asiatic Society of Great Britain and Ireland* 3 (1835), p. 390.

34   C.A. Bayly, *Imperial Meridian: The British Empire and the World, 1780–1830* (London: Longman, 1989), p. 194.

35   There are many accounts of this affair based on thin evidence. For an even-handed account see Théodore Monod, *De Tripoli à Tombouctou: le dernier voyage de Laing: 1825–1826* (Paris: Sociétae française d'histoire d'outre-mer, 1977).

36   Although the Laing affair is not explicitly discussed, Davide Rodogno's excellent *Against Massacre: Humanitarian Interventions in the Ottoman Empire, 1815–1914* (Princeton: Princeton University Press, 2011) provides a key analytical framework.

37   Hamdan Khodja and Abdelkader Djeghloul, *Le miroir: aperçu historique et statistique sur la Régence d'Alger* (Paris: Sindbad, 1985).

38   For a discussion of the book in relation to European liberal ideas, see Jennifer Pitts, 'Liberalism and Empire in a Nineteenth-Century Algerian Mirror', *Modern Intellectual History* 6 (2009), pp. 287–313.

39   See Linda T. Darling, 'Mirrors for Princes in Europe and the Middle East: A Case of Historiographical Incommensurability', in Albrecht Classen (ed.), *East Meets West in the Middle Ages and Early Modern Times: Transcultural Experiences in the Premodern World* (Berlin: De Gruyter, 2013), pp. 223–42, http://public.eblib.com/choice/publicfullrecord.aspx?p=1249779.

40   'Mémoire remis par Sidi Hamdan à la Commission d'Afrique de 1833', reprinted in Michel Habart, *Histoire d'un perjure* (Paris: Editions de minuit, 1960), pp. 229–30.

41   See Rodogno, *Against Massacre,* esp. chap. 2.

42   Robert Greenhow, *The History and Present Condition of Tripoli, with Some Accounts of the Other Barbary States* (Richmond: T.W. White, 1835), p. 76.

43 See Kola Folayan, *Tripoli during the Reign of Yūsuf Pāshā Qaramānlī* (Ile-Ife, Nigeria: University of Ife Press, 1979), esp. chap. 6. Folayan's account of the 'Manshiyya Revolution' is helpful, but the context of wider Ottoman dynamics is lacking.

44 Horatio Southgate, *Narrative of a tour through Armenia, Kurdistan, Persia and Mesopotamia: with observations upon the condition of Mohammedanism and Christianity in those countries* (London: Tilt and Bogue, 1840), vol. 1, p. 69.

45 Justin K. Stearns, *Infectious Ideas: Contagion in Premodern Islamic and Christian Thought in the Western Mediterranean* (Baltimore: Johns Hopkins University Press, 2011).

46 Georges Yver, 'Si *Hamdan* b. Othman Khodja', *Revue africaine* 57 (1913), pp. 96–138.

47 David Ross, *Opinions of the European Press on the Eastern Question* (London: James Ridgway & Sons, 1836), pp. xvi–ii.

48 L.-P.-B. d'Aubignosc, *La Turquie nouvelle jugée au point où l'ont amenée les réformes du sultan Mahmoud* (Paris: Delloye, 1839), p. 233.

CHAPTER SIX

Imperial Nationalism and Orthodox Enlightenment:

A Diasporic Story Between the Ionian Islands, Russia and Greece, ca. 1800–30

Konstantina Zanou

Il Mar Nero e con esso il Don e il Nieper [sarà] riunito al Mediterraneo . . .
[The Black Sea and with it the River Don and the Dnieper River will be united with the Mediterranean]

IOANNIS KAPODISTRIAS ON THE PROSPECT OF THE LIBERATION OF GREECE WITH RUSSIAN ASSISTANCE, GENEVA (1824?)[1]

Does the Mediterranean border on Russia? By focusing on the strong presence of the Russian Empire in the region during the first decades of the nineteenth century and by examining the movement of people and ideas that such a presence precipitated, this chapter claims that there was a moment when it did. Its basic premise is that Russia's political and military conduct in the Mediterranean, and particularly in the Ionian Adriatic during the first decades of the nineteenth century, had a strong impact on the way national and liberal ideas were developing in the area. The human and intellectual links that were established between the post-Venetian Ionian Islands, Ottoman Greece and the Russian Empire, created a specific brand of Greek nationalism, European liberalism and Eastern Enlightenment, to which historians have paid scant attention.

The conventional view about the origins of Greek national consciousness assumes that it was born out of a binary opposition between secular and religious values, Western Enlightenment and Eastern Orthodoxy, the ecumenism of the Church and a parochial nationalism. The anticlerical and radical ideals of a significant number of late-eighteenth and early nineteenth-century Greek Enlightenment thinkers, as well as the stubborn resistance of the Ecumenical Patriarchate of Constantinople to the ideas of nationalism and liberalism, certainly offered convincing enough evidence to interpret the development of Greek nationalism in terms of a clash between religion and secularism and East and West. The scheme and genealogy of the 'Neohellenic Enlightenment', which dominates Greek intellectual historiography, connects the birth of Greek nationalism and the Greek state with the ideas of the Paris-based intellectual Adamantios Koraes, attributing a central place in it to the heritage of the French Revolution and the radical and secular Enlightenment tradition. However, as this chapter will show, this is only a partial reading of the phenomenon. A new interest in the relationship between religion and the Enlightenment has led scholars in recent years to realize that this relationship was far more complex and interesting than had traditionally been supposed. Scholars are now arguing that the Enlightenment was not at war *with* Christianity, but rather *within* it. It was, in most cases, a 'Christian Enlightenment'.[2] The complexity of the phenomenon has been recently acknowledged also in the context of the 'Neohellenic Enlightenment', in spite of a long tradition in Greek scholarship of maintaining the opposite.[3]

By offering a different geographical and intellectual trajectory, which places Greece in a Mediterranean context, viewing it in relation to the Ionian Islands as well as to the Russian Empire, this chapter will argue that there was a circle of diasporic intellectuals who perceived the Greek nation not as incompatible with the Christian oecumene and the traditional world of the empires, but as part of it. The main characters in this story, namely, Ioannis Kapodistrias, Bishop Ignatius, Giorgio Mocenigo, Andrea Mustoxidi, Spiridione Naranzi and Alexandre Stourdza, have been either ignored or, in the case of Kapodistrias, studied in a different geographical and intellectual setting than the one proposed here. By viewing these figures not as 'pre-formed national subjects' who transmitted their 'enlightened knowledge' to the rest of society, but as Greek patriots under formation *through* their diasporic experience, this chapter likewise challenges the conventional descriptions of Greek diasporas as dispersed pieces of the national core.

I. The setting

Russia and the Mediterranean

Russia's interest in the Mediterranean dates only to the last quarter of the eighteenth century. During that time there was an ever-growing sense that Ottoman decline, along with the increasing debility of Venice, had left a power vacuum in the region, which Russia, the Tsarina Catherine II thought, had every right to fill. This plan was lent further credence by the outcome of the Russo-Ottoman war of 1768–74, which ended in the utter humiliation of the Ottomans, ratified by the Treaty of Küçük-Kaynarca. The Treaty recognized for the first time Russian control of part of the Black Sea coast and secured the right of Russian merchant ships (often manned by Greek sailors) to travel through the Bosphorus into the Ottoman waters of the Aegean. Another clause of the Treaty gave the Tsar the right to intervene on behalf of the sultan's Orthodox subjects and to protect Christian worship, especially in the areas of Moldavia and Wallachia.[4]

During the course of the same war, the Russian fleet sailed for the first time in Mediterranean waters. The Russians occupied briefly several Aegean islands and, in 1770, instigated a major but unsuccessful Greek revolt in the Peloponnese, which provoked harsh reprisals from the Ottoman army. During the same period, Catherine II's preferential treatment encouraged thousands of Greeks from the Ottoman Empire to settle along the coastline of the Sea of Azov. The links between the Mediterranean and Russia would subsequently be strengthened, especially after 1783, when the tsarina annexed the Crimea, thereby establishing a base for commercial and naval ventures in the direction of the Mediterranean.[5]

These Russian activities formed part of a grander idea: Catherine II envisaged conquering the Ottomans and founding a great Orthodox Christian empire centred on Constantinople. In this plan, the religiosity of the Balkan peoples played a crucial role. Luckily for the Russians, their dreams of territorial expansion were matched by the 'mystical exaltation' of the age. Among the most popular 'prophecies', triggering waves of enthusiasm among the population of the Greek lands, there featured the so-called *Vision of Agathangelus*, concerning a 'Blond Race' that would come to the Balkans to assist the Orthodox Christians in their battle against the Ottomans. During the eighteenth century, this 'Blond Race' came to be identified with the Russians.[6]

The Ionian Islands

The Russians tended to play the religious card both in Ottoman lands and in those of the Republic of Venice. The seven Ionian Islands, in the southeastern corner of the Adriatic Sea (Corfu, Zakynthos, Lefkada,

Cephallonia, Ithaca, Cythera and Paxi), had been part of the ancient Greek world but followed a profoundly different historical path when they were conquered by the Venetians in the fifteenth century. Five centuries of partial or total Venetian rule (from 1402 until 1797, when the islands were liberated by the advancing French democratic army) transformed this insular extension of the Greek peninsula into a culturally Italian land. The local aristocracy of the cities, educated at the universities of Padua, Pavia and Pisa, spoke the Italian language, while the peasantry still used the local Greek idiom. Likewise, the world of the countryside remained Orthodox, while the religion of the upper echelons in the towns and the official religion of the state was Catholicism.[7] From the beginning of the eighteenth century onwards, however, the Orthodoxy of the inhabitants served more and more to differentiate them from their Venetian rulers and created links instead with their coreligionists from Russia, who started to give Ionians career opportunities as public servants and in trade.[8]

Napoleon's seizure of the Ionian Islands in 1797, his expedition to Egypt in 1798 and the consequent British takeover, as well as the opportunistic diplomatic games that he played with Ali Pasha of Yiannina in Epirus, convinced Russia and the Ottoman Empire to set their historical mistrust aside and, in 1799, to enter into an alliance. Their differences apart, both powers could agree on a double objective: first, to prevent the spread of revolutionary ideas in the Balkans; second, to conquer the Ionian Islands. By early March 1799, the combined forces of the two powers had taken control of the seven islands. The outcome of this process was the 'Septinsular Republic', an aristocratic constitutional, semi-independent state, which united the islands in a federation under the sovereignty of the Porte and the direct political and military protection of Russia. The Republic would last only seven years (1800–7). In 1806, the Russo-Ottoman alliance collapsed and a new war broke out between the two powers. Following the reverses in Europe, the new tsar, Alexander I, made his peace with Napoleon at Tilsit in 1807 and sealed it by ceding the Ionian Islands to imperial France.[9]

II. The cast

The men of the Septinsular Republic

Very brief though Russia's presence had been in the Mediterranean, and particularly in the Adriatic, it had nonetheless left its mark on the way national and liberal ideas were developing in the region. The encounter between the post-Venetian reality of the Ionian Islands and the Russian Empire fostered a particular type of proto-nationalism and proto-liberalism that bore its own distinctive characteristics. This was a version of Ionian patriotism, transformed later into Greek nationalism, which arose in the minds of people who spent their lives between the Ionian Islands, Russia, the

Ottoman Danubian Principalities (Moldavia and Wallachia) and, later, the Greek state; who believed that the Greek Revolution, which was destined to break out in 1821, embroiling thousands of Ionians who crossed over to the Greek continent to join the insurgents, was different from the other revolutions that shook the European continent and compatible with the principles of the Restoration; who thought that philhellenism could be built on conservative and religious foundations and that the rise of the Greek state could be explained in eschatological terms; who were convinced that the Enlightenment was religious in nature and believed that Greek nationalism could exist within Christian ecumenicity. It is the circle of people entertaining these beliefs that I now wish to consider. This circle included, first of all, the political and intellectual leaders of the Septinsular Republic.

The Zakynthian noble Giorgio Mocenigo (ca. 1762–1839), the actual 'boss' of the Septinsular Republic and Russia's omnipotent Imperial Proxy on the islands, created around himself an effective team of political and intellectual leaders. First of all, he entrusted the twenty-seven-year-old Corfiot Ioannis Kapodistrias with the office of the secretary general of the Septinsular Republic, a position second only to his own in the administrative hierarchy of the new state. Kapodistrias (1776–1831), subsequently foreign minister of the tsar and the first governor of the Greek state, was to become certainly the most famous among the characters in this story.[10] The Septinsular Republic found, in addition, its official historiographer in the shape of another young and promising Corfiot, Andrea Mustoxidi (1785–1860). An unabashed Russophile, Mustoxidi would later make a name for himself on both shores of the Adriatic as an eminent philologist, translator and archaeologist, and as one of the first historians to contribute to the construction of Greek national history. He was also to become the first minister of education of Greece in Kapodistrias's government.[11] Somewhat older than Mustoxidi was Spiridione Naranzi (1760–ca. 1833), a Zakynthian who was summoned to the islands from Padua to offer his juridical expertise in the drafting of the various constitutions of the Republic, becoming also its financial administrator.[12] The last to join the cast of the principal characters of the Septinsular Republic – but in terms of intellectual weight indubitably the most important – was Bishop Ignatius (1766–1828). Ignatius was a self-made man from the island of Lesvos, in the eastern Aegean, who studied in Constantinople and distinguished himself alongside Ali Pasha, serving for several years as Bishop of Arta and Nafpaktos in Epirus, a metropolitan seat falling within Ali's domain.[13]

These men were intellectually indebted to the two major representatives of the Septinsular Enlightenment, namely, Eugenios Voulgaris (1716–1806) and Nicephorus Theotokis (1731–1800). These two Ionian clergymen, who had constructed their lives in the selfsame geographical landscape – comprising Venice, the Ionian Islands, the Ottoman Principalities and Russia – half a century earlier, took the view that philosophy and religion belonged to two separate spheres of human experience and could develop along parallel lines without interfering with each other. Voulgaris went so far as to claim that anything which militated against religious doctrines could not deliver authentic philosophical knowledge. Enlightenment, in this view, was considered to be part of Divine Providence and was treated as a separate but equally valid source of knowledge, existing alongside the eschatological tradition. In accordance with this, Voulgaris believed that a revival and refinement of learning within the Orthodox Church, which would include a substantial training in the classics and greater familiarity with modern European philosophy, was necessary. Theotokis, on the other hand, advocated the creation of an 'Orthodox commonwealth' as a continuation of the 'Byzantine commonwealth', which would link the Greek to the Slavic world under the umbrella of ecumenical eastern Orthodoxy.[14] Part of the broader Adriatic Enlightenment of the Venetian imperial framework, the Septinsular Enlightenment had as its key features not only a concern with education and the Orthodox tradition, but also history (especially Byzantine and modern history, as well as local history) and popular poetry.[15]

The new imperial Russian political environment of the Ionian Islands, with its reorganization of the geopolitical realities of the area and its marked emphasis on the Orthodoxy and Greekness of its inhabitants, was the context within which the main characters of our story would acquire a more solid sense of patriotism that transcended the Ionian space, thereby becoming more broadly 'Orthodox' and 'Greek'. At a time when language and religion were becoming increasingly identified with the emerging national consciousness, the Septinsular Republic, in its constitution, did indeed declare the Greek language to be the official language of the state and Christian Orthodoxy the official religion. This sense of Ionian patriotism, developing gradually into Greek nationalism (cultural and religious rather than political – at least at this stage), would be further enhanced by the meeting in Russia of these men with others with a Phanariot and Boyar background from the Danubian Principalities. We shall see now how this encounter occurred, and what the distinctive elements of the proto-national ideology that it produced would prove to be.

Refugees in the bosom of Russia

When, in July 1807, the Septinsular Republic was dissolved and Napoleon seized control of the Ionian region, the leaders of the Republic were left with little choice. 'I am leaving; and I am asking yours' and my mother's blessing', Kapodistrias wrote in a short note to his father in late 1808, before embarking upon his journey, as a volunteer exile, to St Petersburg – a journey that would lead him after some years to the highest ranks of Russian diplomacy.[16] If Kapodistrias had to wait for about a year in order to quit the islands, the same was not true of the other central characters of the Septinsular Republic. Mocenigo and Ignatius left in haste as early as November 1807. They went first to Italy and from there they headed, some months later, to St Petersburg. Their fates would thereafter be inextricably linked to the Russian Empire and particularly to its presence and interests in the Mediterranean. With the passing of time, however, a second focal point of identity emerged, namely, the 'Greek nation' – still, of course, a vague cultural construction which was not associated with any clear political plan. Mocenigo served for many years as the tsar's consul in Naples and then in Turin. On his retirement in 1825 he went to Venice and became actively involved in the local Greek community and its philhellenic activities. Naranzi was appointed Russian consul to Venice, while Mustoxidi was named attaché to Mocenigo's consulate in Turin. As for Ignatius, he stayed in the Russian capital for some time, until a new opportunity arose when, during the Russo-Ottoman War, Russia briefly annexed the Danubian Principalities (1809–12). He was then elected Bishop of Ungrovlachia (the ecclesiastical term for Moldavia and Wallachia) and, in 1810, moved to Bucharest. Ignatius remained there for a couple of years only, since the restitution of the Danubian Principalities to the Ottoman Empire forced him to leave his metropolitan seat again. He then spent some time in Vienna, moving finally to Pisa, and becoming, during the years of the Greek Revolution, a coordinator of sorts of the European philhellenic movement.[17]

In the chilly corridors and salons of St Petersburg, Kapodistrias and his friends had an encounter that proved to be decisive for the development of their ideas: they met with the circle of Boyar and Phanariot exiles, the most important of their number being Alexandre Stourdza (1791–1854). Coming from one of the oldest and most influential Boyar (noble) families of Moldavia and from a leading Greek Phanariot family of Constantinople, which in 1792 had left the threatening atmosphere of the Danubian Principalities to seek a safe haven in Russia, Stourdza held various offices in the tsar's Ministry of Foreign Affairs. He also became known for his published writings, his name chiefly being associated with the history of the Holy Alliance and of counterrevolutionary thought in general. Regarded as 'the Maistre of the East', he is best remembered for his reactionary essay 'Mémoire sur l'état actuel de l'Allemagne' (1818), where he maintained that German universities were hotbeds of atheism and revolution and should be placed under police control. On the other hand, like his friends from the Ionian Islands and other Phanariots in the Danubian Principalities, Stourdza was also a man of the Enlightenment, who tried to reinterpret and adapt the ideas of Montesquieu and Rousseau to an Orthodox and Oriental environment.[18] Indeed, in the activities of this circle, the Septinsular Enlightenment came to meet the Phanariot Enlightenment of the Principalities, part of the broader framework of the Ottoman Enlightenments, an intellectual tradition which was closely connected to the reforms undertaken by the Patriarchate of Constantinople from the seventeenth century onwards as an answer to the penetration of Catholicism in the area. Unlike the Septinsular Enlightenment, which was mostly Italian-speaking, the Phanariot Enlightenment endorsed Greek education and Orthodox culture and supported the foundation of schools for the Christian populations within the political establishment of the Ottoman Empire. A Jacobin and republican version of the Phanariot Enlightenment would develop, in the years around the French Revolution, in the writings of Rigas Velestinlis-Feraios (1757–98), too radical though for the tastes of this circle.[19]

Stourdza and Kapodistrias were bound not only by their commitment to Orthodox Enlightenment ideals, but also by their sharing the same vision of the 'regeneration' of what they more and more perceived to be their common patria, Greece. Around the years of the Greek Revolution, the two of them led the so-called 'War Party', an unofficial political lobby within the Tsarist court which advocated Russian military intervention in favour of the Greek insurgents.[20] This mingling of the Ionian and Phanariot element in St Petersburg would produce, as we will now see, its own peculiar system for interpreting the Greek Revolution and for understanding Greek nationalism in general.

III. The plot

Russian great expectations and the Philomousos Eteria

In the immediate post-Napoleonic years the moral influence of Russia on European politics was immense. These were the years in which many European liberals, particularly in Italy but also in the Balkans, invested boundless hope in Tsar Alexander I, especially after his granting of constitutions to Poland and to the Ionian Islands.[21] Kapodistrias, who was representing the tsar at the Congress of Vienna, had then his moment of glory. The new order of things in restored Europe appeared indeed to be on his and his Russophile friends' side. The messianic atmosphere that prevailed after the fall of the Napoleonic Empire, which led to the creation of the Holy Alliance; the mystic dimensions that this Alliance assumed, perceived as it was to be a holy pact binding all Christians together in mutual respect and everlasting peace; Alexander I's personal sense that it was his divine mission to save the Christians from the sufferings that revolutionary ideas had brought down on their heads; his abstract endorsement of Enlightenment ideals and the belief in man's capacity to improve and be morally elevated through education; even his conservative liberalism, which seemed at first to prevail over Metternich's zeal to restore absolutist order; all these looked to be in perfect sympathy with Kapodistrias' and his friends' world view.[22]

In this moment of absolute harmony with the tsar and with the new world that was unfurling its countless promises, these people thought that the time for the 'regeneration' of Greece might also be fast approaching. Greek hopes were boosted in this context by the Russian imperial couple's decision to give their backing to the *Philomousos Eteria* (Society of the Muses). Co-founded by Kapodistrias, Ignatius and Stourdza on the margins of the Vienna Congress, the *Philomousos* was the project that brought together all the principal characters of our story, becoming the most enduring bearer of this circle's ideology, the hallmark, it might be said, of their intellectual milieu. It was born as a 'charitable' association which aimed particularly at giving financial assistance to those Greeks who were studying in Europe. In the long term, however, the association aspired to lay the foundations for the creation of a Greek intellectual elite, which would be ready to govern Greece when, 'after a happy coincidence of factors', it had been liberated.[23] Of course, these aspirations were abstract at the time. It was only after the outbreak of the Greek Revolution and the inevitability created by the course of the war that this mainly cultural and religious nationalism would be transformed into a more concrete political vision about the formation of an autonomous and even independent Greek state. The *Philomousos* became extremely important in the years 1827–9, when Kapodistrias, soon after his election as governor of Greece – and with the collaboration of Ignatius, Mocenigo, Naranzi and Mustoxidi – brought into effect an ambitious plan for the hospitalization and education of the orphan and refugee children from Greece found in the cities of Venice, Trieste and Ancona. He believed that the reorganized schools of these cities ought to function as a model for the establishment of similar schools in other places of the Greek diaspora.[24] The *Philomousos* epitomized this circle's profound concern with education, a quintessentially Enlightenment ideal. It was only through an extended and invigorated education system, rather than through political activism and revolution, that, according to these intellectuals, the progressive amelioration of society could hope to be realized.[25]

The Holy Alliance: a pan-Christian utopian moment

The framework for the development of an enlightened society resting upon the solid foundations of religion was provided, so far as these men were concerned, by the Treaty of the Holy Alliance (1815). Expressing the tsar's pietistic perception of international relations, the Holy Alliance was meant to be – as Kapodistrias and Stourdza wrote in their apology of 1817 – 'the surest guarantee of a well-ordered liberty, the true safeguard of law, and the most implacable enemy of arbitrary power'.[26] Combining the traditions of Christianity and international law, the Holy Alliance represented the application of a political theology based on the principle of 'Christian fraternity'. 'Thanks to a sublime conception of [the tsar] . . ., Europe has become almost one Republic, the various parts of which are governed through mutual vigilance and alternate harmony, and are sustained and conserved independent under the auspices and the empire of Our Lord Jesus Christ' – reads a note found among Kapodistrias' papers, which bears the handwriting of Mustoxidi (probably a result of a collaborative endeavour between the two men in 1824).[27] What is more interesting, though, is the second part of the note, where the two friends maintain that the states of the Holy Alliance should turn their attention towards Greece: 'But there is still a portion of the children of this Christ who stretch out their hands to their brothers, and yearning to be joined to this family, recall that the Religion of the Man-God has spoken their language.' The allied powers should turn towards Greece, not to suppress the revolution, but to uphold it. For the two men, the Greek revolutionary cause was not incompatible with the spirit of the Restoration. Greece should be liberated, they believed, in order to join the system of the Holy Alliance.

This belief was founded upon the idea that the Holy Alliance represented the first step towards a future of fraternity between European Christian peoples. This pan-Christian utopian vision does indeed often feature in the writings of this circle. In the same note from Kapodistrias' papers, this vision is presented as a plan to reunify the European Churches, with Orthodoxy mediating between the Catholics and the Protestants. In the reunified Christian family of Europe, Oriental Orthodoxy would become the third power that would balance the other two. Then, according to the authors, 'one sole faith and one sole law will unify the souls of all peoples; and the European Republic will become also a Christian Republic'.[28] Since the Congress of Vienna, the aspiration to make of Europe a 'Corpus Christianum' that would embrace and protect all its children, whether Catholic, Protestant or Orthodox, had indeed been a widespread motif among conservative philhellenes. It found its most evocative expression in a text entitled *Mémoire sur l'importance religieuse et politique de réunir les deux Eglises grecque et latine et sur les moyens d'y parvenir*, which was written in 1814 by the French abbot Henri Grégoire, a hugely important figure, noted for his role during the French Revolution, his battles for the emancipation of slaves, the Jews and all oppressed peoples.[29] The memoir – which, as Grégoire acknowledged, was inspired by Ignatius' historical account of *The current state of the Orthodox Oriental Church* (1809) – was delivered through Kapodistrias' mediation to Alexander I during the proceedings of the Congress.[30] In addressing the tsar, Grégoire argued that the union of the two Churches, Catholic and Orthodox, would not only guarantee the liberation of Greece but would also benefit Europe as a whole.[31]

For its part, Stourdza's version of a pan-Christian utopia did not include the whole of Europe. It was instead a pan-Orthodox utopia. He envisaged the creation of a 'post-Byzantine Orthodox commonwealth' that would include all Balkan peoples, with Russia having the leading role. It was a vision of an 'Oriental Christian oecumene' based on the Byzantine tradition and on the Enlightenment teachings of Theotokis. Unlike the Byzantine Empire, however, Stourdza's 'Orthodox oecumene' was not a-national, but multi-national. It was an oecumene constituted by nation-states. He clarified, of course, that there was a hierarchical relationship that should be maintained between the supra-national Church and the national states: 'It is the state that is part of the Church, and not the Church of the state.'[32]

It has been argued that ecumenism was an ideological system bound to the empire and thus incompatible with the ideology of nationalism.[33] The characters discussed here point to a different story, however. There was clearly a cohort of European conservative liberals who, in the years around the Congress of Vienna and inspired by the mystical atmosphere of the Holy Alliance, believed that nationalisms could exist within the oecumene, and that the religious and traditional world could be combined with the reality of the Europe of nations. It was through this combination of the 'familiar' with the 'unfamiliar' that these figures faced the Greek Revolution and tried to make sense of it.

Russia and the outbreak of the Greek Revolution

Regrettably enough, the idyllic relationship between the liberals and Alexander I did not endure. All too soon the 'enigmatic tsar's' conservative liberal phase ended, and he came down to earth – to Metternich's earth, to be precise. From 1820 onward, and as revolutionary movements broke out one after the other in Europe (Spain, Naples, Portugal, Piedmont and finally Greece), Alexander I could no longer play the part of the Russian despot 'speaking vaguely of the rights of man and of nations'. He became increasingly convinced that his own conservative liberal solutions to the political problems of the period – supported as they were by his foreign minister, Kapodistrias – had to be sacrificed to the preservation of the alliance system. If peace and order were to be maintained in Europe, constitutions, national self-determination and any other 'Enlightenment project' had to be temporarily set aside.[34] By 1822 – and following the Congresses of Troppau, Laibach and Verona, at which the powers decided to send troops and suppress the revolutionary movements in Spain and Italy – whatever 'holiness' there had been in the Holy Alliance disappeared under the militaristic and anti-spiritualistic shadow of Metternichian politics.

Only in its attitude toward the Greek Revolution did the Russian government vacillate for a moment. As regards this issue, in particular, matters were much more complicated. On the one hand, the revolution of the Greeks was connected to a basic component of Russian politics from the times of Catherine II – the promise, that is, of a Russian crusade to restore Orthodoxy throughout the Near East. In addition, the eventual defeat of the Greeks' Ottoman oppressors would allow Russia to pursue a number of strategic goals in the Balkans and the Mediterranean. On the other hand, Russia at that juncture was committed to the support of the status quo in

Europe. Any dismantling of the Ottoman Empire along ethnic lines would pose a dangerous precedent for the break-up of the tsar's own multi-ethnic domains and encourage other assaults against the stability of Europe.[35] Torn between these two options – whether to intervene in support of the Greeks or to declare his neutrality and denounce them as insurgents – Alexander I wavered for some time, trying to maintain an illusory balance. In the end, he chose the second option, dashing the hopes of his Greek entourage.

Caught between his Greek patriotism and his personal loyalty to the tsar, Kapodistrias chose nationalism over his imperial allegiances, resigning in August 1822 (officially in 1826). In any case, the prevailing atmosphere in the Russian court was no longer favourable to him. He therefore retired to the more welcoming ambience of Geneva where he applied himself to supporting the Greek Revolution by writing and organizing political activity, until the moment he was elected governor of the newly established Greek state (1827). His example was followed by his friend Stourdza who, in 1822, likewise resigned from the Russian diplomatic service (officially in 1829) and relocated to Odessa, where he lived until the end of his life, pursuing a career as an independent intellectual and philhellene.[36] By the same token, the revolution had a major impact on refashioning Bishop Ignatius's loyalties. During the last years of his life, he abandoned his faith in Russia and reshaped his 'regenerative' vision for Greece within an Anglophile framework.

Conservative philhellenism and religious nationalism

For these servants of the tsar who became attuned to the nascent nationalist feelings of the period, the outbreak of the Greek Revolution in 1821 signified an almost existential dilemma: how was it possible to adhere to the principles of national liberation and, at the same time, remain loyal to the tsarist order? How could one be a philhellene without contesting the European Congress system?

One solution was by disassociating the Greek Revolution from the other revolutionary movements that upset Europe in 1820–1. In international diplomatic circles, especially during the Congresses of Laibach and Verona, the Greek insurgents were seen as no different from the rest of the 'revolutionary troublemakers' in Europe. This association placed the Greek insurrection within a genealogy of radical movements that went back to the French Revolution and which were related to the Carbonari and other secret societies. If philhellenism was generally associated with radical liberalism and revolution, these people wanted to show that it was also related to a thread of thought which was moderate liberal and counterrevolutionary.[37]

Bishop Ignatius thought that one way to do this would be to re-examine the relationship of the Greeks to the French Revolution. The latter, he argued, was never considered as an example to imitate by the Greeks, who detested the French because of their alliance with the Ottomans. It was not the Greeks, Ignatius said, that the French Revolution had influenced, but the Ottomans. Islam contains elements which are republican and democratic – for example, all believers are equal before God, before the law and before the authorities – and therefore resemble the French republican system. This similarity created, according to the bishop, a seedbed of revolutionary ideas among the Muslims of the Ottoman Empire. Thus, the influence of the French Revolution on the Greeks, if there was any, was only collateral, and passed through the Ottoman channel.[38]

The most effective response to the association of the Greek Revolution with the revolutionary movements in Spain and Italy was, however, to maintain that the Greeks, unlike the Jacobin-influenced Carbonari, were fighting a religious war against slavery and tyranny imposed upon them by non-European infidel rulers. Besides, these intellectuals argued, the Greek Revolution was an event of an altogether different historical quality. Stourdza claimed that it was an event that transcended history, touching the sphere of theology. In his interpretative scheme, the survival of the Greeks and their regeneration was considered to be a miracle, the only historical event with messianic dimensions after the Jewish exodus. 'With the exception of the people of Israel', he wrote, 'whose future renaissance is foreseen at the end of time, history does not furnish any other example like the miraculous event that is today accomplished on the soil of Greece.'[39] In Greece, Stourdza argued, it was God who spoke through the insurgents. The revolution was not displacing God's plans but, on the contrary, it was the first step towards their realization.[40] Besides, in a note among Kapodistrias' papers (written again by Mustoxidi), the Greeks are presented as enduring a plight still more terrible than that of the Israelites, because 'it is not in the land of the Pharaohs that they groan, but in their own land, the heritage of their fathers'.[41]

If there is one source where the references to Jewish history abound it is the aforementioned *Vision of Agathangelus*. As we have seen, in prophesying the deliverance of Eastern Orthodoxy through a crusade led by the Russians, *Agathangelus* compared the Ottoman domination of Greece to the Babylonian captivity of the people of Israel. This biblical parallel and the explanation of the past in apocalyptic terms gives *Agathangelus* the ground to predict the future with considerable accuracy: if it is all prescribed in God's plans, then the end of the story, the restoration of the Byzantine Empire, is already known.[42]

In a somewhat similar way, Kapodistrias believed that historical developments, and particularly the events in Greece, are prescribed in the plans of Divine Providence and, for that reason, they can be fully predicted. Another note among his papers (bearing his own handwriting on this occasion), entitled 'De la Grèce en 1823', reads: 'The Restoration of Greece is in God's will. And because of that, time, Politics, and everything, will be in favour of it, and they are in favour of it, despite the malevolence and the egoism of human affairs.'[43] The conviction that history moves with the mediation of the invisible hand of God does indeed often appear in Kapodistrias' writings. It is traceable, for example, in a long and important letter to Bishop Ignatius in April 1823, where he unfolded his proposal to write a history of Greece – a proposal which was attached, some years later, to a draft by the Phanariot historian Jacovaky Rizos Neroulos, producing eventually a book signed only by the latter.[44] This 'inevitability' interpreted the revolution and the foundation of the Greek state as the product-culmination of a divine and deterministic process. Despite their disappointment at Russia's stance as regards the Greek Revolution, these men continued thus to understand politics within the religious and ecumenical framework they had endorsed in the previous two decades. The Russian Empire was perhaps by that date politically out of the picture, but intellectually it was still there.

Conclusions

The reconstruction of these diasporic intellectual trajectories, which developed far from the Parisian nuclei of Greek thought and the democratic ideological tradition of the French Revolution, allows the historian to tell a markedly different story about the Greek diasporas and their Enlightenments, one which, in terms of the circulation of ideas, is less obviously derived from the West and offers a more polycentric account, geographically and intellectually, of the origins of Greek nationalism and of the Greek Revolution. This chapter has shown how multi-levelled Mediterraneans and their extensions – the small patria of the Ionian Islands, the big patrias of the Venetian, Russian and Ottoman Empires, and the emerging new patria of the Greek state – coexisted in the consciousness of a circle of intellectuals who were gradually becoming 'Greek' through their diasporic experience. The sense of nationalism cultivated by these figures embraced all of these smaller and bigger patriotisms and was engendered by their previous cultural and political affiliations.

By describing the epoch in which these figures lived as a transitional period with an unknown future, when empires and nation-states were not yet mutually exclusive, and when the nation-state was not the most obvious solution either, this story also challenges teleological narratives of the emergence and triumph of nation-states. Like most of their contemporaries, Kapodistrias and his friends were trying to make sense of the changes they were living through by experimenting with new forms of imperial nationalism and transnational patriotism. If they were forced by Russia's last-minute disavowal of the Greek Revolution to choose nationhood over their imperial allegiances, they nonetheless never abandoned the ecumenical and religious framework of their political world view and remained loyal to Orthodoxy as the foundation of their national agenda.

Overall, by presenting this panorama of lives and ideas spanning Europe, the Balkans, the Adriatic, the Aegean and Russia, this chapter has tried to show that Greece, rather than being the result of the (incomplete) diffusion of Enlightenment ideals from Western Europe to its south-eastern periphery, was the product of a Mediterranean geography of the 'in-between', where different traditions met and conversed, producing new local realities at every turn.

Notes

1   Autograph note n.d. (1824?). Benaki Museum, Athens: Ioannis Kapodistrias Archive, No. 41, 130/31.

2   Helena Rosenblatt, 'The Christian Enlightenment', in Stewart J. Brown and Timothy Tackett (eds), *The Cambridge History of Christianity*, vol. 7: *Enlightenment, Reawakening and Revolution 1660–1815* (Cambridge: Cambridge University Press, 2006), pp. 283–301; Mark Curran, '*Mettons Toujours Londres*: Enlightened Christianity and the public in pre-revolutionary Francophone Europe', *French History* 24/1 (2009), pp. 40–59; Knud Haakonssen, *Enlightenments and Religions* (Athens: Institute of Neohellenic Studies, 2010); David Sorkin, *The Religious Enlightenment: Protestants, Jews, and Catholics from London to Vienna* (Princeton: Princeton University Press, 2008).

3   Paschalis M. Kitromilides, 'Orthodoxy and the west: Reformation to Enlightenment' and 'The legacy of the French Revolution: Orthodoxy and nationalism', in Michael Angold (ed.), *The Cambridge History of Christianity*, vol. 5: *Eastern Christianity* (Cambridge: Cambridge University Press, 2006), pp. 202–6, 229–30; Effi Gazi, 'Revisiting religion and nationalism in nineteenth-century Greece', in Roderick Beaton and David Ricks (eds), *The Making of Modern Greece: Nationalism, Romanticism, and the Uses of the Past (1797–1896)* (London-New York: Ashgate, 2009), pp. 95–106.

4   Norman E. Saul, *Russia and the Mediterranean 1797–1807* (Chicago: University of Chicago Press, 1970), p. 9ff.; Nicholas Charles Pappas, *Greeks in Russian Military Service in the Late Eighteenth and Early Nineteenth Centuries* (Thessaloniki: Institute for Balkan Studies, 1991), pp. 86–8.

5   Franco Venturi, *La rivolta greca del 1770 e il patriottismo dell'età dei lumi* (Rome: Unione Internazionale degli Istituti di Archeologia, Storia e Storia dell'Arte, 1986); Thomas W. Gallant, *The Edinburgh History of the Greeks, 1768 to 1913: The Long Nineteenth Century* (Edinbuirgh: Edinburgh University Press, 2015), pp. 1–23.

6   Dimitris Michalopoulos, 'The vision of Agathangelus: An 18th-Century Apocalyptic Weltanschauung', in Plamen Mitev, Ivan Parvev, Maria Baramova and Vania Racheva (eds), *Empires and Peninsulas, Southeastern Europe between Karlowitz and the Peace of Adrianople, 1699–1829* (Berlin: Lit, 2010), pp. 265–70; John Nicolopoulos, 'From Agathangelos to the Megale

Idea: Russia and the emergence of modern Greek nationalism', *Balkan Studies* 26 (1985), pp. 41–56.

7   Peter Mackridge, 'Venise après Venise: official languages in the Ionian Islands, 1797–1864', *Byzantine and Modern Greek Studies* 38/1 (2014), pp. 68–90.

8   Nikos Karapidakis, 'Ta Eptanisa: Evropaikoi antagonismoi meta tin ptosi tis Venetias' [The Heptanese: European rivalries after the fall of Venice], in Vassilis Panagiotopoulos (ed.), *Istoria tou Neou Ellinismou, 1770–2000* [*History of Modern Greece, 1770–2000*] (Athens: Ellinika Grammata, 2003), vol. I, p. 155.

9   Pierre Cabanes et al., *Histoire de l'Adriatique* (Paris: Seuil, 2001), pp. 397– 416; Nicholas V. Riasanovsky, *A History of Russia* (New York: Oxford University Press, 1969), pp. 254–75.

10   C.M. Woodhouse, *Capodistrias, the Founder of Greek Independence* (Oxford: Oxford University Press, 1973); Christos Loukos, *Ioannis Kapodistrias* (Athens: Ta Nea-Istoriki Vivliothiki, 2009).

11   Konstantina Zanou, *Expatriate intellectuals and national identity: Andrea Mustoxidi in Italy, France and Switzerland (1802–1829)*, PhD thesis, University of Pisa, 2007.

12   Leonidas Zois, *Lexikon Istorikon kai Laografikon Zakynthou* [*Historical and Folkloric Dictionary of Zakynthos*] (Zakynthos: Trimorfo, 2011), vol. I, p. 467.

13   Emmanuil G. Protopsaltis, *Ignatios Mitropolitis Ouggrovlachias (1766–1828)* [*The Bishop of Ungrovlachia Ignatius (1766–1828)*] (Athens: Academy of Athens, 1961), 2 vols.

14   Stephen K. Batalden, *Catherine II's Greek Prelate: Eugenios Voulgaris in Russia, 1771–1806* (New York: Columbia University Press, 1982); Gregory L. Bruess, *Religion, Identity and Empire: a Greek Archbishop in the Russia of Catherine the Great* (New York: Columbia University Press, 1997); Paschalis M. Kitromilides, *Enlightenment and Revolution, The Making of Modern Greece* (Cambridge, Massachusetts-London: Harvard University Press, 2013), pp. 43–53, 120–33.

15   Paschalis M. Kitromilides, 'Eptanisiakos Diafotismos: ta oria tis idiomorfias' [Septinsular Enlightenment], in *VII Panionian Conference, Proceedings* (Athens: Society of Leucadian Studies, 2004), vol. I, pp. 241–57; Konstantina Zanou, 'Pros mia synoliki theorisi tou ethnikou hronou: Pnevmatikes zymoseis ston italo-eptanisiako horo kata to a' miso toy 19ou aiona' [Intellectual activity in the Italian-Ionian space in the first half of the 19th century], in *IX Panionian Conference, Proceedings* (Paxi: Soxiety of Paxian Studies, 2014), vol. II, pp. 319–44.

16   Kostas Dafnis, *Archeion Ioannou Kapodistria* [*The Archive of Ioannis Kapodistrias*] (Corfu, 1976–86), vol. III, p. 3 [originally in Italian].

17   Artemis Xanthopoulou-Kyriakou, *I Elliniki Koinotita tis Venetias (1797–1866), Dioikitiki kai oikonomiki organosi, ekpaideytiki kai politiki drastiriotita* [*The Greek Community of Venice (1797–1866), Administrative and economic organization, educational and political activity*] (Thessaloniki: Aristotelian University of Thessaloniki, 1978), pp. 60, 131–2; Vassilis

Panagiotopoulos, 'Kati egine stin Pisa to 1821' [Something happened in Pisa in 1821], *Ta Istorika* 5 (June 1986), pp. 177–82.

18 Stella Ghervas, *Réinventer la tradition, Alexandre Stourdza et l'Europe de la Sainte-Alliance* (Paris: H. Champion, 2008).

19 Ariadna Camariano-Cioran, *Les Academies Princieres de Bucarest et de Jassy et leurs professeurs* (Thessalonica: Institute for Balkan Studies, 1974); Christine M. Philliou, *Biography of an Empire: Governing Ottomans in an Age of Revolution* (Berkeley: University of California Press, 2011); Kitromilides, *Enlightenment and Revolution*, pp. 200–29.

20 Theophilus Prousis, *Russian Society and the Greek Revolution* (DeKalb: Northern Illinois University Press, 1994), pp. 26–54.

21 Giuseppe Berti, *Russia e stati Italiani nel Risorgimento* (Turin: Einaudi, 1957), pp. 366, 374–5, 486–9.

22 Patricia Kennedy Grimsted, *The Foreign Ministers of Alexander I, Political Attitudes and the Conduct of Russian Diplomacy, 1801–1825* (Berkeley: University of California Press, 1969), pp. 39, 57–9, 46–9, 60–1, 226–8; idem, 'Capodistrias and a "New Order" for Restoration Europe: The "Liberal Ideas" of a Russian Foreign Minister (1814–1822)', *Journal of Modern History* 40/2 (June 1968), pp. 166–92.

23 John Capodistrias, *Letter to the Tsar Nicholas I* (London-Athens: Doric Publications, 1977), p. 32; C.W. Crawley, 'John Capodistrias and the Greeks before 1821', *Cambridge Historical Journal* XIII/2 (1957), p. 174.

24 E.A. Bétant (ed.), *Correspondance du Comte Capodistrias, Président de la Grèce* (Geneva-Paris: Abraham Cherbuliez, 1839), vol. I, pp. 184–8, 292–303, 317–18, 360–2.

25 [Ioannis Kapodistrias], 'Observations sur les moyens d'améliorer le sort de Grecs' (6/18 April 1819, Corfu), in George Waddinghton, *A visit to Greece in 1823 and 1824* (London: John Murray, 1825), p. xxxviii.

26 The apology was written, at the tsar's request, as an explanation of the treaty and an answer to its critics. In Kennedy Grimsted, 'Capodistrias and a "New Order" for Restoration Europe', p. 190.

27 Benaki Museum, Athens: Ioannis Kapodistrias Archive, No. 41, 130/31 [originally in Italian].

28 Ibid.

29 Michele Lascaris, 'L'abbé Grégoire et la Grèce', *La Révolution française* 3 (1932), pp. 1–16.

30 [Bishop Ignatius], 'Synopsis Istoriki peri tis enestosis katastaseos tis Ortodoxou Anatolikis Ekklisias', *Athina* 1 (January 1831), pp. 6–11 and 26–32; 2 (February 1831), pp. 40–6 and 55–62; 3 (March 1831), pp. 71–7. This is the Greek translation of the memoir *Précis historique sur l'état actuel de l'Eglise orthodoxe (non réunie) d'Orient*, which Ignatius presented in 1809 to Rumyantsev.

31 In Henri Grégoire, *Histoire des Sectes Religieuses* (Paris: Baudouin, 1829), vol. IV, p. 111.

32   Alexandre Stourdza, *La Grèce en 1821 et 1822, Correspondance politique publiée par un Grec* (Paris: Dufart, 1823), p. 90.

33   George Mavrogordatos, 'Orthodoxy and nationalism in the Greek case', *West European Politics* 26/1 (2003), p. 127.

34   Kennedy Grimsted, *The Foreign Ministers of Alexander I*, p. 62.

35   Prousis, *Russian Society and the Greek Revolution*, p. 26.

36   Ghervas, *Réinventer la tradition, Alexandre Stourdza*, pp. 74–6, 82, 84.

37   Stella Ghervas, 'Le philhellénisme d'inspiration conservatrice en Europe et en Russie', in AA.VV., *Peuples, Etats et nations dans le Sud-Est de l'Europe* (Bucarest: Anima 2004), pp. 98–110. On the anti-philhellenic views of the Austrian diplomacy see: Ioannis Dimakis, *O Oesterreichischer Beobachter tis Viennis kai i Elliniki Epanastasis, 1821–1827: Symvoli eis tin meletin toy evropaikou antifilellinismou* [*The Oesterreichischer Beobachter of Vienna and the Greek Revolution, 1821–1827: Contribution to the study of European anti-philhellenism*] (Athens: Papazisis, 1977).

38   [Bishop Ignatius], 'Grèce, Causes de sa Révolution et son Etat actuel' (1/13 October 1822, Pisa – Memoir delivered to Nesserlode). In Protopsaltis, *Ignatios Mitropolitis Ouggrovlachias*, vol. II, p. 333.

39   Stourdza, *La Grèce en 1821 et 1822*, p. 7.

40   Ibid., p. 8. See also Ghervas, *Réinventer la tradition, Alexandre Stourdza*, p. 103.

41   Benaki Museum, Athens: Ioannis Kapodistrias Archive, No. 41, 125/27 [originally in French].

42   Marios Hatzopoulos, 'Oracular prophesy and the politics of toppling Ottoman rule in South-East Europe', *The Historical Review/La Revue Historique* VIII (2011), pp. 95–116.

43   Benaki Museum, Athens: Ioannis Kapodistrias Archive, No. 41, 27 [originally in French].

44   Jacovaky Rizos Neroulos, *Histoire Moderne de la Grèce depuis la chute de l'Empire d'Orient* (Geneva: Abraham Cherbuliez, 1828); Konstantina Zanou, 'O Ioannis Kapodistrias, o Iakovakis Rizos Neroulos kai i *Neoteri Istoria tis Elladas*' [John Kapodistrias, Jacovacy Rizos-Neroulos and the *Histoire Moderne de la Grèce*], *Mnimon* 30 (2009), pp. 141–78; Giannis Koubourlis, *Oi istoriografikes ofeiles ton Sp. Zambeliou kai K. Paparrigopoulou (1782–1846)* [*The historiographical debts of Sp. Zambelios and K. Paparrigopoulos (1782–1846)*] (Athens: Institute of Neohellenic Research, 2012), pp. 222–60.

CHAPTER SEVEN

Away or Homeward Bound?

The Slippery Case of Mediterranean Place in the Era Before Nation-states

Dominique Kirchner Reill

With the new transnational turn, scholars of nationalism have looked to the experience of the physical displacement of activists and intellectuals as a prime means to reassemble the international circulation of ideas: For, after all, Gottfried Herder wrote some of his most stimulating work while sailing across the north seas,[1] Mazzini debated in England longer than he ever resided in Italy,[2] Kossuth spent over half of his life everywhere but Hungary,[3] Mickiewicz attracted world attention not from the medieval burgs of Lithuania, but from Parisian university podiums,[4] and, finally, Garibaldi regularly fell off the peninsular grid, explaining the global commemorations of his stays in New York City, Taganrog (Russia) and Garibaldi (Brazil).[5] Scholars of exile and diaspora have given us the necessary reminder of how transnational nationalism was (and is). However, much remains unclear in trying to ascertain the contours of displacement. Though there can be no doubt that travel and living 'abroad' informed the shape and texture of nineteenth-century activists' ideas and the strategies they chose to make their ideas real, what remains unclear is how far 'home' and 'away' really extended in a world of mini-city-states, broad continental (and transoceanic) empires, tariff unions, and the introduction of railways and steamships. Were you always 'displaced' when you moved? Can we discuss a Mediterranean 'diaspora' if the movement of peoples along and across the Mediterranean followed new and/or old traditions of mobility? Is a historical figure 'abroad' if she or he travels along imperial infrastructures that do not cohere to the map of the imagined national communities of early- and mid-nineteenth-century activists? This chapter argues that 'place' in the Mediterranean before nation-states should not be treated as a stable category, but instead should be read against the modern geographical grain, especially when analysing the mental world of the Mediterranean's provincial imperial subjects. To do this I will compare the travels, intellectual transformations and senses of 'home' and 'away' of three mid-nineteenth-century activists born off the shores of the Adriatic Sea during or immediately after the Napoleonic Wars. These three men lived a total of 236 years between them and spent those years writing well over fifty books as well as thousands of articles, pamphlets and manifestos. I will then conclude by indicating what a comparative analysis of these three figures reveals about the complications of using terms such as 'exile', 'diaspora', and/or 'displacement' in the era before nation-states, especially along the shores of the Mediterranean. All in less than twenty pages. Such an ambitious itinerary requires pretty painful leaps and bounds through the life and minds of this group of complex characters. But what we will lose in nuance, hopefully we will gain in trying to understand the bigger picture of place for nineteenth-century Mediterranean provincials. So off we go.

Niccolò Tommaseo: many homes, rarely away

Of the three figures under discussion, Niccolò Tommaseo is the most likely to be familiar to a reader well-versed in the literary and political history of nineteenth-century Europe, as the fanciful and sometimes frightful publications that his too-active pen authored have made their way into most histories of the Italian Risorgimento and many of the mid-nineteenth-century Balkans. But just to make sure we are all familiar with the same life and professional trajectory of this famous, prolific crank, a little background is necessary.[6]

Niccolò Tommaseo was born in the third tier port town of Šibenik, Dalmatia, in 1802 to an Italian-speaking father and an illiterate Slavic-speaking mother. Both born as subjects of the Venetian Republic that had ruled most of Dalmatia since the fifteenth century, mother and father conversed throughout their marriage in the local Italian dialect of their hometown, though Tommaseo's mother opted to sing her son the Slavic-language lullabies of her girlhood to put him at ease when he fussed. Hoping that their little 'Nico' (Tommaseo's nickname) would grow up to be a lawyer, instead of a small-store owner like his father, Tommaseo's parents first had him educated by his uncle, a fairly well-placed Catholic priest, and then sent young Nico off to the best schools Dalmatia had to offer: first in the provincial capital Zadar to the north and then to the Split seminary in the south (that also claimed Ugo Foscolo as one of its prior alumni). At the ripe old age of fifteen, Tommaseo was then packed off to university in Padua, where he had to voyage due northwest across the Adriatic Sea to attend his university lectures. Once in Padua he was given strict orders from his family to study hard, spend little, keep his head down, and come home to take up a career in law as soon as possible. The only one of these orders Tommaseo followed was that he studied hard, and after several years of torturing his parents during his summer vacations home he finally forced them to concede that he was not meant for their world: not meant for a comfortable bourgeois existence, not meant for Šibenik, and not even meant for Dalmatia.

Even in his early teens, Tommaseo was ambitious: he wanted to be a man of letters and he wanted to de-Slavify himself or, as he put it, to 'deillyrianize myself and make myself Italian, all the way to my nerves, fibres, bones, and the makeup of my soul ... all completely Italian'.[7] Here his ambitions did not end, for not only did he want to make books, and make himself Italian, he also hoped to play a hand in making the Italian peninsula 'Italy' as well. After years of family arguments, his parents let him go, shaking their heads and refusing to financially support him in his pursuits. He shook his head right back and left.

It is important to note here that even before alienating himself from the paternal nest, Tommaseo was not 'outside' his home sphere. Instead he was following the tides of upper-mobility that any Dalmatian family with some sort of means would set for a promising son. Travelling north to Zadar, then south to Split, then northeast across the Adriatic to Padua, were all voyages required for the upperwardly mobile within the confines of the Venetian Republic that had closed its eyes just five years before Tommaseo's birth. And until the very last years of Tommaseo's life, all of these places were conjoined within the infrastructures and administrations of the Adriatic's new hegemon: the Habsburg Empire. To travel back and forth across the Adriatic, Tommaseo had to get a passport, but not one of those hard-to-get ones that permitted travel outside the empire. Instead his travel required at most permission to reside within another Habsburg province besides his own. This sort of passport could be obtained from the local Dalmatian police headquarters, and Tommaseo spent much of his time home during summer vacations coddling friends who had chosen a bureaucratic career in order to ensure his papers were in order without too much hassle. Travelling up, down, and across the Adriatic was no exile. And though freed from the confining desires of the paternal nest during and after university, Tommaseo was not 'away'. He lived briefly in Padua, in Venice, in the Venetian countryside, in Milan, and then finally moved to Florence for about ten years. But the new homes he made himself were not 'abroad'. Instead they followed the spatial transitions that first the Venetian and then the Habsburg Empire laid out for its striving sons. All these new 'homes' were within the same conglomerate and the sail-ships, steamships, carriage trips, and finally train trips he took to make a name and profession for himself were administered by the same monarchy no matter whether it was a Dalmatian, Venetian, Lombard or Tuscan local police force that checked his documents. He was moving among the many Italian-speaking 'home fronts' of the Habsburg Monarchy.

The astronomical rise of this fifteen-year-old Dalmatian to become one of the leaders of the Catholic-Romantic strain of the Italian Risorgimento, the second-in-command of the 1848–9 Venetian Revolution, and the author of what I consider the best Italian dictionary of the nineteenth century, is well documented. And though it is a fascinating tale, there is not the time here to tell it. What there is time for is to discuss exile and Tommaseo. As many have noted before, Tommaseo was a man who narrated himself through the lens of exile.[8] He published one of his memoirs under the heading of exile, imaginatively coining it 'My second exile', indicating thereby that there had been a first. But even in Tommaseo's mind, this first exile was not his 'escape' from Dalmatia when he went off to university. Nor was it his periods in Milan and Florence where he sought to disentangle himself from the provincial Venetian circles he felt were constraining him. None of these forays, though precipitated by what he believed were the compulsion of circumstance, were exile in his mind. It is not just the historian who notes that he moved within the confines of the state in which he was considered a domestic subject. Until he left Habsburg lands for Paris in 1835, he, too, considered himself 'within', even though he was consistently regarded as a 'Schiavone' or a 'Slav' by chauvinistic locals in Padua and Venice and as a 'Dalmatian outsider' in Milan and Florence. Outsider, but not foreign, Tommaseo's time away from the hilly seascape of Šibenik was spent in a mostly monolingual Italian environment within Habsburg lands, an environment he believed was bringing him closer to 'deillyrianizing myself' so that he could help make his 'homeland' a unified *Italia*.

His first foray outside the Habsburg Empire, and his first identification with 'exile', was triggered by his political activities in the mid-1830s, which were viewed with increased hostility by the Habsburg administration. Tommaseo had always made clear his mission to help foster the resurgence of an Italian nation. But in 1835 he chose to leave his Habsburg homes so that he could enjoy France's freedom of the press and tell the world exactly how this new Italy needed to be framed. How did it need to be framed? To put it crudely: as a multi-centric federal republic where Italian unity would be founded on a conscious acceptance of Italian diversity.[9] Tommaseo's future *Italia* would not be one of standardization, but instead of negotiation: all the different cultures and traditions of Italy's *cento città* (hundred cities) – whether linguistic, political, economic, or religious – would need to be recognized and harmonized, not whitewashed or streamlined. These opinions were not very popular among the crowded Parisian boarding houses of the Italian nationalist exiles where Tommaseo resided after crossing the Alps. Nor were they popular in the most famous Risorgimento activist circle, Giuseppe Mazzini's '*Giovine Italia*' (Young Italy). Nor were they popular among Habsburg censors. Running to Paris to tell the world what Italy needed to be, Tommaseo quickly found himself isolated and barred from returning to any of the lands he once had called home: not only were Lombardy, Tuscany and Venetia now off limits, but as a Habsburg persona non-grata, so, too, was Dalmatia.

The first self-proclaimed exile in Paris was a nightmare for Tommaseo: he was isolated, he was poor, he caught a nasty case of syphilis, and he spent most of his time in a feverish state fearing the next round of surgeries and mercury 'cures' he was to undertake.[10] In between these pleasant activities he also learned of the death of both of his parents. Being unable to obtain travel papers to Habsburg Dalmatia to mourn them as he wished, Tommaseo's mind moved homewards to be with them. Eventually, Tommaseo's body moved 'homeward', too. But not to the blue waters of the Adriatic where Habsburg police would still not permit him; instead he chose a virtual home, a land as close to Dalmatia and the Italies he once knew where his political status would be accepted: he moved to Corsica.

Corsica in the nineteenth century was a part of France and had never been ruled by a Venetian doge or a Habsburg monarch. However, amid the rugged island mountains, Tommaseo described Napoleon's birthplace in terms reminiscent of his boyhood home. With its 'lemons in the orchards, snow on the hills, mother who salutes me with a smile, a swim in the sea, pure sun, and flowers in my room', Tommaseo in Corsica felt like he had left exile behind.[11] In fact, Corsica's multilingual maritime mosaic with its rough peasantry helped him rediscover Dalmatia. And once he made the acquaintance of a German amateur poet who loved all things Romantic and all things Slavic, Tommaseo was also introduced to the German-language Slavophile writings of Goethe, Ranke and Herder. Diseased, mourning his parents, and stranded with an amateur German poet on the island of Corsica, Tommaseo began reconsidering Dalmatia's Slavic-speaking cultural legacies and the Slavic nations in formation, the same legacies and nation he had spent the first half of his life avoiding.

From the Dalmatian boy who aspired to 'deillyrianize myself and make myself Italian, all the way to my nerves, fibres, bones, and the makeup of my soul ... all completely Italian',[12] after his months in Corsica Tommaseo became a man who began signing his letters in Italian '*Uno slavo* (A Slav)', beautifully encapsulating the multi-national persona he began to inhabit, the same multi-national persona he would continue to attribute to his boyhood home, Dalmatia, and the same multi-national message he tried to imbue on the Italian Risorgimento before, during, and after 1848. A Habsburg amnesty for all political exiles was issued in 1839 and Tommaseo set sail from Corsica and headed straight back to reassemble his new (Corsican-German-Romantic-influenced) discoveries about Dalmatia and its Slavic identity with that of its 1840s day-to-day. He spent a few months in Dalmatia visiting his parents' graves, arguing over wills and testaments, and making new friends among the province's Slavic-oriented intellectuals and activists. By 1840 he had decided to make his new home in Venice, close to Dalmatia, close to the Balkans, close to Italy, and in the fourth largest city of the Habsburg Monarchy of which he was still a subject. For the next nine years in Venice Tommaseo dedicated his life to promoting simultaneously Italian and South Slavic national agendas. And when revolution erupted in 1848–9, he rose to become second-in-command of the new Venetian Republic, where he used his positions as diplomat and Minister of Education and Religion as a podium from which to spread his words of multi-national activism. While armies raged across half of Europe, Tommaseo tried to teach his Corsican-inspired multi-nationalism to all who could hear, begging his fellow Habsburg subjects-in-arms, whether they be mother-tongue Italian, Slavic, German, Hungarian, Polish or what-have-you 'to join together [*affratellare*] peoples, so that they can mutually help each other in acquiring their own liberty'.[13] When the 1848–9 fight for liberty ended in failure, Tommaseo was listed amongst the forty leaders of the Venetian Revolution who would be forced into exile from Habsburg lands if Venice's surrender to the Habsburg armies was to be accepted.

On 27 August 1849 Tommaseo boarded the ship of the forty condemned leaders of the Venetian Revolution with the only known itinerary being 'exile'. Most of his fellow condemned approached their ousting with the same voyage in mind: armed escort steamship to Marseilles, then Paris, and then hopefully back to the peninsula to start fighting again. Tommaseo, however, chose to forego the normal routes of exile: he had learned from his first try at it. And when the ship leaving Venice made its first stop in British-held Corfu (in order to restock and assure the authorities that the exiles were free of cholera), Tommaseo refused to move on. The rest of his fellow Venetian exiles would spread out and populate the Swiss, British, Belgian and French enclaves so beloved by Italian nationalists, but Tommaseo knew better: he chose exile to be another virtual home of Mediterranean mosaics of multi-national influences instead of being an outsider in northern climes. Almost completely blind and with little money to his name, he rented a room in a boarding house, married its widowed proprietor, and spent the next few years writing his memoirs of 1848 and lecturing Corfu's Orthodox and Catholics, Greek- and Italian-speakers to learn to love one another and live together. When Corfiotes made it clear that they preferred him to make his multi-national home elsewhere, he spent the last years of his exile in Turin, a city he found even less appealing than Paris. With the unification of Italy he returned to the hillsides of Florence, where he ended his life. But to the end, he refused to take on Italian citizenship. In the heart of Italy, he died an exiled subject of Habsburg Dalmatia and an oft-hallowed 'founding father' of the Italian Risorgimento.

The twists and turns of Tommaseo's travels and the resulting transformations of his political and intellectual understandings of nationhood defy a clear pattern at first glance. Until his mid-thirties, Tommaseo moved incessantly, living in three radically different port-towns along the eastern Adriatic

(Šibenik, Zadar, and Split), three different towns in Venetia (Padua, Venice, and Rovereto), one in Lombardy (Milan) and one in Tuscany (Florence), but in these travels he never left the Habsburg Monarchy. Instead, until his mid-twenties, he moved along the traditional pathways of achievement as any eastern-Adriatic subject of the Adriatic would do: schooling in provincial centres until secondary education brought the Adriatic's brightest to the Venetian metropole. And once he had made a name for himself within the traditional centres of the Venice-oriented metropole system to which his provincial parents had sent him, he set out to make a name for himself in the new Italian-language publishing centres of the Habsburg Monarchy: Milan and Florence. Much travel, no doubt. But it is hard to call these itineraries anything other than those of a provincial trying to make it big. Once big, Tommaseo chose to defy his state, and to do so he sought out 1840s Paris with its freedom of the press. There he suffered much and felt alone, but no large intellectual transformations dawned on him. He moved to Paris to write a book outlining a plan for a future multi-centric federal Italy filled with an array of different dialects and traditions. And in Paris he wrote just what he had planned.

Homesickness in Paris pushed him to the Mediterranean island of Corsica and there his whole worldview of nationhood, Dalmatia, Italy, Croatia-Slavonia-Serbia, the Balkans and the Mediterranean changed. At 'home' among the fruits of a Mediterranean clime and its political economy but outside the structures of Venetian- and/or Habsburg-dominated traditions and expectations, Tommaseo re-evaluated his entire understanding of the world that had produced him. At home in the Mediterranean and displaced from the imperial structures he knew, he constructed a new multi-national vision for the homes he loved and Europe as a whole, which he would expand and promote throughout the rest of his life. His return to Dalmatia, Venice, Corfu and Florence over the next thirty years did not budge his Corsica lessons much. He was back to the ex-Venetian and soon-to-be-ex-Habsburg worlds he thought he knew.

Pacifico Valussi: few homes, unexpectedly away

Whereas Tommaseo's movements spanned from Paris in the north to Corfu in the south, from Corsica in the west to Split in the east, Pacifico Valussi's trajectory never ventured further west than Milan, further north than Friuli, further east than Trieste or further south than Rome. In fact, Valussi – who headed the three most influential newspapers in Trieste throughout the 1840s, served as deputy to and secretary of the Venetian provisional government during the 1848–9 revolutions, and was elected senator to the Kingdom of Italy – never lived outside of what was to become Italy. And he only lived outside the southern provinces of the Habsburg Empire when he was named a senator of the Kingdom of Italy. Nonetheless, compelled to move throughout his life from economic and then political necessity, Valussi, too, experienced a sense of displacement that significantly transformed his understanding of nationhood to perhaps a greater degree than Tommaseo.

Pacifico Valussi's small-landholding parents had been raised to expect peace under the Venetian Republic's centuries-long care of their Friulian valleys and hillsides. And when a son was born to them in 1813 (eleven years after Tommaseo) they celebrated by naming him 'Pacifico' to mark what they hoped would be a return to an era of peace after the last round of Napoleonic treaties were signed. Though their hopes were clearly soon dashed, their son was raised under the shadow of other Venetian-informed expectations. Young Pacifico's schooling was overseen by his father and the local priest until he was sent to Friuli's Venetian-built provincial capital, Udine, where he received his secondary training. In his memoirs he noted that as a boy he was weaned on Jean-Jacques Rousseau, Silvio Pellico, Ugo Foscolo and a host of other favourites from the Italian nationalist cannon, but whether we should believe what he wrote in his early seventies about the upbringing that made him the Italian senator he would one day become I leave up to you. What we do know for sure is that before arriving in the university town of Padua to take a degree in engineering, Valussi was fluent in Italian and German and could read French, Spanish and Latin with little difficulty. He also had a passion for local history, especially of the early-modern Venetia. What we also know is that with one brother slated to carry on the family farm and another taking orders in the priesthood, Valussi felt free enough to sow some professional oats further afield than those his brothers had sowed for him.

Where those oats led him after graduating from university in his early twenties was the metropole of his parents' generation: Venice. Living within a stone's throw of the Accademia bridge, Valussi decided he, too, wanted to be a man of letters and he, too, wanted to use his words to help inspire his fellow speakers of the language of *sì* to push for the creation of a united Italy. Venice's empty *calle*, its deserted marketplaces, its empty palazzi, and its array of Grand-Tour tourists calling out to anyone on a boat '*Monsieur une gondole*' seemed the quintessence of why a national revival was necessary to restore Venice (and the Italian peninsula as a whole) back to a level of prestige rather than pitiful pandering.[14] But no matter how hard Valussi tried, his efforts to write histories, economic tracts, poems, plays and pamphlets landed on deaf ears and continued to secure him less than enough money for rent. Venice was a shadow of what it once had been and the chances for young men to make a name for themselves there were a thing of the past.

Enter Trieste: by the late 1830s Valussi was desperate for a chance to make something of himself, and he got his chance when a fellow Friulian and close friend in Venice wrote to him indicating that there was a job open to edit a newspaper in the nearby port town of Trieste. Valussi arrived to find a job and much, much more. For Valussi, Trieste was a 'city [where] you had to work, and work a lot' but it was also patently ethnically diverse in a way that Udine, Padua and Venice had never been.[15] Valussi was struck by the amalgam of multi-lingual and multi-religious communities that inhabited the quintessentially Habsburg free-port city. In his newspapers, in article after article, he made mention of how Italian, South-Slavic, German, Greek, French, Turkish, Spanish and English speakers converged within the city, practising their respective Catholic, Christian Orthodox, Jewish, Protestant and Muslim rites in the various religious houses sprinkled throughout the urban space. To Valussi, it was not just city living that was different from Venice, but his understanding of the Adriatic Sea had changed, too. In Venice, he resented foreign tongues and foreign ways dominating the economics of St Mark's Square and the lagoon that sat in front of it. In Habsburg-built Trieste, he listened to the port-city's many different tongues while staring out across its sea-soaked piazza and reconsidered the Adriatic as 'a promiscuous, middle, neutral territory, an open field to the commerce of all the Nations of this gulf, which nature pushed inside the land not to divide the Peoples, but to unite them'.[16]

The effect living and working in Trieste for ten years had on Valussi's understanding of how nationalism needed to function was astounding. He went from a man who hoped to re-enliven Italian piazzas to one who proposed that a multi-national borderland system needed to be created for all of Europe, one where each nation needed to be created along its peripheries to ensure it could be harmonized and rendered compatible with the many other national communities that intersected with it.[17] Beginning in 1839, Valussi used his influence as newspaper editor for some of the Habsburg Empire's most important publications to pound home his new Trieste-inspired creed: multi-national spaces were not an accident of history, but an opportunity for commerce and pacification. And 'nationalizing' multi-national and/or multi-ethnic borderland regions promised little more than senseless violence. As Valussi saw it, borderlands were made up of communities 'only fire and iron could break up [disunirsi]' and what was needed to create a peaceful and economically prosperous Europe was one with a multi-national infrastructure, with the Adriatic at its core.[18]

In spring 1848, Valussi left Trieste to join the Venetian Revolution. And though he left his Habsburg newspapers behind in the hopes of helping bring about the unification of Italy, he did not shed his new multi-national creeds when returning to Venice. Instead, he used his position as Secretary to the provisional Venetian government and his editorship of several of its newspapers to promote a Venetian-led multi-national platform for the Adriatic, the Mediterranean and Europe at large. So, while Habsburg and Venetian armies battled it out in the surrounding countryside, Valussi preached that national, linguistic and ethnic diversity required more complex solutions than those derived from the 'sword'. Throughout 1848–9 he proposed that buffer-zone states should be founded between Europe's future nation-states. He hoped that an idealized and expanded version of a multi-national Belgium or Switzerland would replace the Habsburg Monarchy in the mixed lands of Central Europe, arguing that only in this way could nationalist violence be dispelled and European-wide trade promoted. Such inspirations taken from his experiences in Habsburg Trieste were repeated in countless newspaper articles, pamphlets and speeches to participants of Venice's war against the Habsburgs. And though few of Valussi's colleagues recognized the irony of this situation, when in August 1849 Valussi's name was initially added to the list of Venice's political leaders slated for forced exile (alongside that of Tommaseo), Valussi's former Trieste employer Karl von Bruck, now Commerce Minister of the entire Austrian Empire, had Valussi's sentence of exile commuted, a sign of respect for their friendship but also because in many ways Valussi had not betrayed the work he had started in Trieste.

When Tommaseo, Manin and the rest of the Venetian revolutionary leadership were put on a boat headed for Corfu to begin their exile from Habsburg territory, a spared Valussi was 'encouraged' to leave Venice and return to Habsburg-controlled Udine. After the failure of 1848, it was assumed that Valussi would have learned his lesson and would avoid politics upon arriving 'home'. However, once back in Friuli, Valussi continued much as he had before: he kept publishing newspapers, he set up economic and scientific societies and he published pamphlets encouraging any readership he could get to see nations as naturally and inevitably intersecting and overlapping.

Valussi only left Habsburg Europe when the next round of wars over Italian unification began in 1859. Though a vocal multi-nationalist, he had never shed his commitment to the Italian national cause. And when Habsburg and Italian forces began preparing for battle, Valussi no longer felt welcome in Friuli. He packed up his family and fled to Milan, where he spent the next couple of years using his pen to push for a grander Italian unification. When Venetia and Friuli were left out of the newly united Italy in 1861, he found himself an exile in the truest sense of the word. Exiled in Italy, he gave up his multi-national stance and became a fervent irredentist. From arguing in favour of a Trieste-inspired multi-nationalism, now he worked late into the night publishing article after article proclaiming Friuli Italian and only Italian, and calling his brothers to arms so that they could beat the barbarian German hordes back. Once most of Friuli was annexed to Italy in 1866, Valussi became the province's first senator, promising his electorate that he would fight to the last to reclaim for Rome all of the Habsburg regions where Italian was spoken, regardless of how linguistically mixed those regions were. Much had changed.

Looking over Valussi's life and works, two points come to the fore when considering movement and the issue of displacement in the era before nation-states around the Mediterranean. First, if we took a map of the eighteenth-century Venetian Republic and its territories and superimposed upon it a map of the nineteenth-century Habsburg Monarchy we would see that the moments of greatest intellectual change in Valussi's life happened when he ventured beyond the Venetian geographies of his parents' generation and set up shop in traditional Habsburg outposts. In the hillsides of Friuli, in Udine, in Padua and in Venice, Valussi's ideas about his own future and his hopes for political and cultural reform coaligned almost precisely to the 'Risorgimento canon' he himself claimed had nursed him as a youth.[19] In Trieste and then later in Lombardy, Valussi switched gears completely. In Habsburg Trieste, which had never participated in a Venetian order, he questioned the wisdom of imagining the nurturing and development of just one nation to the exclusion of others, especially in seaboard communities where members of different languages and religions lived together as a result of the mechanics of global trade. In Milan – the capital of newly 'liberated' Habsburg Lombardy and also a decidedly un-Venetian urban space – Valussi shed the Trieste-inspired Habsburg multi-national impulses that he had developed and promoted for over twenty years and now learned to prioritize the making of Italy over all else. Milan-inspired Valussi began a twenty-year career of disseminating a message of Italian chauvinism, which denied the rights for equal national development if at odds with Italian interests. The frustrations and sensibilities of exile and war, no doubt, had much to do with this shift. But, nonetheless, when 'home' in Venetian lands such shifts towards multi-nationalism or away from it had never come to the fore.

The second point made clear from analysing Valussi's life and works is the importance of not assuming an 'Italian' geography to understand his movements. Though he never lived outside the lands that would one day become part of the Kingdom of Italy, he did experience a sense of being 'outside' the infrastructures and expectations he was raised to consider natural. Though the Venetian Republic had gasped its last breaths several years before his birth, Pacifico Valussi was home along its contours and displaced for better or worse when he slipped past them. The geography of the Italian nation-state was one he was trying to help define, but not one that defined him.

Matija Ban: away as home

Tommaseo and Valussi both lived out their lives between the contours of the greater Venetian sociopolitical land- and seascapes of their parents and the Habsburg Monarchy of their present. The third and least well known of the figures discussed in this chapter vied between the legacies of the small pre-nineteenth-century Mediterranean city-state Dubrovnik, the Ottoman Empire, the Serbian Kingdom and the Habsburg Monarchy. From the most humble of beginnings, Matija Ban would tutor Serbian royalty, help found the Serbian Academy of Sciences and travel the Balkans in attempts to incite rebellion against Ottoman and then Habsburg overlords.

Virtually unknown to present-day readers, Matija Ban was born in 1818 to a Slavic-speaking family in a village outside Dubrovnik. His father was a barber and his mother an illiterate homemaker. Born just ten years after the Dubrovnik city-state had been dissolved by Napoleon, Ban's family struggled to make a living in a city that still reverberated more of the mores of an oligarchic city-state than the bureaucratic Habsburg etiquettes of the city's new rulers. As such, there were few questions of what would happen to a precocious barber's son in an extremely class-divided city. He was intelligent, he excelled at school, and he was without fortune. Clearly, he was destined for the priesthood.

Unlike Tommaseo and Valussi, who were forced to venture out into Venetian-based provincial centres to obtain their educations, for good or ill Dubrovnik still provided all the infrastructures of a city-state and the barber-son Matija attended the city's fine gymnasium, populated by the sons of aristocrats, sea captains, lawyers, doctors and the few other odd charity cases like himself. After distinguishing himself in school he entered the world of the priests and was trained by Franciscans in philosophy and rhetoric. By the age of seventeen he was fluent in Serbo-Croatian, Italian, Latin, Ancient Greek and French, and had written several Romantic poems and poetic histories celebrating Dubrovnik's illustrious past.

Apparently young Matija Ban's flights of Romantic fantasy inspired him more than Franciscan teachings. It is rumoured he fell in love with a Dubrovnik lady far more comfortable in the regal palaces straddling Dubrovnik's famed *Stradun* than she would have ever felt in Ban's village environs. Rejected in love, Ban decided to reject the Church as well. And he did something the likes of Tommaseo or Valussi would never have considered: he got on a boat and followed the path so many former citizens of Dubrovnik had chosen before. He decided to make his future and fortune in the Ottoman Empire.

Little remains from Matija Ban's early years in the Ottoman Empire. We know that immediately upon leaving the Franciscan order he obtained a job as a scribe within a Dubrovnik law firm and then at the city's tax office. One can only assume that, armed with a superior education and letters of introduction from Dubrovnik city and commercial elites, Ban set forth to make a new life for himself using the centuries-old Ottoman networks available in abundance to any promising son of his hometown. Ban's leap into the Eastern Mediterranean was less blind, therefore, than practised. He was following the footsteps and depending on the credentials of many former ambitious Dubrovnikers before him.

Upon disembarking ship in Istanbul, Ban landed on his feet immediately, ushered into employment by the well-endowed and well-connected Greek seminary on the island of Heybeliada/Halki, just a stone's throw (more or less) from Istanbul itself. There Ban taught Italian language and literature, and in between teaching Dante, he studied Greek and attended courses at the French naval academy also housed on the island. With a spattering of Turkish, a semi-firm knowledge of Greek and a new love of all things French, within a year Ban intensified his relationships with some of the more powerful Istanbul-based commercial circles: he was offered positions in mainland Istanbul teaching history and geography for the city's most prestigious French school, the Lycée Saint Benoît. He was also hired to teach Italian language and literature for the new reform-oriented Armenian college, the Bebek Seminary. In many ways, Ban's first years in the Ottoman Mediterranean minted him as a premiere diaspora tutor: sons of wealthy families hailing from the Greek Orthodox, Armenian and French communities were schooled by him to learn and love the languages of Petrarch and Racine. He thus provided his students with precisely those languages most felt to be de rigueur for success in Mediterranean trade, politics and high society.

Up until the early 1840s, few indicators remain of Ban's worldview. What is clear, however, is that he moved with aplomb in the Ottoman metropolis, displaying few signs of estrangement. The ease with which he introduced himself to Istanbul society and the alacrity with which he was incorporated therein probably had much to do with the Dubrovniker's centuries-long traditional role as the cross-Mediterranean dragoman, acting as interpreter between West and East in politics, commerce and culture.[20] However, this cultural mediator-type figure did little to infuse the Mediterranean with any Slavic character, though that was the language of his birth. So how did such a firmly entrenched Romance-language Mediterranean transform himself into a man whose entire life centred around landlocked Serbia? The answer lies with the fact that Istanbul served not just as an ideal haven for penniless, highly educated Romantics from Dubrovnik. It was also one of the preferred havens for exiled pan-Slavists from the Russian Empire.

Probably through his intensifying relations with Istanbul's French community, Matija Ban met the Polish nationalist Michał Czajkowski, founder of Istanbul's branch of the Paris-based Polish émigré centre 'Hôtel Lambert'. Through Czajkowski's circle, Ban's Romanticism went political and his love of Dubrovnik local history and local (Slavic-centred) literature was now wedded to a new emphasis on all things Slav. Within Czajkowski's circle, Ban was bombarded with the same Slavophile texts that Tommaseo had encountered in Corsica. And amidst discussions about Mickiewicz, Goethe, Ranke and Herder, Ban also devoured the secular nationalist message of the two premier linguists of South-Slavic Europe, the Serbian lexicographer and collector of folk tales, Vuk Stefanović Karadžić, and the Croatian linguist, journalist and political activist, Ljudevit Gaj. The effect these two authors had on Ban cannot be understated, for through their insistence that South-Slavic nationalism should be centred around language instead of religion, Ban imagined a role for himself within the Eastern-Orthodox dominated Serb world: as a Catholic he could help mediate through literature a unification of South-Slavic brothers through words. With Czajkowski's encouragement and connections, a path to participate in the nationalist movement of the heroic upstart Serbia was made possible. And in 1844 Matija Ban took the plunge and left the Mediterranean.

Immediately upon arriving in Belgrade, again thanks to Czajkowski's connections, he was hired to be the new tutor of Prince Alexander Karadjordjević's daughter.

Again, Matija Ban's move to Belgrade was not just a move away from Mediterranean commercial-centred cosmopolitanism towards Slavic nationalism. It also delineated the new mission for his life: to negotiate the relationship between nationhood and religion. Ban's new mission did not play its life out purely in the princely drawing rooms of the Serbian royal house. He was given lectureships on comparative (secular) literatures in Belgrade's burgeoning educational institutions. And during the revolutions of 1848–9 he was even commissioned by Serbia's Minister of the Interior, Ilija Garašanin, to spread this cross-confessional Serbian platform among the Catholic populations of the Balkans. Ban gladly consented and spent much of 1848–50 travelling through Dalmatia, Croatia and Herzegovina arguing that the only liberty for South-Slavic speaking peoples would be available outside the reigns of Habsburg, Russian and Ottoman rule and within a multi-religious Serb-oriented South-Slavic brotherhood. When his 1848–9 efforts ended in failure, he returned to Belgrade, where he took up citizenship. There he penned well over fifteen historical dramas encapsulating the heroic fight for Serbian and South-Slav freedom.[21] He died in 1903 as one of the first four members of the Royal Serbian Academy of Arts and Sciences and a remarkable example of what some historians describe as the 'Serb-Catholic minority' of mid-nineteenth-century Balkan activism.[22]

Conclusion: slipping through Mediterranean imperial, post-state and national geographies

The eclectic life story of Matija Ban flushes out some of the points brought to the fore when analysing the life and works of the other fellow sons of the Adriatic discussed earlier, Niccolò Tommaseo and Pacifico Valussi. Firstly, like Tommaseo and Valussi, Ban is remembered as a nationalist and founding father of the twentieth-century nation-state that would come to life after his death. But just like Tommaseo and Valussi, Ban 'discovered' the national passion that would guide his writings and activism 'outside' the imperial structures for which his upbringing had prepared him. Tommaseo's national ideas fulminated within his 'virtual' Mediterranean home of Corsica precisely because he was within an environment he could understand but without the mental and political strictures that had limited his readings and his interests thus far. Valussi, too, travelled just 100 miles from the Adriatic port-town Venice to the Adriatic port-town Trieste, expecting not much more than to finally land some employment. Instead, living in a Habsburg city not built on Venetian legacies transformed completely his sensitivities about nationalism, multi-nationalism and the challenges of community diversity. And just such a trajectory opened up for Ban. He fled a broken heart and a broken pact with the Catholic Church by plunging himself into the Ottoman metropole where so many Dubrovnikers had made a new life for themselves in the past. But once there, he was brought into the new European-wide waves of nationalist and specifically pan-Slavic nationalist thought that had barely touched his peripheral, newly-dissolved city-state. Negotiating between Turkish, Greek, Armenian, Italian and French communities was the kind of thing he had been led to expect when travelling into the Eastern Mediterranean. Polish and Russian émigrés carrying dictionaries, linguistic tracts, folk tales and pamphlets calling for cross-confessional national union was not; and Ban was shocked into action.

Lastly and relatedly, Ban's story brings to life again how slippery geographies are when considering the nineteenth-century Mediterranean. For to understand 'displacement' we need to consider what movement 'felt' natural, what movement was considered 'domestic' and what movement helped build the world that was to come. For 'feelings' of displacement, Tommaseo, Valussi and Ban's stories act as important reminders that legacy infrastructures of dissolved states had just as much (if not more) to do with perceptions of being 'home' and 'away' as contemporary geopolitical borders along the Mediterranean. Like Tommaseo and Valussi, Ban's life moved along the ebbs and flows of a state that no longer existed and within which he could and did move with astounding ease. In Tommaseo's self-narrative, moving up and down the Dalmatian coast to attend school, crossing the Adriatic to attend university and striving for professional opportunities among Venetian provincial centres was no rupture. For Valussi, leaving Friuli to attend school in Udine, then university in Padua, and then settling in Venice to strive for professional recognition was also par for the course. These were trajectories of upper mobility that subjects of the Venetian Republic had been following for centuries. And just because the Venetian Republic no longer existed, this did not mean that a sense of Venetian 'domestic' or 'settled' space dissolved along with it.

In just such a way, but from the basis of a completely different state, Matija Ban moved through the world until his mid-twenties. Though he was born into the same Habsburg Monarchy as Tommaseo and Valussi, unlike Tommaseo and Valussi, Ban was no Venetian provincial. Instead, he was a lower-class subject of a newly-dissolved self-contained metropole. Ban's parents and his community still worked along the infrastructures and expectations of the Ottoman vassal, oligarchic city-state of Dubrovnik. As such, Ban did not move away to obtain an education; instead he was versed *in situ*. And when he rebelled against all that his family and community hoped for him, he still followed the paths of the shadow-state to which he was born instead of the Habsburg paths of the new state that ruled him. As Dubrovnik had for centuries before, Ban sought his fortunes eastwards and went to his metropole's former metropole, Istanbul. In this Tommaseo, Valussi and Ban all had something in common: they began their lives travelling the lands and waters of the Mediterranean without experiencing displacement. They left their paternal nests looking to realize what they already wanted and in their first travels little challenged their worldview. Perhaps a phenomenon hard for the modern reader to remember, but these post-Napoleonic war babies still moved within geographies of their parents' generation and strove to excel along the paths that felt like 'home'. They moved within a geography of a pre-Napoleonic legacy dismissed from the geopolitical map, yes, but they were 'at home' as they moved, nonetheless.

But the true slipperiness of place reveals itself by the fact that these legacy geographies could be and were bumped by the present tensions of the new states that had come into their own after Napoleon. Tommaseo was jolted into multi-nationalism not when he experienced a Mediterranean outside of Venice's grasp. Instead he lurched into Slavophilia when he was in a Mediterranean space outside the strictures of Habsburg censorship and Habsburg intellectual influences. Pacifico Valussi's convictions in provincial Udine remained the same when he moved throughout Venetia thereafter. His mind reeled, however, when he lived in the expanding Habsburg-faithful imperial port-city of Trieste, whose exponentially growing trade and multiethnic populations felt like a foreign Adriatic for someone raised along Venetian norms. And Matija Ban's story, too, is one of displacement with new state players in the game, for in the Ottoman world Ban had been led to expect no Polish-Ukrainian-Czech-French coalitions were on his radar to tout that all things Serb are great, no matter what the religion. Dubrovnik had always been the Ottomans' 'Athens of the South Slavs', not Belgrade. But times had changed and all these actors and the hundred more who made such journeys felt the jars, jerks and jolts that inspired as they displaced the imperial legacies that had comforted them into their convictions thus far. As modern readers of the nineteenth-century Mediterranean past we need to keep all these different slippery senses of place in mind if we hope to understand how and why these actors pushed to make the nation-state world we are living in today.

Notes

1   Johann Gottfried Herder, 'Journal of my voyage in the year 1769', in F.M. Barnard (ed.), *J.G. Herder on Social and Political Culture*, Cambridge Studies in the History and Theory of Politics (Cambridge: Cambridge University Press, 2010), pp. 63–117.

2   Mazzini's British career has been written on extensively. For some examples see: Maurizio Isabella, *Risorgimento in Exile: Italian Émigrés and the Liberal International in the Post-Napoleonic Era* (Oxford: Oxford University Press, 2009); Lucy Riall, *Garibaldi: Invention of a Hero* (New Haven: Yale University Press, 2007); Denis Mack Smith, *Mazzini* (New Haven: Yale University Press, 1994).

3   István Deák, *Lawful Revolution: Louis Kossuth and the Hungarians 1848–1849* (London: Phoenix, 2001).

4   Roman Robert Koropeckyj, *Adam Mickiewicz: The Life of a Romantic* (Ithaca: Cornell University Press, 2008).

5   Lucy Riall, *Garibaldi: Invention of a Hero* (New Haven: Yale University Press, 2007).

6   For a more in depth discussion of Tommaseo and his political and intellectual importance see Dominique Kirchner Reill, *Nationalists Who Feared the Nation: Adriatic Multi-Nationalism in Habsburg Dalmatia, Trieste, and Venice* (Stanford: Stanford University Press, 2012); Jože Pirjevec, *Niccolò Tommaseo tra Italia e Slavia* (Venice: Marsilio, 1977); Raffaele Ciampini, *Vita di Niccolò Tommaseo* (Florence: Sansoni, 1945).

7   Ciampini, *Vita di Niccolò Tommaseo*; Pirjevec, *Niccolò Tommaseo tra Italia e Slavia*.

8   Among publications that have emphasized the 'exile persona' that Tommaseo referenced when contextualizing his life and work, see: Niccolò Tommaseo, *Il primo esilio di N. Tommaseo (1834–1839), Lettere di lui a Cesare Cantù*, edited by Ettore Verga (Milan: L.F. Cogliati, 1904); Susanne Lachenicht and Kirsten Heinsohn (eds), *Diaspora Identities: Exile, Nationalism and Cosmopolitanism in Past and Present* (Frankfurt: Campus, 2009); Renate Lunzer, ' "Esule in casa mia, ma concittadino di più nazioni": Der Italokroate Niccolò Tommaseo', in Olaf Müller (ed.), *Exildiskurse der Romantik in der europäischen und lateinamerikanischen Literatur* (Tübingen: Narr Verlag, 2011), pp. 191–209. Morana Čale, Sanja Roić and Ivana Jerolimov (eds), *I Mari di Niccolò Tommaseo e altri mari* [Studia romanica et anglica zagrabiensia] (Zagreb: FF Press, 2004); as well as Konstantina Zanou's upcoming monograph on early-nineteenth-century nationalists and exiles in the Mediterranean.

9   Tommaseo published his political tract on his vision of how and why Italy should be unified in Niccolò Tommaseo, *Dell'Italia: libri cinque* [epilogue by Francesco Bruni] (Alessandria: Edizioni dell'Orso, 2003). *Dell'Italia* was originally published in 1835.

10 For a concise description of Tommaseo's Paris experience see: Gustavo Balsamo-Crivelli, 'Introduzione', in *Dell'Italia di Niccolò Tommaseo*, pp. vii–xxxi. Important letters and diary entries from this period can be found in Tommaseo, *Il primo esilio di N. Tommaseo (1834–1839)*; Niccolò Tommaseo, *Diario intimo*, edited by Raffaele Ciampini (Turin: Einaudi, 1938).

11 Tommaseo, *Diario intimo*, pp. 206–7.

12 Ciampini, *Vita di Niccolò Tommaseo*; Pirjevec, *Niccolò Tommaseo tra Italia e Slavia*, pp. 43–4.

13 Niccolò Tommaseo, 'Lettera di N. Tommaseo', *La Fratellanza de' Popoli* (1 April 1849), pp. 2–3.

14 Pacifico Valussi, 'Capitolo I. La nostra educazione', in *Dalla memoria d'un vecchio giornalista dall'epoca del Risorgimento italiano* (Udine: Tip. A. Pellegrini, 1967), pp. 17–32.

15 Pacifico Valussi, 'Capitolo II. A Trieste', in *Dalla memoria d'un vecchio giornalista*, pp. 33–48.

16 Pacifico Valussi, 'Ancora del Litorale italo-slavo', *Il Precursore* (14 January 1849), pp. 165–7.

17 For more on this see: Reill, *Nationalists Who Feared the Nation*; idem, 'Bordertopia: Pacifico Valussi and the Challenge of Borderlands in the Mid-Nineteenth Century', *California Italian Studies* 2/1 (2011), pp. 1–25.

18 Pacifico Valussi, 'Bibliografia', *La Favilla* VII/2 (27 January 1842), pp. 29–35.

19 For a discussion of a Risorgimento canon and the dissemination of a shared, prototype 'national Italian consciousness' see Alberto Mario Banti, *Il Risorgimento italiano* (Rome: Laterza, 2004); idem, *La nazione del Risorgimento: parentela, santità e onore alle origini dell'Italia unita* (Turin: Einaudi, 2000).

20 Vesna Miović-Perić, 'Dragomans of the Dubrovnik Republic: Their Training and Career', *Dubrovnik Annals 5* (2001), pp. 81–94.

21 Ban's literary production has not survived the test of time. Some of the more available collected publications of his work include: Matija Ban, *Djela* (Belgrade: Kraljevsko srpska držama štamparija, 1889); idem, *Tragovi* (Zagreb: Forada, 1995); idem, *Dva svijeta* (Zagreb: Print, 1989); idem, *Različnih Pisma* (Belgrade: Kraljevska srpska državna štamparija, 1861), 2 vols.

22 Ivo Banac, 'The Confessional "Rule" and the Dubrovnik Exception: The Origins of the "Serb-Catholic" Circle in Nineteenth-Century Dalmatia', *Slavic Review* 42/3 (1983), pp. 448–74; Ivica Šarac, 'The Catholic Serbs: a Hidden Minority on the Adriatic Coast', in Christian Promitzer, Klaus-Jürgen Hermanik and Eduard Staudinger (eds), *(Hidden) Minorities: Language and Ethnic Identity between Central Europe and the Balkans* (Berlin: Lit, 2009), pp. 177–88.

CHAPTER EIGHT

The Strange Lives of Ottoman Liberalism:

Exile, Patriotism and Constitutionalism in the Thought of Mustafa Fazıl Paşa

Andrew Arsan[*]

There remains, still, a blank spot on the global map of nineteenth-century liberalism. Our understanding of liberal thought and practice has expanded significantly in recent decades, as scholars have reconstructed, and dissected, the distinctive liberal languages that took hold in Southern Europe, Latin America and South Asia over the course of the long nineteenth century.[1] As C.A. Bayly has argued, these decades witnessed the global circulation of novel political and economic ideas of liberty and justice, representation and popular sovereignty, redistribution and land reform, which were evaluated and recast in the light of often longstanding traditions of ethical propriety, virtue, righteousness and political consultation.[2] There is, however, a notable absentee at this party, for historians of the Ottoman lands remain reluctant to trace the lives and transmutations of liberalism in the well-protected

[*] The author wishes to thank Maurizio Isabella and Konstantina Zanou for their patience, generosity and careful readings of this chapter, and Chris Bayly and Chris Clark for enlivening and helpful discussions of some of these themes. The errors, as always, are my own.

domains. Liberal thought thus retains an ambiguous place in the historiography of the *Tanzimat* – the momentous succession of reforms through which mid-nineteenth-century Ottoman sultans and functionaries attempted to refurbish the sprawling structures of the state and to recast the foundations of imperial community. These began, in the conventional chronology, with the Gülhane imperial edict of 1839, which sought to provide renewed 'guarantees' that the empire's 'subjects' would enjoy 'perfect security for life, honour and property', and culminated in 1876 with the promulgation of an imperial constitution and the opening of a representative assembly.[3] On the face of it, then, the *Tanzimat* would seem a good place to look for the application of liberal principles.

An older generation of scholars might have been tempted to agree.[4] Its admiration for the pioneering endeavours of *Tanzimat* statesmen, however, was tinged at once with condescension for the naivety and unoriginality of their thought, and with sympathy for their resilience in the face of obscurantist clerics and obstructionist provincial notables. The men of the *Tanzimat* failed, in these accounts, to meet many of their objectives. Despite this, they did succeed in bringing the inchoate beginnings of political modernity to a state that had hitherto been in, but not of, the nineteenth century, a ruined leftover of a revolute time. Such ambivalent praise is reserved, in particular, for the group of young men who gathered in the Belgrade forest on the outskirts of Istanbul one pleasant Saturday evening in June 1865 to found the *İttifak-i Hamiyet*, or 'patriotic alliance'. This coterie, which included such brilliant polemicists and publicists as Âli Suavi, Namık Kemal, Ziya Paşa and Şinasi, had come to be known by 1867 as the *yeni osmanlılar*, or Young Ottomans.[5] Despite their differing backgrounds and dispositions, they were united in their antipathy for the 'despotism' of Fuad and Âli, the two ministers who dominated the upper echelons of Ottoman government for much of the 1860s; their dissatisfaction with the baleful consequences of the 1856 Treaty of Paris, which had made of European intervention in Ottoman affairs a routine occurrence; their dismay at the continuing provincial unrest which culminated in the Cretan rebellion of 1866–7; and their growing disquiet at the mismanagement and indebtedness of the Ottoman exchequer, which had brought the Sublime Porte to the edge of bankruptcy.[6]

The historical accounts of the 1960s treated the Young Ottomans as at once the symbols and the vectors of modernization. On the one hand, their writings were considered inert objects of inquiry, which could be used – in the scientistic language of post-war modernization theory – to 'gauge the rate of change of political beliefs', and to assess the West's 'impact' on the Ottoman Empire.[7] On the other, they were depicted as consequential agents of historical change, Pygmalion-like sculptors who attempted to chisel the timeworn structures of the Ottoman state into the image of Europe. Though 'no giants of political theory', they had performed a useful service by beginning the difficult task of adapting 'Western European political ideas to suit the needs of the Ottoman Empire', assisting in its transformation 'from a medieval theocracy to a constitutional republic'.[8]

It is upon one of the members of this loose coalition that this chapter focuses: the Turco-Egyptian prince Mustafa Fazıl Paşa, now best known as the financial and political patron of the Young Ottomans. This chapter examines his political ideas, encapsulated in a pamphlet published under his name in Paris in 1867, and which served as a clarion call for Ottoman constitutionalism; setting them in their intellectual and political contexts, it argues that we can see in these the evidence of a liberalism which, while distinctively Ottoman in its particular preoccupation with alleviating the pressures of foreign intervention and financial instability, shared much with its contemporary European counterparts. In doing so, it strives to put the Ottoman world on the map of nineteenth-century liberalism, and to suggest that its political thinkers moved in time with developments elsewhere. For too long, historians have treated nineteenth-century Ottoman thought as a derivative product, a home-grown substitute whose exponents were forever fated to remain lagging behind the latest developments in the European heartlands – a little like those provincial ladies in the novels of the time, who went proudly about their evening strolls in fashions which had long since fallen out of favour in Paris. The Ottoman liberalism of Mustafa Fazıl, this piece contends, was very much of its time.

In making the case for synchrony, this chapter breaks not just with earlier assessments of the Young Ottomans, but also with the preoccupations of much current scholarship. Historians of the Ottoman Empire have, in recent years, largely turned away from the diffusionism of the 1960s. Returning, not without reason, to the Gülhane edict, scholars have argued that this declaration was founded upon Islamic principles of the good life and the virtuous ruler.[9] There is much to be said for such work, which has reminded us of the dynamism of an autochthonous tradition of political thought which hardly needed the impetus of European liberalism to arrive at this resounding statement of munificent imperial justice. These efforts, however, have largely focused on the inaugural moments of the *Tanzimat*, leaving unexamined later developments, such as the growth of the Young Ottomans. Scholarship on the later nineteenth century, meanwhile, has increasingly focused on the manner in which reform played itself out in the provinces, creating new expectations and resentments, and transforming the relations between Istanbul and its dependencies.[10] But, in doing so, it has largely abandoned the high ground of intellectual history for the brambly terrain of provincial political and social life, leaving us with a poorer sense of the ways in which Ottoman literati and public men made sense of their state's circumstances, and elaborated schemes for the reform of state and society which, they hoped, might rescue the empire from the twin threats of internal disarray and external encroachment.

*

This piece shifts the focus back towards political thought, and the writings of Mustafa Fazıl Paşa. Born in 1829 in Cairo, Mustafa was the son of Ibrahim Paşa and the grandson of Mehmet Ali, the founder of the dynasty which had ruled Egypt as an autonomous province since 1805.[11] However, he spent much of his adult life as a servant of the Ottoman state. Appointed minister of education in 1862, he moved on to the Ministry of Finances in 1864, and the chairmanship of the *meclis-i hazain*, or Council of the Treasury, in 1865, before being pushed into exile in April 1866 – apparently for having spoken out in his audiences with Sultan Abdülaziz against Fuad and Âli, the powerful ministers who held, in his view, undue sway over affairs of state.[12] Barely a month after Mustafa's sudden departure for Paris, Fuad stripped him of his claim to the Egyptian viceroyalty by introducing hereditary succession in a break with Ottoman custom, which had long favoured the most senior male relative of the incumbent. This was a reform the ruler of Egypt, Mustafa's estranged half-brother Isma'il, had long pined for, in the hope of putting his own son on the khedivial throne. The decision dealt Mustafa a bitter blow, and set him on a course of open opposition with Fuad and Âli, whose executive monopoly he had long deplored.[13] On 5 February 1867, less than a year into his Parisian exile, Mustafa declared himself the representative of 'the great party of Young Turkey', composed of 'all the men of progress and good patriots' intent upon reforming the empire and staving off the domestic disarray of which the 'Cretan insurrection' was such a forceful, and worrying, reminder.[14] Then, in early March, came Mustafa's open letter to Abdülaziz, calling for the introduction of an imperial constitution. Published in pamphlet form in the French capital, this impassioned plea for reform rapidly made it to Istanbul, where it circulated clandestinely, helping to give a fleeting sense of common purpose to the group of liberal public men who would briefly cohere around Mustafa in Paris.[15]

A few days after Mustafa's letter was first disseminated in Istanbul, a handwritten tract espousing the same constitutionalist ideas appeared in the Ottoman capital – the work of Halil Şerif Paşa, another member of the Egyptian viceregal family, who had served as Ottoman ambassador to Russia. Others, too, were emboldened by the appearance of Mustafa's letter. Though Âli Suavi had initially been reluctant to side with Mustafa, the newspaper he edited, the *Muhbir*, soon began to attack the Sublime Porte's stance on foreign loans and its decision to evacuate Belgrade, which Suavi deemed a humiliating capitulation. Namık Kemal, meanwhile, inveighed in his *Tasvir-i Efkâr* against the foreign intervention and official ineptitude that had inflamed the Cretan situation. Such stances, though, earned these men nothing but official opprobrium. Namık, Suavi and the latter's sometime collaborator, Ziya, were all sent out to pasture in the provinces. Invited by Mustafa – through the intermediary of the French publisher Giampetry, a fixture of the liberal world of Istanbul – to join forces in Paris, they chose foreign flight over domestic exile, leaving the Ottoman capital in May 1867. On 10 August, Suavi, Namık, Ziya and others met in Mustafa's *hôtel particulier*, where they decided to found a 'Young Ottoman' society under Mustafa's aegis, dedicated to the promulgation of liberal ideas – not least through the *Muhbir*, which was to begin publication again in London.[16]

Mustafa's letter has commonly been read as a distant echo of the *lumières* or the Risorgimento, an epiphenomenal product of self-interest, or a piece ghost-written by one of the European schemers and intriguers who swarmed around him in Paris. For his own part, Mustafa is considered an 'Egyptian prince', whose background and concerns were far from those of the 'young intellectuals' to whom he lent his patronage. Regarding Mustafa's epistle as 'reminiscent' of Mazzini's 1831 letter to the ruler of Piedmont, Roderic Davison argued that, while intellectually accomplished, it was ultimately driven by his desire to 'overthrow the Ottoman administration that had denied him the Egyptian throne'. Intelligence and intrigue were, in this account, difficult to disentangle. More generously, Şerif Mardin saw the letter as both 'evocative of Rousseau' and having 'the moralistic tinge' of Gioberti's *Primato*, and as demonstrative of a 'strand of genuine, if somewhat naïve, universalism'. Both scholars, however, cast doubt on Mustafa's authorship, citing contemporary rumours that the letter was in fact the work of the Wallachian exile and political entrepreneur Grégory Ganesco, who had established himself in Paris in the wake of 1848.[17] Such readings effectively relegate this text to the margins of Ottoman political thought, whether because its contents are a disingenuous cover for baser motives, largely cribbed from European models, or because its author was not fully Ottoman, and reliant on the hired hand of a ghost-writer.

The present chapter runs against the current of such interpretations. Treating Mustafa as an Ottoman thinker concerned with the fate of the empire in its totality, it strives not just to reconstruct the arguments of his letter, but also to situate them within the political languages and debates of his own moment. For its central contention is that Mustafa's letter was simultaneously shaped by the pressing concerns of Ottoman imperial administration in the 1860s, and largely consonant with a particular strain of liberalism which developed across Europe in the wake of the 1848 revolutions. This text, with its powerful depiction of a polity brought to its knees by bureaucratic despotism and a man pushed into exile by the callous intrigues of courtiers, presented the constitution as the only means of ensuring the sound functioning of the state, the progress of society, and the preservation of the Ottoman Empire's sovereignty in the face of foreign encroachment and domestic disturbance. Indeed, the letter – written as it was against the backdrop of the Cretan rebellion – was marked by a strong, if ill-defined, insistence on the primacy of the Muslim elements of Ottoman society. Though it sat somewhat uneasily with Mustafa's stress upon the need for concord between the empire's various religious communities, this emphasis served to buttress his case for the constitution. Untrammelled administrative centralization, Mustafa argued, had corroded the virtue and liberty of the Ottoman 'race', hereditary attributes which had proven so precious in its rise to pre-eminence. Thus, the reforms implemented after 1839 had allowed the empire's 'countless' administrators to act as 'subaltern tyrants', whose rapaciousness had dampened the native initiative of a population that could see no point in 'industrious' undertakings, and bred 'turpitude' in the hearts of subjects who had once been so morally sound.[18] The growth of administrative power alone, then, could not prevent the stagnation and fragmentation of Ottoman society – quite the contrary. Only an imperial constitution could provide a remedy to these ills. It would allow for free public debate and a measure of representation – if one that stopped well short of universal suffrage. And, moreover, it would provide a powerful countervailing check upon both excessive executive power, and the narrow and self-interested individualism this had bred in the hearts of Ottoman subjects, facilitating the emergence of a felicitous equilibrium between subject and state, and the one and the many. It was this happy balance that Mustafa strove for above all else, insisting vigorously that the interests of the commonweal should be privileged over those of the individual.

These were claims that chimed with those of mid-century liberals in Britain, France or Italy, many of whom were concerned more with political order and social cohesion, the primacy of legal process and the adequate representation of the community, than with the liberties and rights of the individual. Scholars of mid-Victorian British liberalism have largely discarded the once-dominant notion that this was an essentially 'libertarian' body of thought, concerned above all else with the protection of individual freedom from the state's depredations.[19] Far from being incompatible, liberty and 'the legitimate authority of the state' were largely complementary. While the state had a 'responsibility to improve . . . national character and morality' – not least through constitutional reform – its subjects' freedom was contingent, in turn, upon their 'obedience to just laws'. British liberalism was thus sustained by a long tradition of thought which 'sought to elevate the power of the State, . . . by making it more . . . accountable', and to strengthen the bonds of political society by chipping away at sectional interest.[20] Historians of French political thought, meanwhile, have increasingly taken apart older accounts which contrasted the individualistic, democratic vision of citizenship which purportedly appeared with the Third Republic with an older, more authoritarian, and more communitarian understanding of political subjectivity. On the contrary, they now argue, a powerful strand of liberal thought, as critical of the pitfalls of centralization as it was of the perils of individualism, developed under the Second Empire.[21] Likewise, scholars of post-1848 Italy have discerned the growth of a conservative liberalism whose proponents, bridging the gap between Tocqueville and Guizot, saw the creation of a constitutional regime as the best means of warding off the dangers of democracy, ensuring a centralized but responsive state built around a consultative monarchy, and demonstrating the peninsula's entry into the circle of civilized states.[22] Like liberals across Europe in the two decades after 1848, Mustafa denounced at once the dangers of unchecked central power and those of social disintegration and atomization.

Mustafa's tract was also of its moment in its reliance upon a range of European comparisons. His, it should be stressed, was an argument from analogy. It did not so much seek to find influences to lean upon and precedents to emulate, as frame the eminent viability of an Ottoman constitution through a set of illustrations. Thus, the latter stages of his letter drew much of their effect from the evocation of constitutional experiments and reformist undertakings in a broad range of European states, from France and Britain to Austria, Piedmont and Prussia. In adopting this wide-angled political vision, Mustafa was in a sense no different from other Young Ottomans, who were both well informed of the train of European political events and ideas, and strongly inclined to situate themselves as one of the patriotic, reformist movements that had swept across the continent over the nineteenth century. Suavi, for one, recalled that 'Young Spain, Young France, [and] Young Italy' had provided specific models for the 'patriotic alliance' established in 1865, while Namık cited Garibaldi and Silvio Pellico alongside Voltaire, Condorcet and Montesquieu.[23]

Indeed, several of the Young Ottomans frequented – and, it would seem, sought to build alliances with – other political exiles and émigrés living in the French capital. It would thus appear that Ziya Bey established contact in 1867 with Marian Langiewicz, one of the leaders of the Polish uprising of 1863 who, upon his release from prison in 1865, sought refuge in Switzerland before finding military employment in the Ottoman Empire. Langiewicz, in turn, helped Ziya to secure the support of Count Wladyslaw Plater, who had fled Poland after the revolt of 1830, and of the Austrian socialist Simon Deutsch – a veteran of the revolution of 1848 and a member of the First International, who would go on to participate in the Paris Commune before finding favour in Istanbul, where he died in 1877.[24] These men, it was said, were – along with Mustafa, Ziya, and Namık – signatories of the statutes of the Young Ottoman society, finalized in Paris on 30 August 1867. Indeed, one of the striking features of this document was its commitment to 'the destruction of Russian influence . . . in the East' by a two-pronged attack, one focusing on 'the emancipation of the Christian populations in Turkey from the Muscovite protectorship', and the other on the 'reestablishment of the heroic Polish nation in its former independence'.[25] At such moments, the Young Ottomans seem a part of that second 'liberal international' which came into being after the revolutions of 1848, as a host of disenchanted radicals, exiled democrats and cosmopolitan nationalists attempted to regroup, creating new networks and alignments in the name of liberty, nationality and equality.

However, neither Mustafa nor his missive can be assimilated quite so readily to this émigré world, with its admixture of ardent patriotism and cosmopolitan fraternity. We thus have no way of verifying the seemingly far-fetched claim of Frederick Millingen – one of those who entered Mustafa's circle of 'émigrés and discontents' in Paris – that he was tasked with meeting Garibaldi, from whom Mustafa hoped to obtain 'officers and transports' to lead an 'expedition against Tripoli of Barbary'.[26] Nor is there any firm evidence to suggest that Grégory Ganesco was the author of Mustafa's letter, as David Urquhart and his close ally Suavi, who had come to look upon Mustafa as a traitor to the cause of Ottoman reform, would later allege.[27] A canny operator, Ganesco rapidly established a foothold in the turbulent world of Parisian journalism after fleeing his native Wallachia in 1848. But, while he shared the hostility of Mustafa and the other Young Ottomans for Russia and its designs in the Eastern Mediterranean, his view of the Crimean War was starkly at odds with their bleak assessment of the Treaty of Paris and its consequences for Ottoman sovereignty. This conflict, he wrote in its immediate aftermath, had presented an opportunity to check Russia's 'universal domination', that potent threat to European 'progress'. What's more, it held out hope of a lasting 'great peace', whose foundations had been laid by the collaboration between England, France and the 'young peoples' of Italy, Poland and Romania, whose earnest 'belief in the solidarity of the entire human family' had led them to assist the Ottoman Empire.[28] By contrast, many in Istanbul saw the treaty, and the imperial edict which accompanied it, as a threat to the 'integrity and independence of our empire'.[29] It is difficult, too, to square Ganesco's staunch commitment to Wallachia's administrative autonomy with Mustafa's marked distaste for the experiments in decentralization which had become rife in the Ottoman realm after 1856. While Mustafa inveighed against bureaucratic despotism, which handed power to unaccountable and corrupt administrators, he reserved equal scorn for the foreign meddlers who encouraged the empire's Christian subjects to rise up in rebellion. His vision, then, was not one of decentralization, but of consultation; rather than loosening the ties between province and capital, he sought, on the contrary, to strengthen them.

Moreover, the cases Mustafa did cite – post-1789 France; Prussia; Italy – were often ones of newfound or restored national greatness. His letter was written, it should be remembered, in the wake of Italian unification, in the immediate aftermath of Prussia's victory at Sadowa, and just as the details of Austro-Hungarian dualism were being worked out. It is perhaps no surprise, then, that he took it as axiomatic that a constitution was necessary to the social stability and political survival of a state. Such a document was not, to Mustafa, the embodiment of an emancipatory ideal, but a stabilizing social compact and a geopolitical survival strategy, warding off future territorial losses; without such a charter, nations were simply fated to disappear. In this sense, too, the letter was a document of a quite specific moment. Though it restated arguments frequently rehearsed after 1848, as liberals across Europe set about recasting constitutionalism in more conservative terms, the letter bore the immediate, hastily considered traces of contemporary events. It was a child of its time, born of the particular circumstances of the late 1860s. In treating it as more generally derivative of European thought, we lose sight of this chronological specificity.

By the same dint, we cannot understand Mustafa's letter without taking into consideration the administrative questions that preoccupied him for much of the 1860s, as he grappled with the Ottoman Empire's domestic travails and diplomatic predicament. He should not simply be considered an Egyptian prince, whose primary concern remained securing the reins of power in Cairo, and whose relationship with his Turkish protégés was destined to remain a volatile and fleeting marriage of convenience. As recent scholarship on nineteenth-century Egypt has persuasively demonstrated, Mehmet Ali and his successors remained firmly anchored in a broader Ottoman world.[30] Mustafa seems a case in point, whose occupancy of high office in Istanbul gave a particular inflection to his arguments for political reform. His stint as minister of education may, it could be argued, have reinforced his deep-seated sense of the importance of learning in fostering liberal dispositions and setting the wheels of progress turning. He certainly put theory into practice in his own household, 'giving ... as liberal a European education as was compatible with the rules of the *harem*' to his daughter, Nazlı Hanım, who 'spoke both French and English perfectly, read a good deal – mostly English novels, which had made her familiar with English life – and was a fairly good musician'.[31]

More important still was his tenure as minister of finance. Appointed in 1864, Mustafa found the public finances in disarray, due to a disastrous emission of paper currency, which had forced another foreign loan. On taking office, Mustafa energetically set about reducing expenditure in an attempt to ease the growing financial burden on the Ottoman exchequer. Implementing particularly stringent cuts to the civil list and to defence and naval spending, he succeeded in bringing the budget into the black, and proposed wide-ranging fiscal reform to lighten the indirect load on the poorest, and to tax property and foreign trade directly.[32] Though these measures remained a dead letter, Mustafa continued to show a concern for fiscal matters in his open letter. 'Everywhere', he wrote, 'we battle the monster of misery'; crippled by administrative abuse and venality, the empire's subjects 'had become incapable of meeting public charges which everywhere else would appear light'. Its coffers empty, the empire was unable to pay its soldiers and administrators. This led only to further abuses, for 'in Orient a functionary who is not paid enough is a functionary who holds the population to ransom'.[33] The problem, Mustafa concluded, was not an excessive fiscal burden, but the impecuniousness of the empire's subjects. And this, in turn, was a consequence of misrule.

*

Indeed, Mustafa's open letter can be read as a text pre-eminently concerned with explaining the causes and consequences of despotism. Exile – more even than poverty – was the surest sign of the maladministration which had befallen the Ottoman Empire. As Mustafa noted in the very first sentence of his open letter: 'that which enters with the greatest difficulty into the palaces of princes is the truth'. For 'those who surround' these rulers 'hide it even from themselves', going so far as to 'throw into exile' those brave enough to 'reveal . . . the vices of . . . government and the wounds of the Empire'. There is no doubting the considerable personal animus for Fuad which underwrote such words. But, from the particular, Mustafa sought to extract a more general lesson. In his eyes, political liberty hinged upon the existence of a realm of untrammelled public discussion, in which those who sought to speak truth to power might proceed without fear of sanction. This was a view shared by other Young Ottomans and, in particular, by Şinasi, who stressed in his writings the beneficent effects of the 'political gazettes of those people the limits of whose understanding have been enlarged by the power of knowledge'.[34] For Mustafa, the absence of such 'public opinion' did not simply leave the people uninformed of the affairs of state; it also freed the 'innumerable members of Your Government' from political responsibility: 'unaccountable before [public] opinion, they are therefore unaccountable to Your Majesty'. For their part, those who strove to 'confront head-on the ills besieging us', and to 'suggest, as faithful subject[s]' should, 'the remedy which can save us' from a perdition precipitated by despotism, were consigned to live abroad, far from the state they sought to defend.[35]

The conclusions to be drawn were clear. Those who remained in the employ of the sultan, 'living amidst the pleasures of power', showed neither concern for the wishes of the people nor understanding of the workings of the state. Imagining 'that the people suffer only because of their own indolence, and that empires decline only because of the unhappy consequences of painful events', they remained immured in their own self-indulgence. Those who were forced to leave the lands of their birth, meanwhile, were the veritable servants of the sultan, his state and subjects, selfless truth-seekers willing to compromise their own comfort and happiness in the pursuit of the well-being of the many. As Mustafa insisted, he had asked for little: 'soliciting neither positions nor favours', his 'sole ambition . . . was to pass on to Your Majesty the wishes and complaints of the great majority of the empire's . . . inhabitants'. The political exile was a figure of singular courage and virtue, willing to sacrifice his own welfare for that of the body politic. A true intermediary between the people and the ruler, he embodied the traits – 'virtue', 'moral virility', intelligence, industry and initiative – of the ideal political subject.[36]

By contrast, Mustafa saw little worthy of praise in the 'revolts' that had broken out 'amongst the empire's Christian populations'. These were not, as some European observers insisted, the stirrings of a deep-seated desire for liberty, but the 'work of our external enemies'. The only means of stemming the 'perpetual interference of the European powers in our internal affairs' and its 'disastrous consequences' was the introduction of a constitution. This, Mustafa argued, would grant 'all [the empire's] populations' equal access to 'the same tutelary justice'. Doing so would enable the Ottoman state to roll back the regime of exceptions, foreign protectorates and local autonomies which had spread across the empire over the nineteenth century, thus putting 'an end to all external meddling' and leading 'to a salutary improvement in our international relations'.[37] These ideas were echoed by Halil Şerif Paşa, who argued in his own pamphlet of 1867 that the only means of outdoing 'Muscovite Machiavellism' was to introduce a constitution which would demonstrate the Ottoman Empire's 'moral superiority over Russia' by 'erasing social and political distinctions between Christians and Muslims'.[38] But Mustafa went further still. The distinctions drawn by European observers between the empire's various populations were specious. There could not be one policy for Christians and another for Muslims, 'for there is only one justice, and politics is justice put into practice'. While 'Europe imagined that the Christians alone are subjected to arbitrary abuses . . . the Muslims, precisely because no foreign power is interested in their fate', suffered just as much from the oppressive practices of corrupt administrators.[39]

This was not an argument free of inconsistencies. On the one hand, Mustafa called for an end to the distinction European opinion drew between the empire's Muslims and its Christians, to whose defence politicians and propagandists rushed so eagerly, proclaiming high-minded 'principles of civilisation and humanity' which often barely disguised their baser 'interests'. This, he maintained, was detrimental to the empire's cohesion; all its inhabitants should have the same 'rights and duties', irrespective of religion. On the other hand, Mustafa himself differentiated between Muslims and Christians, 'victors and vanquished'. Even as he spoke of a single 'people', united in its loyalty to the emperor and thirst for constitutional rule, he regarded the 'Turkish race' as the empire's dominant element. This, ultimately, was 'the Empire of our ancestors'. Mustafa's patriotism, despite its apparent openness, was in the end distinctly proprietorial, insisting upon the primacy of the empire's Muslim 'Ottoman' inhabitants, related by ties of kin to its founders and rulers. But this was no simple bigoted grandstanding. Rather, Mustafa's vision of his own 'race' was instrumental to his case for the constitution, for the notable decrease in its own 'pride, honour, and dignity' was a particularly worrisome indication of the 'incurable moral cowardice' which had gripped the empire. Should the 'Ottoman' element give out, 'there would be no remedy . . . for our decadence'.[40]

The only cure for these ills was a constitution. The 'ignorance' and 'intellectual degeneration' of Ottoman subjects had become impossible to avoid. These were all the more worrying because states across Europe were 'busy with the instruction of the people'. One would be hard pressed, for instance, to 'find a single inhabitant' of Switzerland who could not read or write, while 'Prussia had perhaps only triumphed over Austria at Sadowa because its population was more educated than that of its rival'. Even England, whose aristocracy was only slowly and reluctantly doing away with its own 'privileges', had made 'gigantic' efforts to spread 'elementary knowledge'. Could the Ottomans really afford to 'decrease in intelligence when most European states' were working to raise standards of education? But educational endeavours alone were not enough. 'The first teacher of peoples', 'that which creates all others, and which no other can replace, is *liberty*!' And the only means of winning liberty, and securing the empire's salvation, was a '*Constitution*! A real, large, and fecund Constitution'. By taking the bold step of promulgating such a document, the sultan would not just ensure that he would be gratefully remembered as the 'regenerator' of his people; he would also make of his dejected and dispossessed subjects 'active, energetic, industrious citizens' who would 'enrich the Empire, cultivate their spirit, [and] regain their forefathers' virtue'.[41] In this vision, the constitution was a veritable panacea to the empire's manifold political, social and economic ills. Ample evidence for this could be found with only the most cursory of glances at political developments across Europe. But Mustafa strove not to make a case for blind emulation of European precedent – for taking on something borrowed and something new – but rather to remind the Ottoman people of their own intrinsic abilities, their immanent capacity to move in step with the times.

For, while acknowledging that any '*constitutional government*' should be tailored to the 'traditions and needs of Turkey', Mustafa insisted that the Ottoman Empire could not be seen as an exception, standing outside the stream of progress. It was simply wrong to differentiate, as Europeans did, between the empire and other states. If the Ottomans had initially distinguished themselves by their 'military heroism', it was not because of any inherent disposition towards the martial arts, which led them to neglect other human faculties; it was merely because they needed, like the 'Franks, the Germans, and the Arabs', to 'find a spot in the sun'. The veritable cause of the Ottomans' failure to 'become an active and industrious people at the same time as others was . . . our political system'. A state lacking laws and liberties was one which bred universal indolence. While some would inevitably 'exploit' others, rather than devote their energies to cultivating 'their soil and spirit', the ensuing 'tyranny and exaction' would dissuade even the most well-meaning and industrious, 'no longer . . . certain of enjoying the fruits of their labours'. The surest guide to the value of liberty was France. Before 1789, peasants in many of the country's provinces 'wandered through the woods dressed in animal hides', their humanity hidden beneath layers of deprivation and dirt. But a mere 'thirty years after the emancipation of 1789, everything had changed! France, thanks to *liberty*, had taken its place amongst the richest and most industrious nations of the two Worlds', its peasants, scrubbed of their filth, full participants in progress.[42]

Equally compelling examples could be found in Piedmont, Austria and Prussia. 'When the little king of Piedmont had wanted to become the king of a great Italy', his first step was not military mobilization, but the declaration of a 'liberal *constitution*'. Austria, meanwhile, was saved from extremity by '*constitutional liberty*'. Perhaps the most telling example of all was Prussia. Its resounding victory over Austria, Mustafa insisted, owed as much to 'the civilization of its people as to the needle-gun'. It was incontestable, then, that granting freedom of one's people was a sure way of strengthening the workings of government. 'Why should Turkey deviate from the norm?' Was 'the Turkish race ... a monstrous exception to the human race'? Was it, perhaps, 'our religion which condemns us to live' poor and unfree? Here Mustafa was categorical: religion was best left where it belonged, in the 'sublime domain of eternal truths'; it could play no part in determining 'the rights of peoples' – a view which marked him off from Namık, who remained convinced that 'with us good and evil are determined by the Şeriat', the 'binding thread' holding together political society.[43] Thus, Mustafa insisted it was high time to prove to the newspapers and 'public opinion' of 'Paris, London, and Florence' that 'neither our race nor our religion compel us to remain in this state of weakness and corruption', and to embark upon a constitutional 'Revolution'. After all, those 'provinces which had broken free of metropolitan power', like Wallachia, Serbia, Moldavia, Egypt and Tunisia had already proven that constitutional practices could travel east. Indeed, inspiration could be taken from their experiments. While Mustafa provided scant detail of his scheme, he did suggest that each province should have a 'freely-elected assembly'; its delegates' chief responsibility would be to 'inform' the sultan of the 'situation' and 'desires' of his subjects.[44] This should not be seen as a decentralist scheme, allowing greater powers to the provinces. On the contrary, the introduction of these representative assemblies would tie the provinces closer to the centre; transforming the empire into a consultative regime, it would make the sultan and his administration at once more knowledgeable of provincial circumstances and more accountable to provincial demands. This brought Mustafa into line with Namık, who saw *meşveret*, or consultation, as the central underpinning of just government.[45] But Mustafa went further. The constitution was not simply a means of renewing the contractual vows between the Ottoman people and their sultan; it was also the only means of staving off the empire's collapse. There was no time for laborious preliminary reforms. Only a constitution could guarantee progress – and survival.

*

What, in the end, came of all of this? Historians' assessments of Mustafa's role have remained decidedly ambivalent. After all, his time as the Young Ottomans' leader-in-exile was brief. Having met Abdülaziz during the latter's visit to France in the summer of 1867, he rapidly patched up his differences with the sultan. By the autumn, he was back in Istanbul, his relations with Namık, Ziya, and Suavi, if not entirely broken, then increasingly strained. But the point of this piece has not been to measure the impact of Mustafa's publication, and to trace his political vagaries. And nor has it been to trace his influences back to their European origins, finding the fount from which his words flowed like an explorer in search of the source of the Nile, or to compare his construct with its European blueprints to detect and disparage derivations and departures. It seems difficult, of course, to deny that Mustafa's vociferous attack upon despotism may have owed something to eighteenth-century antecedents or to hive off his writings from their European context. And nor would this chapter want to do so. On the contrary, it has sought to find a place for Ottoman political thought in our accounts of nineteenth-century liberalism.

On the one hand, it has set out the particularly Ottoman contingencies and concerns which shaped Mustafa's writings, from financial disarray and increasing dependence on foreign loans, to the growing fear that Ottoman sovereignty was compromised by intervention and local rebellions. On the other hand, it has situated Mustafa's thought within its European context. While Suavi found common ground in London with the Russophobe David Urquhart and Namık and Ziya fraternized in Paris with the cosmopolitan exiles of 1848, whose hatred for despotism and desire for a more equitable international order meshed with their own, Mustafa remained distinctly aristocratic in his social frequentations and conservative in his thought. A 'welcome guest', thanks to his 'rank and intelligence', of the 'most select *salons*' of the French capital, Mustafa regarded the constitution not just as a check upon the administrative despotism of the pen-pushers and intriguers to whom the *Tanzimat* had given such power, but also as a guarantor of social stability and progress, a glue which would hold an increasingly fissiparous imperial society together.[46] The Young Ottomans' thought may have been 'strange' in its exilic strains or its desire to engage on equal terms with Europe. But, like the apparent demise of liberalism in early twentieth-century England, there is nothing inexplicable about its emergence and intellectual vitality.[47] Rather, it can be accounted for by careful consideration of its content and reconstruction of its contexts.

Mustafa's examples, this chapter has argued, were very much of the moment; they included not just the revolutionary France of 1789, but also the unifying Italy, victorious Prussia and reforming Austria of the late 1860s. And, significantly, they spilled well over the confines of the Mediterranean world to encompass the entire European continent. This is a salient point of the liberalism of Mustafa and his fellow Young Ottomans. While they were all too aware of the pressing weight of the Eastern question, they seemingly showed little concern for the middle sea as a distinct geopolitical space, in marked contrast to contemporary Italian, French or British thinkers who increasingly thought of the Mediterranean as a discrete sphere of operation and competition.[48] For Mustafa, the continental mass of Europe, not the maritime expanses of the Mediterranean, was the point of reference. But this Europe was neither a suspended mobile, made up of single, disembodied texts, detached from their context, inspirational documents which could blow the cleansing air of liberalism into Ottoman lands, nor a reified construct, whose uncontested synonymity with the Enlightenment should be apparent to all comers. Europe was not just Rousseau, Mazzini or Montesquieu; but nor was it a lodestone, an enlightened mass exerting an irresistible attraction on Ottoman thinkers. Rather, to men like Mustafa, it was a changing continent whose varied states were at different stages of progress, and whose rulers had confronted – and, in some cases, continued to confront – many of the same issues bedeviling the Porte. And the Ottoman Empire was, to Mustafa, a part of Europe; its statesmen had no reason not to implement constitutional rule, for its subjects were eminently capable of the political advances much of the rest of the continent had witnessed since 1789. Much earlier scholarship on nineteenth-century Ottoman political thought took, it is true, an abstracted image of an enlightened Europe as its constant, looming referent. But to place Ottoman public men like Mustafa firmly within the mainstream of contemporary European political thought is not to give in to the temptations of diffusionism. On the contrary, it is to continue the task of provincializing Europe – treating it not as a norm, a universal benchmark by which other societies and thinkers must be measured, but as a place subject to the push and pull of history, and as a region whose boundaries might be open to reconsideration.[49]

Notes

1   C.A. Bayly, *Recovering Liberties: Indian Thought in the Age of Liberalism and Empire* (Cambridge: Cambridge University Press, 2012); Maurizio Isabella, *Risorgimento in Exile: Italian Émigrés and the Liberal International in the Post-Napoleonic Era* (Oxford: Oxford University Press, 2009); Gabriel Paquette, 'Introduction: Liberalism in the Early Nineteenth-Century Iberian World', *History of European Ideas* 41/2 (2015), pp. 153–65.

2   C.A. Bayly, *The Birth of the Modern World 1780–1914: Global Connections and Comparisons* (Oxford: Blackwell, 2004), chaps. 8–9.

3   Akram Khater (ed.), *Sources in the History of the Modern Middle East* (Boston: Houghton Mifflin, 2011), p. 12.

4   Niyazi Berkes, *The Development of Secularism in Turkey* (Montreal: McGill University Press, 1964); Roderic Davison, *Reform in the Ottoman Empire 1856–1876* (Princeton: Princeton University Press, 1963); Bernard Lewis, *The Emergence of Modern Turkey* (Oxford: Oxford University Press, 2002 [1961]); Şerif Mardin, *The Genesis of Young Ottoman Thought: A Study in the Modernization of Turkish Political Ideas* (Princeton: Princeton University Press, 1962).

5   Ebüzziya Tevfik, 'Yeni Osmanlılar', *Yeni Tasvir-i Efkâr* (20 June 1909).

6   Nazan Çiçek, *The Young Ottomans: Turkish Critics of the Eastern Question in the Late Nineteenth Century* (London: IB Tauris, 2010).

7   Berkes, *Development*, p. 3; Mardin, *Genesis*, p. 8.

8   Mardin, *Genesis*, p. 9; Lewis, *Emergence*, pp. 173–4, 481.

9   Butrus Abu-Manneh, 'The Islamic Roots of the Gülhane Rescript', *Die Welts des Islams* 34 (1994), pp. 173–203; Frederick Anscombe, 'Islam and the Age of Ottoman Reform', *Past & Present* 208 (2010), pp. 159–89.

10   Zeynep Çelik, *Empire, Architecture and the City: French-Ottoman Encounters, 1830–1914* (Seattle: University of Washington Press, 2008); Selim Deringil, ' "They Live in a State of Nomadism and Savagery": The Late Ottoman Empire and the Postcolonial Debate', *Comparative Studies in Society and History* 45 (2003), pp. 311–42; Thomas Kühn, *Empire, Islam, and Politics of Difference: Ottoman Rule in Yemen, 1849–1919* (Leiden: Brill, 2011); Ussama Makdisi, 'Ottoman Orientalism', *American Historical Review* 117 (2002), pp. 768–96; Milen Petrov, 'Everyday Forms of Compliance: Subaltern Commentaries on Ottoman Reform, 1864–1868', *Comparative Studies in Society and History* 46 (2004), pp. 730–56.

11   Blanchard Jerrold, *Egypt under Ismail Pasha* (London: Samuel Tinsley, 1879), p. 19.

12   Mehmet Zaki Pakalın, *Tanzimat Maliye Nazırları* (Istanbul: Kanaat Kitabevi, 1940), p. 6.

13   Georges Douin, *Histoire du Règne du Khédive Ismail* (Rome: Société Royale de Géographie d'Egypte, 1933–34), vol. 1, pp. 207–19.

14   *Le Nord* (5 February 1867).

15   Davison, *Reform*, pp. 202–6.

16   Ibid., pp. 207–9; Mardin, *Genesis*, pp. 38–45.

17   Davison, *Reform*, pp. 201–3; Mardin, *Genesis*, pp. 282, 281, 278.

18   [Mustafa Fazıl Paşa], *Lettre Adressée au feu Sultan Abdul Aziz par le Feu Prince Moustapha Fazil Pasha 1866* [*sic*] (Cairo: A. Costagliola, 1897), pp. 10, 7.

19   Eugenio Biagini (ed.), *Citizenship and Community: Liberals, Radicals, and Collective Identities in the British Isles, 1865–1931* (Cambridge: Cambridge University Press, 1996); J.P. Parry, *The Politics of Patriotism: English Liberalism, National Identity, and Europe, 1830–1866* (Cambridge: Cambridge University Press, 2006).

20   J.P. Parry, 'Liberalism and Liberty', in Peter Mandler (ed.), *Liberty and Authority in Victorian Britain* (Oxford: Oxford University Press, 2006), pp. 72, 82, 97–8.

21   Sudhir Hazareesingh, *From Subject to Citizen: The Second Empire and the Emergence of Modern French Democracy* (Princeton: Princeton University Press, 1998); Jeremy Jennings, *Revolution and the Republic: A History of Political Thought in France since the Eighteenth Century* (Oxford: Oxford University Press, 2011).

22   Maurizio Isabella, 'Aristocratic Liberalism and Risorgimento: Cesare Balbo and Piedmontese Political Thought after 1848', *History of European Ideas* 39/6 (2013), pp. 835–57; Roberto Romani, 'Reluctant Revolutionaries: Moderate Liberalism in the Kingdom of Sardinia, 1848–1859', *Historical Journal* 55 (2012), pp. 45–73.

23 Mardin, *Genesis*, pp. 21–2.

24 Adam Lewak, *Dzieje Emigracji Polskiej w Turcji (1831–1878)* (Warsaw: Gebethner & Wolff, 1935), pp. 211–14; Michael Miller, 'From Liberal Nationalism to Cosmopolitan Patriotism: Simon Deutsch and 1848ers in Exile', *European Review of History* 17 (2010), pp. 379–93.

25 Davison, *Reform*, p. 214; Lewak, *Dzieje Emigracji*, p. 214, n. 62.

26 Frederick Millingen, *La Turquie sous le Règne d'Abdul-Aziz (1862–1867)* (Paris: Librairie Internationale, 1868), pp. 345–6.

27 See Çiçek, *Young Ottomans*, pp. 57–69.

28 G. Ganesco, *La Valachie depuis 1830 jusqu'à ce Jour. Son Avenir* (Brussels: Charles Muquardt, 1855), pp. 242–3, 249; Ganesco, *Diplomatie et Nationalité* (Paris: Librairie Nouvelle, 1856), pp. 19, 35–6.

29 Çiçek, *Young Ottomans*, p. 113.

30 Khaled Fahmy, *All the Pasha's Men: Mehmed Ali, his Army and the Making of Modern Egypt* (Cambridge: Cambridge University Press, 1997); Ehud Toledano, *State and Society in Mid-Nineteenth Century Egypt* (Cambridge: Cambridge University Press, 1990).

31 Horace Rumbold, *Recollections of a Diplomatist* (London: Edward Arnold, 1902), vol. 2, pp. 330–2.

32 Vicomte de la Jonquière, *Histoire de l'Empire Ottoman depuis les Origines jusqu'à nos Jours* (Paris: Hachette, 1914), vol. 2, pp. 21–5.

33 *Lettre*, pp. 9–10.

34 Mardin, *Genesis*, p. 263.

35 *Lettre*, pp. 3, 6.

36 Ibid., pp. 18, 5, 6.

37 Ibid., pp. 4, 12–13.

38 Edouard Engelhardt, *La Turquie et le Tanzimat* (Paris: Cotillon, 1882), vol. 1, p. 231.

39 *Lettre*, p. 17.

40 Ibid., 5–8.

41 Ibid., pp. 7–9, 17.

42 Ibid., pp. 18, 10–11.

43 Mardin, *Genesis*, pp. 292–3.

44 *Lettre*, pp. 16, 14, 17.

45 Mardin, *Genesis*, pp. 308–13.

46 Edwin de Leon, 'The Old Ottoman and the Young Turk', *Harper's New Monthly Magazine* 44 (1872), p. 612.

47 George Dangerfield, *The Strange Death of Liberal England, 1910–1914* (London: Serif, 1997 [1935]).

48 Andrew Arsan, ' "There Is, in the Heart of Asia . . . an Entirely French Population": France, Mount Lebanon, and the Workings of Affective Empire in the Mediterranean, c.1830–1919', forthcoming; Maurizio Isabella,

'Liberalism and Empires in the Mediterranean: The View-Point of the Risorgimento', in Silvana Patriarca and Lucy Riall (eds), *The Risorgimento Revisited: Nationalism and Culture in Nineteenth-Century Italy* (Basingstoke: Palgrave, 2012), pp. 232–54.

49 Dipesh Chakrabarty, *Provincializing Europe: Postcolonial Thought and Historical Difference* (Princeton: Princeton University Press, 2000).

CHAPTER NINE

From Southern Italy to Istanbul:

Trajectories of Albanian Nationalism in the Writings of Girolamo de Rada and Shemseddin Sami Frashëri, ca. 1848–1903

Artan Puto and Maurizio Isabella

What is the Albanian nation, and when was it first conceived? The mid-nineteenth-century Albanian-speaking populations included a variety of religious communities – Muslim, Orthodox and Catholic – that spoke a range of different dialects and until the early decades of the twentieth century did not have a recognized official written language. Indeed, use was made of several different alphabets: Latin, Greek and Arabic. It was in this period that the educated elites speaking Albanian, and Albanian-speaking intellectuals living both within and outside the Ottoman Empire, tried for the first time to establish common ties within an 'imagined' Albanian community, which was otherwise scattered across different regional, religious and cultural contexts, attempting to single out its distinctive cultural features. The lands inhabited by Albanian-speaking populations were situated in the western part of the Balkans, extending along the Adriatic and Ionian coast and its hinterland, zones that today are located within the territory of Albania proper, and within the borders of Greece, Macedonia and the new offshoots of the former Yugoslav Federation, namely, Montenegro and Kosovo. Before the Congress of Berlin (1878), the territories of the Ottoman Empire inhabited by Albanians were divided into four *vilayets* (provinces): Shkodër, Yiannina, Monastir and Kosovo. They included not only Albanian-speaking populations, but also predominantly Slav, Greek and Turkish ones. Yet significant Albanian-speaking minorities existed in other regions. The Albanian diaspora included populations in southern Italy, in Greece, as well as immigrants in Romania, Bulgaria and Egypt. The most significant, however, was that of the Italo-Albanians, who had settled mainly in the southern Italian regions of Calabria and Sicily in the fifteenth century, following the Ottoman seizure of the Albanian homeland. The importance of this community lay not in its size, since it consisted of no more than approximately 200,000 people, but rather in the precocious and influential attempts by its intellectual leaders to recover its culture.

While in its early decades intellectuals had been primarily concerned with the historical and cultural features of an 'Albanian nation', in the last quarter of the nineteenth and the early twentieth century, Albanian nationalism became more politicized. The Congress of Berlin (1878), which assigned to the newly founded Balkan states, such as Montenegro, Serbia and Greece, Ottoman territories inhabited by Albanian-speaking populations, prompted more nationally-minded Albanian activists to present demands on behalf of 'an Albanian nation', calling for an autonomous Albanian *vilayet* inside the Ottoman Empire, instead of various 'Albanian' lands scattered across a number of different *vilayets*. The Sublime Porte supported these claims by Albanians, its judgement being that Albanian nationalism might prevent further Ottoman territories from being annexed to the newly formed Balkan states.[1]

This chapter explores the birth and evolution of the cultural and political idea of the 'Albanian nation' through the biographies of two leading Albanian intellectuals of the second half of the nineteenth and the early twentieth century, namely, Girolamo (Jeronim in Albanian) De Rada (1814–1903), an outstanding political and cultural exponent of the oldest Albanian diaspora, that of Italy, and Shemseddin Sami Frashëri (1850–1904), a distinguished Ottoman and Albanian intellectual born in southern Albania. While showing the disparate geographical origins of Albanian nationalism, an analysis of their lives will also demonstrate the extent to which this latter was the product of reflections by individuals far from the nation they were imagining. De Rada in fact lived his entire life in his native region in Calabria, in southern Italy, never visited the Albanian territories of the Ottoman Empire and remained attached to, and proudly defended, the cultural peculiarities of the Albanian community in Italy to which he belonged; Frashëri, for his part, although born in southern Albania, lived and worked for most of his life in Istanbul, the capital of the empire which he never ceased to regard as the cultural as well as the political centre of his world. As a result, their idea of Albania was in fact polycentric, reconciling loyalties to different nations and polities, both men being at one and the same time imperial, national and regional patriots. Their deep attachment to Albanian culture and language was compatible with other cultural and linguistic affiliations that made them at once Albanian, Italian, Ottoman and Turkish: De Rada continued to write in both Italian and Albanian all his life, while Frashëri was both a prominent Turkish linguist and an activist within the 'Albanian National Movement'.[2] In addition, their contribution to the definition of an Albanian national culture was the result of the interaction of different traditions and intellectual influences. This chapter focuses on the evolution of their thought, and the formulation of their idea of the Albanian nation in relation to the geopolitical transformations of the period, and in particular to two important features of Ottoman and Mediterranean history in the second half of the nineteenth century. Their lives coincided with those decades, between the Crimean War and the Treaty of Berlin of 1878, when the Ottoman Empire was failing, a number of Ottoman Balkan territories were lost, and the political sovereignty of new Balkan states, such as Serbia, Montenegro and Bulgaria, came under Russian protection, at the same time as European influence in the region grew. This period was also marked by increasing competition between the various national movements of the Balkans. Conversely, the empire itself passed through a period of modernization, resulting in the reforms of the *Tanzimat*, which culminated in the proclamation of the first Ottoman Constitution of 1876 and the intellectual and political activities of the Young Ottomans aspiring to revitalize the empire with new institutions in a bid to ward off the threats to its territorial integrity coming from Europe.[3] As this chapter will demonstrate, while the evolution of De Rada and Frashëri's solution to the 'Albanian question' was very much the result of a reaction to these external transformations, as intellectuals they tried to remain loyal to the multicultural and pluri-national world from which they had issued.

Girolamo de Rada and the defence of a federal and multicultural Albanian nationalism in Italy and the Ottoman Empire (1814–1903)

Italo-Albanian intellectuals had made a pioneering contribution, in the late eighteenth and early nineteenth century, to the study of the language and culture of their 'motherland'. Writers like Angelo Masci (1758–1821), Emanuele Bidera (1784–1858), De Rada's mentor and teacher, Demetrio Camarda (1821–82), Giuseppe Crispi (1781–1859) and Vincenzo Dorsa (1823–85) were thus among the first to entertain the prospect of an autonomous Albanian nationality, collecting local folklore, turning their ancient Albanian dialect into a written language at a time when Albanian still lacked a written form, and building a national pantheon, which included Philip and Alexander the Great of Macedonia, King Pyrrhus of Epirus (fourth century BC) and Gjergj Kastrioti Skanderbeg (1405–68).[4] They did so under the influence of works by Western scholars on Albania, and, more importantly, in the context of the cultural revival associated with the rise of southern Italian patriotism.[5] Calabria and Sicily, where the main Albanian diaspora was settled, were the theatre of major social and political changes in the first decades of the nineteenth century. The shift of power in the Kingdom of Naples from Napoleon to the Bourbons, and back again, created a revolutionary context for liberal movements. Italo-Albanians took an active part in the anti-Bourbon revolts, as they saw in the restoration of the absolutism of Ferdinand IV (1816) a threat to their traditional regional privileges.[6] Thus the Albanian cultural revival coincided with, and was closely intertwined with, the Italian Risorgimento, which represented at the same time a regional and local reaction against the Neapolitan centralized state.

It is this context, combining involvement in southern Italian revolutionary culture and acknowledgement of Italian language and culture with an interest in Albanian popular literature, that accounts for the idiosyncratic nature of Girolamo De Rada's Albanian nationalism. Born in 1814 in Macchia, close to the town of Cosenza, in the southern Italian province of Calabria, De Rada came from an Uniate Catholic family following the Greek Byzantine rite.[7] De Rada's cultural formation owed much to his father Michele De Rada, who was a teacher of Ancient Greek and Latin at the Sant' Adriano College and 'a Carbonaro and an admirer of the liberties of the Classical world', while his mother's forebears had been distinguished scholars of humanities and collectors of Albanian folklore.[8] In the 1830s De Rada himself started to write about, and build up, a corpus of a 'national' literature, by collecting folk songs and publishing his own verse, and by studying the language and history of what he perceived to be the Albanian nation. His first important contribution to the rescue and reinterpretation of Albanian folklore was the *Collezione di poesie albanesi* (1834), written in Italian and heavily influenced by a variety of literary sources that had nothing to do with the Albanian tradition, ranging from Homer to Ariosto, and to the Italian national poet Ugo Foscolo.[9] While De Rada in later years cultivated the Albanian language, his literary works continued to be influenced by Italian literature, and throughout the rest of his life he persevered with the written use of both languages.[10]

The college of Sant' Adriano, where De Rada studied, had been since the end of the previous century an important centre of dissemination of liberal and democratic ideas. As De Rada himself observed, 'the College was a centre of freedom and light'. Along with other students and professors from the college, he was involved in the insurrection of 1837 in the Calabrian city of Cosenza.[11] It comes as no surprise that during one of the most important moments of the Italian Risorgimento, the 1848 uprisings, De Rada, like many other southern provincial liberals, was drawn to the centre of the revolution, Naples, where he published the first ever Albanian newspaper, *L'Albanese d'Italia*, in which some articles were written in the dialect of the Albanian diaspora of southern Italy.

De Rada's own political ideas were moulded by a variety of intellectual influences drawn from Risorgimento political culture. He in fact favoured the creation of a federation of Italian states, convinced as he was that the interests of the Italo-Albanians (their religious rites and their particular cultural traditions) would be better preserved in a multicultural setting protected by a federal structure. These ideas made his brand of the Risorgimento similar to that of the great federalist Carlo Cattaneo (1801–69), and also, given the religious and Christian overtones of his ideals, to that of Vincenzo Gioberti (1801–52). Like the vast majority of Risorgimento patriots, De Rada imagined the regeneration of the Italian nation within a European framework. As early as 1840, in his poem *Giovanni Uniade*, he made the case for a federal Europe made up of self-governing peoples, and capable of guaranteeing the peace and progress of the continent.[12]

It was precisely this belief in a multicultural and tolerant idea of the nation that caused De Rada to be disappointed by the structure and nature of the newly founded Italian liberal state after 1860, when he saw Italo-Albanian cultural and religious specificity as being under threat within a nation-state apparently intent upon promoting ever more cultural homogeneity.[13] As he argued in his *Lettera a Stamile*, written in 1865, and in his *Quanto di libertá*, drafted in 1882, federalism as a system of government, being designed to grant a substantial degree of autonomy to regions and communes, was more respectful of cultural diversity. This was also the principle De Rada envisaged for the future organization of the territories of Albania proper.[14]

In fact, De Rada's dedication to the 'Albanian question' went beyond the defence of the rights of the Albanian communities in Italy, since he also considered the plight of the Albanian provinces in the Ottoman Empire. In correspondence with Shemseddin Sami Frashëri in 1880, De Rada advocated the creation of a tripartite Albanian federation, whose component parts would mirror the religious division of Albanians into Muslims, Catholics and Orthodox.[15] Disappointed as he was with the nature of the new Italian state, he nonetheless envisaged an important role for Italy in the solution of the Albanian national question in the Ottoman territories. After Italian unification and the gradual dissolution of Ottoman dominion in the Balkans, Albanian-inhabited lands entered into the sphere of influence of Rome, which planned to use the Albanian lands as a bulwark for its future expansion towards the East. Although by now critical of the internal structure of the state and its potential intolerance of diversity, De Rada saw Italian irredentist aspirations in the Balkans as offering a means to preserve Albanian autonomy inside the Ottoman Empire against the threats posed by other national movements within the empire.[16]

It was the Greek national movement that seemed to pose the most serious challenges to the claims of Albania. The Italo-Albanians had as early as the late eighteenth and early nineteenth century sought to differentiate themselves from the Italo-Greek community in order to preserve their specific Uniate ecclesiastical-educational privileges in the Kingdom of

Naples. However, Greek nationalism continued to be a source of concern for Albanian nationalists later on in the century. After the creation of the Greek state in 1830, and in the light of its mounting expansionist ambitions in the second half of the nineteenth century, the Albanian desire to assert a separate cultural identity represented also a reaction against Greek nationalists, who coveted territories inhabited by Albanians in the Ottoman Balkans, especially in the fiercely contested *vilayet* of Yiannina, a province containing a mixture of different populations.

De Rada's contribution to the formulation of a theory about the historical origins of the Albanian nation reflected both his concern to emphasize the close association between Italy and Albanian nationalism, and his preoccupation with the distinctiveness of the Albanian nationality as against the Greek. The Italo-Albanians identified the origins of the Albanian nation in the Pelasgian or Pellazg people (otherwise known as *Pelasgi* in *Risorgimento* literature), whose history could be traced back to 2000 BC, and whose territories covered parts of Greece, Albania itself, and, further to the west, Italy and Sicily; they stressed the sheer antiquity of the Albanian language, deeming it to be the oldest in the region, older than Greek even, in order to justify their claims to political and cultural emancipation.

In an article published in Italian in 1864 on the 'Antiquity of the Albanian nation and its affinity with the Hellenes and the Latins', De Rada provided evidence of an old Latin-Pellazg cohabitation, based on the assumption that old Albanians had lived on both coasts of the Adriatic Sea, and argued that the ancient Albanian language could also account for Latin place names. More importantly, he claimed that the Albanian nation was older than the Greek. Although the Pellazgs had given birth to all Balkan 'races', he contended that the Albanians alone were the direct heirs of this ancient population.[17] While Albanians had remained in a 'pure' state of primitiveness, resembling their predecessors far more closely, the Greeks had developed into a separate population with a different culture, and at a later stage of development. In order to demonstrate how Greek culture derived from Albanian, De Rada used Albanian words to 'decipher' the meaning of ancient Greek deities and to explain the polytheism of Greek mythology as the systematization of more ancient natural concepts.[18]

De Rada reiterated his argument about the antiquity of the Albanian nation in the following decades but, given the new political context, his erudite historical disquisitions reflected different preoccupations. In the article 'Pellazgs and Hellenes', published in 1885, both in Italian and old Albanian, De Rada employed linguistic arguments to distinguish the Greek and Albanian nations, and to confirm the antiquity of the Albanians, as heirs of the Pellazgs.[19] He explained the fact that Albanians had remained without a written language in terms of their having always lived in the remotest corners of the region, while the Greeks had developed into an urban civilization, and he therefore emphasized the Albanian presence along the Apennines.

In the political context of the 1880s, however, emphasis on the antiquity of the Albanian nation served new political purposes, since Greek nationalism was no longer the sole threat to Albanian nationalism. In fact, it was designed to counter also the Slavic national movements, several of which in the 1880s were planning to create a Balkan federation as a means to liberate themselves from the dominion of the Sublime Porte.[20] De Rada saw in these plans a threat to the political future of the Albanians, since their territories might be partitioned by the Balkan countries once the Ottoman Empire had retreated. By now, he had also come to the conclusion that the Italian nation-state was no friend to the Albanians, and accused Italy of aspiring, like the other nationalities in the Balkans, to take over the Albanian territories.[21]

While many Italo-Albanian intellectuals, Demetrio Camarda and Vincenzo Dorsa among them, supported a Greek-Albanian federation in the context of an anti-Ottoman alliance, De Rada advocated a kind of autonomous status for the Albanian territories inside the Ottoman Empire. Against those who favoured taking up arms against the Ottomans, De Rada and others espoused more cautious solutions. In order to preserve his peculiar multicultural vision against the multiple threats of different and ever more aggressive nationalisms, whether Italian, Greek or Balkan, the protective umbrella of the Ottoman Empire seemed to him to be the best possible guarantee of the rights of the Albanians. He argued that Albanians were familiar with Ottoman rule, and that more time was needed for the 'awakening' of the national consciousness of Albania.[22] He held on to this belief until the very end of his life. In his political testament written in 1902, one year before his death, De Rada reaffirmed his belief that while Albania was a nation 'scattered and exhausted on different shores', its centre remained in the *vilayets* in the Ottoman Empire. For De Rada, the Adriatic and Ionian Seas, whose names, he claimed, had an Albanian origin, represented the connecting element of the Albanian world: 'Adriatico from *Atërisë* (seat of the ancestors) and Jonio from *Jonë* (ours)'.[23] Politically, however, the empire offered the best shelter against the threats and aggression of other nations to Albania, as 'it never had in mind the extinction of our nationality'. This association would ultimately strengthen both Albania and the empire itself in a brotherhood, as De Rada saw it, similar to the bond that united Scotland and England, or Austria and Hungary, and one that 'could give the Empire of Constantinople the happy primacy among States, to which its geographical and natural primacies contribute'.[24] While he hoped that Christianity would thrive and even expand in this context, and win back the Muslim Albanians, he remained loyal to an idea of the Albanian nation based primarily on language.

Thus it was not in the creation of a nation-state, an event that De Rada projected into a distant future, but in the cultivation of their culture and language within a reformed and multi-national Ottoman world that he saw the best hopes for the survival of his tolerant idea of the Albanian nation, which earlier in his life he had hoped to protect and advance through a particular brand of multicultural and federal Italian *Risorgimento*.

Shemseddin Sami Frashëri: the making and unmaking of an Ottoman, Turkish and Albanian intellectual

While De Rada's peculiar brand of Albanian patriotism had been marked by his origin as a member of the southern Italian diaspora, Shemseddin Sami Frashëri's intellectual trajectory and contribution to the solution of the 'Albanian question' can only be understood in terms of its original Ottoman and Muslim context. Born in June 1850 in the small town of Frashëri in the south-eastern part of Albania, and into a family of small landowners, Frashëri studied in the Greek Zosimea gymnasium of Yiannina, the capital of the *vilayet* of Yiannina where the family had moved in 1865.[25] The years spent at Zosimea gymnasium furnished Sami with a solid grounding, classical and modern, and a firm grasp of both western and eastern languages, whereas with private tutors he had learned Persian, Arabic and Turkish.[26] In 1872, Sami went to Istanbul, where, except for short intervals, he lived and worked until his death in 1904.

Although Sami has been described as being by turns a Turkish and an Albanian nationalist, his intellectual interests and political beliefs since his early years in the capital of the empire demonstrate in essence the shaping of an Ottoman intellectual, committed to the advancement of both cultures within a reformed empire. While his major intellectual work was produced in Turkish, forty-five books having been written by him in that language, he also produced six books in Albanian.[27] His sense of 'being an Ottoman' also derived from the combination of his various cultural affiliations. This stance was compatible with that of the *Tanzimat* leaders, who considered that the preservation of a common 'fatherland', symbolized in the existence of the Ottoman state, could be achieved by keeping together diverse Ottoman 'races'. Since the 1860s, *Tanzimat* statesmen aimed at achieving a political fusion between Muslims and non-Muslims, by virtue of a secular education through which the equally secular concept of 'Ottoman nationality' would be formed and propagated.[28]

Being influenced by Muslim reformism, Sami perceived the Islamic community as composed of various ethnic groups whose advancement would be achieved through the use of the vernaculars. It is not by chance that Sami made an enormous contribution to Albanian and Turkish linguistics, and to the respective cultures.[29] Through the simplification of Ottoman Turkish, which was based on a combination of Arabic, Persian and Turkish lexicons, Sami shared with other intellectuals of the *Tanzimat* a commitment to spread knowledge to as broad an audience as possible.[30] His intellectual endeavours were devoted in large part to purging the Turkish language of foreign words and to turning it into a written language based on the vernacular and, therefore, into a language easily understood by the common people.[31] To this end, he wrote seven books on Turkish and Arabic grammar, and published various studies on the first documents written in Turkish in the Middle Ages and on Turkish dialectology and its relations to Arabic.[32] In Istanbul in 1873 he also wrote the first ever novel in Turkish, *Taassuku Taalatve Fitnat* (*Love between Talat and Fitnete*), while one year later, in 1876, he wrote the first ever drama in the Turkish language, *Seyyit Yahja* (*Mister Yahja*).[33]

This commitment to Turkish language and culture was associated with support for the modernization and political reform of the empire, and an alignment with the Young Ottomans that attracted the suspicions of the Ottoman authorities. At the age of twenty-three he became editor-in-chief of the *Hadika* (*Garden*) newspaper, founded by Namik Kemal, one of the most prominent of the Young Ottomans, and one year later, on account of his liberal opinions, he was exiled to Tripoli (Libya), where he stayed for one year. In 1877, when the Russo-Turkish War broke out, he was exiled yet again, this time to Rhodes, the Greek island in the Aegean Sea, where he served as the secretary of the Ottoman *vali* (governor), Sava Pasha. When, at the end of the eastern crisis in 1878 and the abrogation of the constitution, the conservative turn of the empire made journalistic activities impossible to pursue, Sami's commitment to the dissemination of a Turkish written language continued in different forms. Convinced as he was that science and technology represented the foundation of modern education, he began publishing a series of booklets designed to propagate scientific knowledge, under the title *Pocket Library*; the series continued until 1895. While Sami was acutely aware of the fact that the Muslim people of the empire were lagging behind in education and progress, in comparison with the people of European Christian civilization, he advanced at the same time the idea that Islam itself was a source of progress and that it could set the empire on the road to development.[34]

It is in association with these literary, journalistic and political activities in favour of reform of the empire and the Turkish language that Sami was engaged also in advancing the cause of Albanian culture. Sami's commitment to the Albanian national cause may be dated to a specific conjuncture, after the Treaty of San Stefano and the Congress of Berlin (1878), when the Albanian question acquired particular urgency, due to the risk of the Albanian lands being partitioned among the new Balkan states. His involvement in the 'Albanian cause' started when he became a member of the Albanian patriotic 'Committee for the Defence of the Rights of the Albanian Nation', founded in Istanbul in December 1877, and of the 'Society for the Printing of Albanian Writings' (1879).[35] These associations were created on the eve, and in the aftermath of, the Congress of Berlin. As the 'League of Prizren' (1878–81), the main intention of the 'Committee' was to prevent the European powers from ceding Albanian-speaking territories to Montenegro and Serbia, its fear being that this would happen at the Congress of Berlin.

It was in this context that Sami spelled out his views on the relationship between his loyalty to the empire and his commitment to the Albanian nation. In response to an anonymous journalist accusing the 'League of Prizren' of striving for the independence of the Albanian-inhabited lands at the expense of Ottoman territorial integrity and of betraying Muslim Ottoman brotherhood, Sami confirmed his allegiance to both the empire and his own nationality of origin.[36] He insisted that the Ottoman dominions would be safer if Albanians were able to keep all their territories in the framework of a single and autonomous province inside the empire. He did so by making a distinction between his general fatherland, or *Vatan*, the Ottoman Empire, and his 'personal *vatan*' or 'mother *vatan*', namely, Albania:

> There is nothing more beloved to a man than his homeland [Albania] and nothing more sacred than his nationality and race (origin). If he loves his general fatherland once [the Ottoman Empire], he loves his personal motherland twice. No matter how much he may love his province (Vilayet), he loves the place where he was born and grew up twofold. There is therefore no need to express here how wounded I am by the defamations and lies against my motherland [Albania] and against my co-nationals, not least because the people of my general homeland [the Ottoman Empire] may be misled by these defamations and lies.[37]

Sami propounded a double discourse about the nature of the Albanian nation, which varied depending on the public he was addressing. When writing for the Ottoman press about Albania, he stressed the Muslim nature of its population, viewed as part of the great Muslim commonwealth of the Ottoman Empire – Muslim Albanians, he conceded, constituted a majority of the Albanian-speaking populations. At the same time, when addressing Albanian audiences, and in order to avoid potential religious conflicts or divisions, he sought first and foremost to give legitimacy to the rights of the Albanian nation through the creation of a national written language. To promote Albanian language and culture, Sami also edited the first magazines in the Albanian language, *Drita* (*Light*) and *Dituria* (*Knowledge*) (1884–5), and became the main patron of the first school using the Albanian language, inaugurated in Korça (the south-east of present day Albania) in 1887, where his works were used as textbooks. In these magazines and books the emphasis was on culture and language as the distinctive features of Albania as a nation.[38] Sami had headed an Albanian 'Society for the Printing of Albanian Writings' created in the aftermath of the Congress of Berlin, with a view to defining a distinct Albanian alphabet for publications in the Albanian language. This society stood for the principle that 'all enlightened nations have been ... civilized by writings in their own language'.[39] The Society accepted in 1879 the alphabet devised by Sami, the so-called 'Istanbul alphabet', based upon Latin script mixed with some Greek and Cyrillic characters. This alphabet 'became the only Latin-based alphabet adopted by a largely Muslim people in the Ottoman Empire'.[40] In the multi-ethnic setting of the Ottoman Empire, a distinct alphabet would mean also a distinct Albanian 'nation', not to be confused either with the Greeks, or with the Slavs and, at the same time, a 'European' nation.

Sami's allegiance to the Ottoman Empire, and his purely cultural and religious understanding of the Albanian nation was subject to a major revision towards the end of the century, in the context of the Macedonian crisis (1899–1904), when the European powers were trying to divide up the Ottoman *vilayet*s that included modern Macedonia – Kosovo, Monastir and Thessaloniki – along ethnic and religious lines, turning it into a bone of contention among various different nationalisms. Such divisions were expected to favour the Balkan Christian populations, while the Muslim populations of the region, predominantly Albanian-speaking in fact, were in danger of being categorized as 'Muslim Turks', and, as such, were at risk of being deported from the Balkans. This had already been the case with those Muslim populations expelled from their territories after the granting of independence to Christian Balkan states, especially Serbia and Montenegro, in the wake of the Congress of Berlin.

It was in this context that Sami came to reformulate his view of the relationship of the Albanian with the Ottoman world, firstly expressing strong doubts regarding the long-term survival of Ottoman dominion in the Balkans, and arguing for full political emancipation of the Albanians in the event of the disintegration of the empire. As a consequence, he revised his earlier notion of Albanians as primarily a religious community within the Muslim Ottoman Empire. He did so in his principal, and most influential, contribution to the discussion and solution of the Albanian question, the book entitled *Albania what it was, what it is and what it will be*, published in 1899 in Bucharest with the financial assistance of the Albanian diaspora in Romania.

Sami followed the same path as De Rada and other Balkan intellectuals of the second half of the nineteenth century in describing the Albanian nation as the oldest in the Balkans, or even in Europe.[41] Under the influence of western scholars, who listed the Albanians, together with Illyrians, Macedonians and Greeks as heirs of the Pellazgs, Sami argued that the Albanians, due to their isolated and wild existence in the mountains, had preserved intact their language, which was a kind of fossil of the prehistoric people. The subchapter on the Albanian language is very indicative of the importance which Sami gave to language, the title being simply 'Albanian nationality'.[42] Given the organization of the Albanian populations into three millets, Muslim, Rum (Orthodox) and the Austro-Hungarian *Kultus Protektorat* for the Catholics, the Albanian language was the most effective means of fostering a national consciousness and helping to forge the Albanian 'imagined community'. The treatise laid down demands for the protection and cultivation of Albanian language and culture, through the establishment of Albanian schools, which until that moment had not been accepted by the imperial government, for fear of their producing an upsurge in Albanian nationalism.

Although this emphasis on language and culture was not new in his thought, Sami's book did in fact mark a shift in the way in which he conceived the relationship between his Ottomanism and its Albanian and Turkish components. Whereas in his earlier work Sami had stressed that the main bond between the empire and the Albanians was that of religion, he now pursued a different line of argument, one that reflected the geopolitical transformation then under way, and the influence of European public opinion on the solution to the Balkan crisis. Unlike Albanian intellectuals of the earlier generation, De Rada among them, who had stressed the distinction between Greeks and Albanians, Frashëri, in line with many other nationalists of the day, now sought to distinguish the Albanian Muslims from the Turkish, and to argue for the 'European nature' of the Albanian Muslims.

As Maria Todorova has written, European public opinion up until the second half of the nineteenth century supposed that all Balkan lands were inhabited by Turks and Greeks, adding to this picture, at a later date, other 'nations' such as the southern Slavs, lumped together with Greeks within the category of 'non-Muslims'.[43] Albanian nationalist intellectuals likewise felt that European public opinion did not perceive the Albanians to be a 'nation' as such, but saw them only as Muslims, who in general were identified with the Turks. In his text, Sami put the blame on the Turks and the Greeks, who in his judgement were intent upon dividing the Albanians.[44] A sharp distinction between European Albanian Muslim and Turkish Muslim was introduced also in the light of another risk, namely, that this confusion might in due course consign the Albanians to the same fate as was suffered, after the granting of independence to Serbia and the occupation of Bosnia-Herzegovina by Austro-Hungary in 1878, by the Muslims of those countries, who had then migrated en masse to Anatolia. By means of this distinction Sami aimed to carve out a legitimate place in Europe for Muslim Albanians, in the event of a future withdrawal of the empire from its Balkan possessions.[45]

As a consequence, in his work Sami argued that the Albanian Muslims were of European origin and indigenous, whereas the Turkish Muslims were from Asia and latecomers to the region. Moreover, he characterized the Albanians as 'civilized' and the Turks as 'backward-barbarian'. For this purpose, Sami referred to the important role of the Bektashis, a heterodox Muslim sect, mainly present among the southern Muslim Albanians, and, according to him, representing a moderate version of Islam that might serve as a force binding together all Albanians. By so doing, he was attempting to legitimize Albanians in the eyes of Europe as a single nation, and to portray the Albanian Muslim population as religiously 'tolerant' and different from the more 'fanatic' Turks.[46] Sami described Albanians as a warrior people, who did not 'pay much heed' to religious matters, and might be prepared to change their faith provided that the new one would serve them better in the business of retaining their weapons, profiting by them and preserving their status as 'equal partners' with the Turks in their conquests. In addition, he highlighted the fact that no religious struggles had ever divided the Albanians.[47]

Another important shift in Sami's view of the mutual relationship between the empire and its nationalities to be manifested in this book was the voicing of new political demands for the Albanian provinces, accompanied by an increasingly critical attitude towards Ottoman government. Convinced as he was that Ottoman rule would not last for long in the Balkans, he argued that the Sublime Porte should temporarily serve as a shield against the Albanians' Balkan neighbours, and imagined an Albanian government under the auspices of the sultan that would nonetheless be ready to govern itself as an independent state once the empire had withdrawn from the region.[48]

However, even in this new political context, Sami did not lose interest in his Turkish studies, nor did he relinquish his allegiance to both languages and cultures. In 1900, one year after the publication of *Albania*, Sami prepared a new edition of a monolingual Turkish dictionary (*Kamus-iTurki*), in which he described the Turks as a 'race' to which he belonged, among many others under Ottoman rule.[49] Consequently, notwithstanding the changes in his political views, and his conviction that the end of Ottoman rule in the Balkans was inevitable, he remained loyal to what had been the essential element of being an Ottoman intellectual, namely, a simultaneous allegiance to several different nationalities and the cultivation of a number of different cultures.

Conclusions

Nineteenth-century Albanianism was not by any means a separatist project based on the desire to break with the Ottoman Empire and to create a nation-state. In its essence Albanian nationalism was a reaction to the gradual disintegration of the Ottoman Empire and a response to the threats posed by Christian and Balkan national movements to a population that was predominantly Muslim. In this sense, its main goal was to gather all 'Albanian' *vilayet*s into an autonomous province inside the Ottoman Empire. In fact, given its focus on the defence of the language, history and culture of a population spread across various regions and states, from Italy to the Balkans, it was not associated with any specific type of polity, but rather with the protection of its rights within the existing states. This was due to the fact that, culturally, early Albanian nationalists belonged to a world in which they were at home, though poised between different languages, cultures, and at times even states. As this chapter has demonstrated, in spite of their differences in religious background and origin, De Rada and Sami's nationalisms displayed some striking commonalities. Both De Rada and Sami conceived the Albanian motherland from a distance, without however feeling displaced or *déraciné*. For De Rada, southern Italy was also the place to which he belonged, and for Sami, Istanbul was the capital of the empire which made him at the same time an Ottoman, an Albanian and a Turkish intellectual. At the end of their lives, both men had become convinced that the solution to the Albanian question had to be found further away from the places in which they lived. But it was the belief itself in the equal rights of different languages and nationalities that served to convince the Italo-Albanian and Christian De Rada, disappointed as he was with the nature of the newly constituted Italian state, that the Ottoman Empire was the best shelter for the rights of the Albanians, and by the same token to persuade the Ottoman Sami that, in the light of the inevitable disintegration of imperial rule in the Balkans, Albania would be better off as an independent state. Forced by external circumstances to revise their early ideals, De Rada and Sami nonetheless remained attached until the end of their lives to the multicultural world which had been the roots of their own brand of Albanian nationalism.

Notes

1   Stavro Skëndi, *The Albanian National Awakening* (Princeton: Princeton University Press, 1967), pp. 43–250; Peter Bartl, *Myslimanët shqiptarë në lëvizjen për pavarësi kombëtare* (1878–1912) [*The Albanian Muslims in the movement for national independence*] (Tirana: Shtëpia Botuese Onufri, 2006), p. 146; KristoFrashëri, *Lidhja Shqiptare e Prizrenit* [*The Albanian League of Prizren*] (Tirana: Shtëpia Botuese Toena, 1997), pp. 68–79. See also *Historia e Popullit Shqiptar* [*History of the Albanian People*] (Tirana: Shtëpia Botuese Toena, 2002), pp. 152–3.

2   In each country, Turkey and Albania, he is known by a different name, Shemseddin Sami in Turkish and Sami Frashëri in Albanian. This chapter follows the example of Bülent Bilmez's study on Shemseddin Sami Frashëri who, in order to avoid 'partisanship in this matter', used simply Sami. See Bülent Bilmez, 'Shemseddin Sami Frashëri (1850–1904): Contributing to the Construction of Albanian and Turkish Identities', in Diana Mishkova (ed.), *We, The People. Politics of National Peculiarity in Southeastern Europe* (Budapest and New York: Central European University Press, 2008), pp. 341–66. In Albania national historiography called De Rada with an Albanian first name, but in reality he always used his original Italian name Girolamo.

3   Niyazi Berkes, *The Development of Secularism in Turkey* (London: Hurst, 1998), p. 145; Serif Mardin, *The Genesis of Young Ottoman Thought* (Princeton: Princeton University Press, 1962), pp. 320–31.

4   Nathalie Clayer, *Aux origines du nationalisme albanais* (Paris: Editions Karthalá, 2007), pp. 170–80.

5   Among the most important Western authors to write about the origin of the Albanians and their language were Conrad Malte-Brun (1775–1826) with his *Géographie universelle* (published posthumously); Johann Thunmann, *Untersuchungenüber die Geschichte der oestlicheneuropäischen Völker* (1774); F.C.H. L. Pouqueville, French consul to Yiannina, *Voyage dans la Grèce* (1820–21); W.M. Leake, a British traveller, *Researches in Greece* (1814); J. Xylander, *Die Sprache der Albanesen oder Schkipetaren* (1835); Johann Georg von Hahn, the Austrian consul to Yiannina, who in 1854 published his

Albanesische Studien; C.H.T. Rheinhold, *Noctes Pelasgicae* (1855); and Franz Bopp, *Über das Albanesische in seinen verwandtschaftlichen Beziehungen* (1854).

6 Clayer, *Aux origines du nationalisme albanais*, p. 171.

7 Jeronim De Rada, *Autobiografia* [1899] (Tirana: Shtëpia Botuese Onufri, 2002), p. 53; Jup Kastrati, *Jeronim De Rada* (Tirana: Shtëpia Botuese 8 Nëntori, 1979), p. 14.

8 Kastrati, *Jeronim De Rada*, p. 15.

9 Arshi Pipa, *Hieronymus De Rada* (Munich: Rudolf Trofenik, 1978), p. 35.

10 Among his best known works are: *Canto di morte di Scanderbeg, Milosao* (poems, 1836); *Serafina* (poem, 1837); *Principi di estetica* (literary essay, 1861); *Antichitá della nazione Albanese* (historical study, 1861); *Rapsodie* (folkloric collection, 1866); *Grammatica della lingua albanese* (by Giuseppe De Rada, supervised by his father, 1870); *Pelasgi e Albanesi* (historical study, 1890), etc. See Pipa, *Hieronymus De Rada*, pp. 10–14.

11 Kastrati, *Jeronim De Rada*, p. 16. On the college see also Domenico Cassiano, *S. Adriano, educazione e politica (1807–1923)* (Lungro: Marco Editore, 1999), pp. 93–4.

12 Andrea Varfi, 'Rreth ideve politiko-shoqërore të Jeronim De Radës' [On the political-social ideas of Jeronim De Rada], in *Jeronim De Rada* (Tirana: Shtëpia Botonjëse 'Naim Frashëri', 1965), p. 82.

13 'Lettera a Giovanni Stamile' (Cosenza: Tipografia della Indipendenza, 1865); *Quanto di libertá e di ottimo vivere sia nello stato rappresentativo* (Naples: G. De Angelis e figlio, 1882), now in Girolamo De Rada, *Opera Omnia*, vol. IX, *Opere filosofiche e politiche*, introduction by Anton Nikë Berisha (Soveria Mannelli: Rubbettino Editore, 2005), pp. 97–162.

14 De Rada, *Quanto di libertà*, in *Opere filosofiche e politiche*, pp. 108–11.

15 Letter of Sami Frashëri sent to Jeronim De Rada, Istanbul, 20 February 1881. In the Albanian State Archive (AQSH), Fond 51, file nr. 4, pp. 1–2.

16 Jeronim De Rada, 'Austria and Albania', *Fiamuri i Arbërit* [Flag of Albania], 20 September 1883.

17 De Rada, *Antichitá della nazione Albanese e sua affinitá con gli elleni e i latini* (Naples: Stamperia dell'Industria, 1864), now in De Rada, *Opera Omnia*, vol. XI, *Opere filologiche e storico-culturali* (Soveria Mannelli: Rubbettino Editore, 2009), pp. 52–78.

18 De Rada, *Antichitá della nazione Albanese*, pp. 53–5.

19 *Fiamuri i Arbërit* [Flag of Albania], Cosenza, 20 September 1885.

20 Skëndi, *The Albanian National Awakening*, pp. 307–8.

21 De Rada, 'L'Albania e i giornali italiani', *Fiamuri i Arberit* [Flag of Albania], 20 Novembre 1885.

22 De Rada, *Autobiografia*, pp. 155–6.

23 De Rada, 'Testamento Politico' [1902], in *Opera Omnia*, vol. IX, *Opere filosofiche e politiche*, pp. 167–78, at p. 170.

24 Ibid, p. 178.

25   Kristo Frashëri, 'Sami Frashëri 1850–1904', in *Buletin për Shkencat Shoqërore* [*Bulletin for Social Sciences*] 4 (1955), p. 62. See also Kristo Frashëri, *Abdyl Frashëri* (Tirana: Shtëpia Botuese 8 Nëntori, 1984), p. 42.

26   Shaban Çollaku, *Mendimi iluminist i Sami Frashërit* (Tirana: Shtëpia Botuese 8 Nëntori, 1986), p. 12.

27   Esat Reso, *Sami Frashëri- vepra* [Sami Frashëri-works] (Prishtinë: Rilindja, 1978), vol. 2, p. 7.

28   Niyazi Berkes, *The Development of Secularism in Turkey* (London: Hurst, 1998), p. 179.

29   Hasan Kaleshi, 'Le role de Chemseddin Sami Frashery dans la formation de deux langues littèraires: turc et albanais', in *Actes du II Congrès International des Études du Sud-Est Européen*, vol. IV (Linguistique et Literature) (Athens: 1978), pp. 177–8.

30   Berkes, *The Development of Secularism in Turkey*, p. 279.

31   Bülent Bilmez, 'Sami Frashëri-apo-Shemsedin Sami?' [Sami Frashëri apo Shemseddin Sami?], *Përpjekja* 18 (2003), p. 118. For his important role in Turkish linguistics, journalism and culture in general see also Çollaku, *Mendimi iluminist i Sami Frashërit*, pp. 28–31.

32   For a detailed list of these publications see Kaleshi, 'Le role de Chemseddin Sami Frashery', p.179. Also Bartl, *Myslimanët shqiptarë në lëvizjen për pavarësi kombëtare (1878–1912)*, pp. 167–9.

33   Frashëri, 'Sami Frashëri (1850–1904)', p. 64.

34   Sami wrote two small popular booklets entirely on Islam, respectively *The Islamic Civilization* written in the Ottoman-Turkish language and published in Istanbul in 1879 and *The endeavors of the heroes in the diffusion of Islam*, which was written in Arabic and was published in Istanbul in 1884.

35   *History of the Albanian People*, p. 143.

36   Sami Frasheri, 'Albania', *Terxhuman-iHakikat* V/144 (1878), in idem, *Kush e prish paqen ne Ballkan* [*Who Broke the Peace in the Balkans*] (Peja: Dukagjini, 2000), pp. 308–12.

37   See the letter that Sami sent to the newspaper *Terxhuman-iHakikat*, V/150 (26 December 1878), in Frasheri, *Kush e prish paqen ne Ballkan*, p. 315.

38   Çollaku, *Mendimi iluministi Sami Frashërit*, p. 20.

39   As cited by Skëndi, *The Albanian National Awakening*, p. 120.

40   Francis Trix, 'Stamboul alphabet of Shemseddin Sami Bey: Precursor of Turkish Script Reform', *Middle East Studies* XXXI/2 (1999), pp. 255–72.

41   Sami Frashëri, *Shqipëria si ka qënë, si është dhe si do të jetë* [*Albania what it was, what it is and what it will be*] (Pristina: Botime Rilindja, 1978), p. 21.

42   Ibid., p. 79.

43   Maria Todorova, *Imagining the Balkans* (Oxford: Oxford University Press, 1997), p. 98.

44   Frashëri, *Shqipëria si ka qënë, si është dhe si do të jetë*, pp. 56–7.

45 Ibid., pp. 74–5.

46 Ibid., p. 61. Clayer, *Aux origines du nationalisme albanais*, pp. 433–74.

47 Frashëri, *Shqipëria si ka qenë, si është dhe si do tëjetë*, pp. 34, 54.

48 Ibid., p. 81.

49 For more see Bilmez, 'Shemseddin Sami Frashëri (1850–1904)', p. 355.

CHAPTER TEN

Ottomanism with a Greek Face:

Karamanlı Greek Orthodox Diaspora at the End of the Ottoman Empire

Vangelis Kechriotis

Fictions and narratives on the Cappadocean diaspora

In his movie *America, America*, the late Greek-American director Elia Kazan narrated the story of the young Greek Orthodox Stavros Topouzoglou, who was living in the 1890s in a village somewhere in Cappadocia, a large region in the hinterland of Anatolia, in present-day Turkey.[1] The movie depicts a hard life, made even more difficult by the violence inflicted by the Ottoman authorities upon the local Christian populations. The hero is sent by his family to Istanbul in order to seek out one of his uncles and to set up his own business. After an adventurous journey on a donkey, during which the young boy is robbed of all the family property, he manages finally to reach Istanbul and to enter into the network of the rich Cappadocean merchants resident in the city. However, appalled at the thought of a life of commerce and at the prospect of an unchosen engagement with a merchant's allegedly ugly daughter, the hero abandons Istanbul and sets sail for America, where new horizons would open up for the people of Anatolia. It is not clearly stated if the protagonists of the movie were *Karamanlı*s. The majority of Cappadocean Greek Orthodox were known by that name, however, and the written form of their language – Turkish written in Greek characters – is known as *Karamanlıca* or *Karamanlidika*.[2] Although not all of these Cappadocean migrants became merchants, the stereotype of the *Karamanlı* grocer (*bakkal*) is still widespread in Turkey.

Studies of the Greek Orthodox Cappadocean populations have flourished in the last twenty years. Until the 1980s Greek historiography was preoccupied in the main with proving the Greek origins of these populations, despite their use of the Turkish language. This is a debate dating back to the nineteenth century, when both Greek and nascent Turkish nationalism wished to incorporate these populations into their respective national bodies. Yet this debate would seem in the end to be fruitless. Recent historiography has acknowledged that what is important is not so much the historical reality, which cannot ultimately be recovered, but how these people perceived themselves.[3] As in the case of other populations with a particular historical origin or cultural profile – such as the Circassians, who migrated to Anatolia from the Caucasus in the nineteenth century, or the Laz people, who have been inhabiting areas in the Black Sea region since Byzantine times – the history and literature of the *Karamanlı*s have recently been viewed as the product of a distinct population that deserves to be studied in its own right, and not in terms of their belonging (or not belonging) to the Greek or to the Turkish nation. In this context, many new titles have been added to older bibliographies of publications in *Karamanlıca* while monographs on populations of particular regions of Cappadocia have been published.[4] Although *Karamanlı* studies form a distinct field of research with its own body of literature, they can be creatively combined with other studies of the social, political and intellectual history of Anatolia.

In this chapter, I will explore the biographies of two individuals, Pavlos Carolidis and Emmanouil Emmanouilidis who, like the hero of Elia Kazan's movie, originated in Cappadocia, although, unlike him, they spent much of their lives in Smyrna. During the second half of the nineteenth century, this major port-city of the Eastern Mediterranean experienced rapid demographic growth. The city attracted like a magnet populations both from the West and the East, connecting the Mediterranean basin to the hinterland of Anatolia. The story of these two prominent individuals will allow me to describe mobility networks which extended from Cappadocia to Smyrna and Istanbul and from there, across the Aegean, to Athens. Though in time Pavlos Carolidis and Emmanouil Emmanouilidis would become prominent members of the Smyrniot community, they remained firmly connected to their family or homeland networks. More importantly, their activities in Smyrna, Athens and Istanbul demonstrate the existence of a peculiar brand of Greekness associated with the history and existence of this Anatolian Greek population, which had rallied to the Ottoman Empire. The brand of Hellenism and, more generally, the political ideas of these community leaders, were distinct from mainstream Greek nationalist ideology as represented by the Greek state and endorsed by the Greek migrants from the Aegean or the Ionian Islands who lived in the same city.

The prevailing view in Ottoman historiography regarding the political choices of the Ottoman Greeks during the Second Constitutional Period (1908–18) has been that this community was divided into two groups, those described as the *Yunancılar* (from *Yunan*, the Arabic and Turkish term for Greek), who advocated the incorporation of the 'unredeemed' Greek populations and territories into the Hellenic state, and those referred to as the *Bizansçılar* (a reference to Byzantium), who supported the integrity of the Ottoman Empire, albeit with the explicit purpose of taking over its institutions from within and transforming it into a Christian empire.[5] As the cases of Carolidis and Emmanouilidis both illustrate, however, a number of Greeks were inspired by Ottoman patriotism and a sincere wish to cooperate with the Turkish-Muslim element in order to protect the integrity of the empire in ways that do not fit the categorization mentioned above. The biography of these individuals, who were at the same time community leaders, Greek intellectuals and imperial politicians, shows how the peculiar history of this Turkish-speaking Greek community and their brand of Greekness developed in relationship to local politics and to the political reforms of the Ottoman Empire. As a result of the rising tension between the two opposed Turkish and Greek nationalist ideologies, relations between this brand of Greekness and the two nationalisms became increasingly controversial towards the end of the empire. However, it was only when loyalty to the Ottoman Empire was no longer feasible that figures such as Carolidis and Emmanouilidis had to reshape their public discourse in order to survive in the post-imperial world.

The multiple origins of migration: from the Aegean and Cappadocia to Smyrna

Since the end of the seventeenth century, the western coasts of Asia Minor had attracted Greek Orthodox migrants from the Aegean islands and the Peloponnese, driven there by wars, natural disasters or simply the quest for a better life. The immigration accelerated at the end of the eighteenth century due to the favourable conditions that the Treaty of Küçük Kaynarca (1774) between the Ottoman and the Russian Empires entailed for all Greek Orthodox subjects of the sultan. Population transfer from the Aegean assumed a more systematic character in the 1840s, when relations between the newly established Greek state and the Ottoman Empire were no longer as tense as they had initially been. The Greek Orthodox benefited from the policy of free trade in the wake of the Anglo-Ottoman Agreement of Balta Limanı in 1838 as well. During the period of Ottoman liberal reforms – known as the *Tanzimat* – a new generation of Greek Orthodox with

Ottoman or Hellenic citizenship became involved in the economic life of the empire, sometimes resorting to long-established commercial practices but also exploiting new opportunities when they appeared. In this atmosphere of liberal economic policy and imperial rivalry, where the non-Muslim subjects of the sultan could be granted the status of a protégé or even the nationality of a foreign power, it was difficult for the Ottoman authorities to monitor economic transactions. On the other hand, by the 1850s, many of those who benefited from these favourable conditions endorsed a less aggressive stance towards the Ottoman Empire, to the extent of supporting its integrity and rejecting Greek nationalism.[6]

Bearing in mind this picture of intensive mobility from the West, we need now to consider the flow of migration to the shores of Asia Minor from the East. Mobility from Cappadocia had started in the eighteenth century but assumed a more systematic form from the 1840s onwards. The improvement of infrastructure and, more importantly, the inauguration of the maritime line of Mersina-Smyrna, led to the gradual abandonment of old trade routes on the mainland and the emergence of new, maritime ones, which ended in Smyrna, Istanbul and their environs. Compared to Istanbul, Smyrna became more attractive to Cappadoceans, due to the emergence of the city as a thriving economic centre offering many opportunities for trade.[7] Starting from the 1860s, the further increase in migration especially to the hinterland of Smyrna was the result of the intensification of the cultivation and the commerce of cotton, as well as the construction of the Smyrna-Aydın railway in 1866, which facilitated the circulation of goods and people.[8]

The Greek community of Smyrna was composed of a diaspora coming from every corner of the Greek world. Like other urban 'communities', it was actually a multi-ethnic aggregation of several migrant populations which had moved to the city relatively recently – groups bound by ethnicity, locality, occupation and kinship.[9] Each of these groups had a distinct perception of what a Greek and a Smyrniot was, and such divisions had an impact on debates regarding the right to participate in the administration of the 'community'.[10] Two administrative bodies, the 'Elders' Council' (*Dimogerontia*) and the 'Central Committee' (*Kentriki Epitropi*) competed with one another to impose their authority upon the Greek Orthodox population. The Elders' Council, reflecting the stance of the Greeks of Ottoman citizenship, entertained a legal conception of 'community', whereby it would be integrated into the Ottoman state structure and only Greek Orthodox of Ottoman citizenship would be entitled to belong to it. Conversely, the Central Committee argued that membership of the 'community' should be determined by ethno-religious criteria, and that all Greek Orthodox should be included, irrespective of their citizenship.[11] In this context, Greek Orthodox of Ottoman citizenship who contested the right of their co-religionists of Hellenic or other citizenship to participate in the 'community' structure occasionally complained to the Ottoman authorities. This led to outrage among the Hellenic citizens and a conflict with repercussions as far as Istanbul and Athens. Although the arguments used on both sides were ideological, the cultural dimension and the existence of two distinct ideas of Greekness were important aspects of the conflict also. Ottoman Greeks, in fact, argued that the Hellenic Greeks were foreigners with no legitimate claims to the protection offered by Ottoman institutions, while their opponents accused them of violating national solidarity and committing treason.

Among those Greeks of Ottoman citizenship who spearheaded the struggle against Hellenic citizens in Smyrna in the first decade of the twentieth century, there feature a number of individuals who were in close contact with each other, not only because of their common origin in Cappadocia, but also through family ties. Many among them had failed to profit from the city's expanding commercial activity, which had led to the emergence of new commercial elites. In order to achieve social prominence, they therefore sought to dominate the only arena available to them, namely community administration, which included important charitable foundations, such as the orphanage, the nursery or the community schools. A leading figure in this context was the lawyer Emmanouil Emmanouilidis, a pillar of the Smyrniot 'community', who later forged close relations with the local branch of the Committee of Union and Progress (CUP), the political platform of the Young Turks, and became a deputy in the Ottoman Parliament. Both Emmanouil Emmanouilidis and a history professor at the University of Athens, Pavlos Carolidis, who likewise served as an Ottoman parliamentary deputy, were outstanding examples of Cappadocean diasporic Greek Orthodox who attained social and political prominence. Originating in the same region, they were equally conversant with Ottoman society and culture. They benefited from mobility networks extending from Cappadocia to Smyrna, and from there to Athens, and they contributed, in their turn, to the proliferation of these networks through their official status and positions. Although they followed different professional paths, they were eventually both involved in politics at a time when ideological divisions, in the context of intensive debates on the future of Hellenism within the Ottoman Empire, became unprecedentedly acrimonious.

The history professor: from Cappadocia to Smyrna, Athens and Istanbul

While Emmanouilidis was involved for more than a decade in the 'community' conflicts in Smyrna as a staunch advocate of the Ottoman Greeks, before moving to Istanbul as an Ottoman parliamentarian, Carolidis left Smyrna at an early age and, after completing his studies, spent many years in Athens, as a university professor. Pavlos Carolidis was born in Endürlük (Andronikio), near Kayseri (Kesaria), a town in Cappadocia, in

1849. His family were wealthy Turkish-speaking landowners. His education was typical for a person of his background from Anatolia, studying first in Smyrna, at the most important Greek school in the city, the Evangelical School (*Evageliki Sholi*), and then in Istanbul, at the Patriarchal Academy, known also as the Supreme School of the Nation (*Mekteb-i Kebir, Megali tou Genous Sholi*). After his graduation, in 1867, he moved to Athens, where he studied history at the university. He then continued his studies in Munich, Strasbourg and, finally, Tübingen. After obtaining his doctoral diploma, in 1872, Carolidis taught in Istanbul and in Smyrna. Finally, in 1886, with the encouragement of the Greek prime minister, Charilaos Trikoupis (1832–96), he moved to Athens, where he taught at the university until 1908.

There, in his capacity as a scholar and also thanks to his connections with the political elite in the Greek capital, Carolidis assisted the networks of migrants from Cappadocia and other parts of Asia Minor, who were keen to promote the education of their compatriots. In Vassilios, the metropolitan of Smyrna (1834–1910), he found a natural ally. In a letter to Carolidis, the church dignitary introduced young men from Cappadocia who were, he said, 'deserving of protection' and were going to travel to Athens 'in order to be enlightened . . . as now they live in the darkness and the shadow of death'.[12] Young men from several regions of Asia Minor benefited, in fact, from these social and cultural networks, which offered them financial support and the chance to study either in Smyrna, in Athens or at the school for teachers on the island of Patmos near the southwestern coast of Asia Minor. This school was built by the 'Association of People from Asia Minor – Anatoli' (*Syllogos Mikrasiaton – Anatoli*), founded in Athens in 1891, of whose governing council Carolidis was a member. *Anatoli* undertook the task of providing grants for young people from different regions of Asia Minor and sent them to Athens or elsewhere to study. After graduation, these students would be appointed by their respective communities to positions enabling them to contribute to the promotion and consolidation of Greek language and culture in their locality.[13]

The major concern inspiring such initiatives among educated elites both in the Greek state and in the Ottoman Empire was the perceived loss of Greek language among populations in Asia Minor, notably in Cappadocia and other regions where the Orthodox population was Turkish or even Armenian-speaking. In Macedonia as in Asia Minor, Orthodox populations who did not speak Greek were considered to have lost their Greek tongue due to interaction with other ethnic elements or to foreign suppression, either by the Turks in Asia Minor or by the Bulgarians in Macedonia. However, they were presumed to have retained their Greek consciousness and, therefore, deserved to be included in the national body. Nevertheless, the antagonistic stance of other nationalisms or their proselytizing activities jeopardized the national allegiance of these populations. Hence the preoccupation of educational associations in the Greek state or the Ottoman Empire with founding schools and sponsoring the studies of these 'unredeemed brethren', with a view to promoting their cultural transformation, political integration seeming not to be a viable option, given the inability of the fragile Greek kingdom to expand.[14] Although affinity to Greece and Greek culture was an incentive that attracted many young people from Cappadocia and their patrons to such mechanisms of integration, their eagerness (or that of their families) to pursue such educational opportunities was also no doubt due in part to their concern to safeguard geographical and social mobility. It is sometimes difficult to assess whether the beneficiaries of *Anatoli* had a sense of a broader 'imagined community', national or local, to which they belonged. Yet self-interest would appear to have been involved; they sought a better education, well-paid jobs and social recognition.[15]

This cultural transformation was bolstered by a peculiar version of Hellenic history, differing from the prevailing account in Greece, which for its part cast Athens as not only the political centre but also the cultural and historical cradle of Hellenism, all local identities being dismissed as peripheral and thus secondary. Scholars and writers originating from Asia Minor, like Carolidis, not only incorporated the lands of Cappadocia, Ionia or the Pontus (the Black Sea region) into the mainstream narrative about national continuity, but also credited their own communities with an important role as genuine storehouses of national culture.[16] Carolidis's essay *Cappadocica or a Historical and Archeological Treatise on Cappadocia*, published in Istanbul in 1874, was written with such a purpose in mind. Although it was printed at the printing press of Evangelinos Misailidis, the founding father of journalism and literature in *Karamanlı* Turkish, it was written in Greek – like the rest of Carolidis's essays – because it targeted the Greek-speaking audience on both shores of the Aegean. In the introduction, Carolidis maintained that:

> The real Greece, as one modern philosopher claims, the Greece where the poetry of the Homeric circle flourished, where Philosophy was born, where the noble art of ideals first appeared, the Greece [that was the] mother of science and good taste is the Greece of Asia, Ionia, which received these elements of high civilization from Asia through the mediation of other peoples of Asia Minor.[17]

The last decades of the nineteenth and the early decades of the twentieth century were marked in the Ottoman Balkans by the conflict in Macedonia. Greek, Bulgarian, and also self-proclaimed Macedonian groups, vied with one another in a determined bid to win the allegiance of the local Christian populations. In 1908, as a result of the mounting tension in Macedonia, a coup orchestrated by a clandestine society of young military officers and bureaucrats known as the Young Turks compelled Sultan Abdülhamid II to restore the Ottoman constitution that he himself had suspended in 1878, and to proclaim elections. The Hellenic state had initially discouraged any involvement in the Young Turks' activities, demonstrating its preference for the absolutist regime, not so much as a matter of principle but out of fear that any change would endanger the autonomous status of the Ecumenical Patriarchate and the Greek Orthodox communities. As the policy of the Young Turks became increasingly authoritarian, both the Greek state and many among the Ottoman Greeks rallied in the context of the Parliament to the party of the opposition, the *Entente Liberale*, which endorsed decentralization and guaranteed the rights of all ethno-religious communities. This led to a division among the twenty-four Greek Orthodox Ottoman parliamentary deputies, with eight of their number being more favourably disposed towards the CUP, the political platform of the Young Turks, supporting the latter on many issues.[18]

Sympathies of this sort were evident in the case of Pavlos Carolidis, elected deputy in 1908, though as an independent candidate, for the prefecture of Aydın, whose administrative centre was Smyrna. In 1912 he was re-elected on the CUP's ticket. It seems that Carolidis's origin from a Turcophone region of Cappadocia as well as his thorough knowledge of Ottoman history and language played a role in his endorsement of a peculiar version of Ottomanism. Carolidis strongly believed that the new regime would pave the way for a sincere understanding between the different ethnicities of the empire. This would presuppose respect for the 'national rights' of Hellenism on the part of the Turkish Muslim majority, but at the same time it would entail the absolute compliance of the Ottoman Greeks with the legislation of the Ottoman state. This mutual understanding would be achieved through the joint action of the Greek and the Turkish elements of the empire against what Carolidis considered to be a fatal danger to both, namely, the Slavic or else the Bulgarian threat.[19] In his writings, Carolidis often expressed disquiet at the interethnic violence in Macedonia and the occupation of Greek Orthodox churches and schools by the supporters of the Bulgarian Church (known as the Exarchate), not so much with respect to the overall interests of Hellenism in the empire, but mainly as regards the potentially damaging outcome of the struggle in Macedonia.[20] Macedonia and the Slavic danger were at the top of the political agenda during that period. Indeed, the argument of those politicians and journalists who strongly advocated joint action between Greeks and Turks hinged upon the Macedonian question. Interestingly enough, it was individuals who were not originally from Macedonia, among them Cappadoceans such as Carolidis and Emmanouilidis, who became the most prominent defenders of Greek claims there. On the other hand, between 1910 and 1912 those Greek nationalists who were from Macedonia and who had fought for years against the Bulgarians were the first to cooperate with the latter in the Ottoman Parliament in order to resist what they considered to be the CUP's endeavour to 'turkify' Ottoman society by means of policies designed to curtail the autonomy enjoyed by non-Muslims up until then.

Carolidis's reflections, though, went far beyond political expediency. In his memoirs, he also elaborated on the compatibility that existed between constitutional principles and Islam. He argued that it was possible to discern a correlation between the constitution and the idea of the Islamic polity itself. He explained that:

> This idea is compatible with what is called 'popular sovereignty' (*hakimiyet-i milliye*). The polity of the Prophet had a democratic character. Absolutism emerged during the era of the Umayyad and the Abbasid Caliphates, not as an element of Islam but as a result of the spirit of the old Asiatic Despotism which still survives in these countries . . . Now, we can build our constitutional life relying on the harmony between the Sultanate, the Caliphate and free political life.[21]

In the light of his positive attitude towards Islam, which derived from his deep knowledge of Islamic history, Carolidis sought to offer a justification for his support of the constitutional empire that did not solely depend on the self-interest of Hellenism. By contrast with most Greek scholars and politicians of the day, he proved how much he valued the integrity of the empire not only as the expression of the will of the majority of its population but also as a means to advance the interests of his own nation. In his essay *Nations and Races* (1907), he elaborated his theory on the origins and evolution of the Greek nation. He argued there that the nation-state was not a political context in which Hellenism could flourish. Unlike those Greek intellectuals who claimed that the Greek nation had been separate and distinct throughout its history, Carolidis argued that already in Byzantine times the Greek nation had integrated other Orthodox populations (Albanian, Macedonian, Vlach, etc.). For him these populations did not constitute fully-fledged nations, but races that actually had their origin in the Greek nation and had lost their Greek consciousness due to the vicissitudes of history.[22] What made the Greek nation special, Carolidis went on, was its antiquity and its cultural superiority, which could be said to justify the cultural reintegration of all the aforementioned races into it. The Greek nation could therefore only reclaim and dominate politically 'races' such as the Albanians and the Macedonians, if it succeeded in preventing the emergence of separate nation-states based on misplaced ideas of racial purity. Only the integrity of the empire would enable the Greeks to reintegrate culturally those races that had orginated from them. This stood in sharp contrast with the West, where nations were not the result of political fragmentation, but of the combination into single political entities of different races that had not developed enough to claim their distinct existence as nations. Such was the case with England and France, for instance.

The lawyer: a Greek 'Young Turk' between Cappadocia, Smyrna and Istanbul

A similar brand of Ottomanism was endorsed by Emmanouil Emmanouilidis. The Smyrniot lawyer and politician was born in 1867 in Tavlosun, a small town east of Kayseri in Cappadocia. He was the son of Charalambos Emmanouilidis, a local landowner, and his wife Polyxeni Georgantzoglou. He was also the nephew of the Ottoman bureaucrat and parliamentary deputy Aristidis Pasha Georgantzoglou, in his turn a nephew of a translator and a pioneer of the satirical press in the Ottoman Empire, Todor Kasap.[23] Emmanouilidis studied law both in Istanbul and in Athens, subsequently working in a legal practice in Smyrna for many years. In the aftermath of the Greek-Ottoman War of 1897, he published the journal *Aktis*, whose Greek vernacular language, in marked contrast to the bulk of Greek publications in the city, couched in the purist idiom (*katharevousa*), left him vulnerable to barbed comments.

Emmanouilidis' involvement in Smyrniot politics dates to well before 1908. As already mentioned, Smyrna was wracked by a bitter controversy between the two administrative bodies, the Elders' Council and the Central Committee, each of which sought to impose its authority over the Greek Orthodox population. In this rivalry, in the first decade of the century, Emmanouilidis played a major role, as did a number of other individuals who were closely associated with one another on account of their common origin in Cappadocia and their family ties. Among them was Sokratis Solomonidis, one of the editors of *Amalthia*, a Greek newspaper published in Smyrna, but which had a much wider readership in the Ottoman Empire. The two Cappadoceans were accused of treachery, the charge being that they had appealed to the Ottoman authorities in order to prevent the participation of Hellenic Greeks in the communal institutions, with a view to dominating the community administration themselves. Emmanouilidis had used his skills as a lawyer and his prestige among the members of the Greek Orthodox community to convince them to abide by the Ottoman regulations. By the same token, in 1908, Stelios Tsalouchos, the editor of the Athenian newspaper *Eleftheron Vima*, published a pamphlet entitled *History of the Orthodox Community of Smyrna* in which he provided details regarding specific aspects of the community conflict. Tsalouchos focused his criticism particularly on the editor of *Amalthia*.[24] Solomonidis' chief accomplice, according to the pamphlet, was 'the austere and ungainly fez-wearing lawyer Manologlou' (this is a pejorative Turkish version of the name Emmanouilidis).[25] Tsalouchos accused him of having wrecked the community, and of having through his slanderous pronouncements brought every honourable activity into disrepute. The author referred explicitly to the network of those who originated from Kayseri in Cappadocia, pointing out that the *vali* (governor) of Smyrna Kiâmil Pasha (and obviously himself) had a very low opinion of the *Kayserli*. This was why, according to the Athenian journalist, these people had behaved as they did.

Whereas the press of the Greek state was hostile to Emmanouilidis's activities, the Young Turks were not slow to rally to his support. When, in 1911, Emmanouilidis's uncle Aristidis Pasha Georgantzoglou, was offered a seat in the *meclis-i ayan* (senate) and resigned as a parliamentary deputy, the CUP backed Emmanouilidis, who eventually won the election, receiving an overwhelming majority of both Muslim and Greek votes, especially in the areas where there were no Greek consulates.[26] Soon after his election, Emmanouilidis was elected second vice president of the Parliament, an office that his uncle had also held.[27]

The Young Turks had reasons of their own for offering Emmanouilidis their backing. Upon the restoration of the constitution, the Smyrniot lawyer had published a series of articles in the Smyrniot newspaper *Imerisia,* in which he wholeheartedly endorsed the ideas of the constitutional revolution and urged his Greek Orthodox compatriots to side with the Young Turks.[28] Several of these articles were translated and published by the local daily of the CUP *İttihad* as exemplary cases of loyalty to the Ottomanist ideology. In these articles, he had specifically exhorted his co-religionists to avoid being carried away by the artificially produced tension between Muslims and Christians in Smyrna as elsewhere in the empire.[29] He wrote in 1908:

> If the Parliament and the Constitution are suspended by the reactionaries, who is going to prevent them? The Young Turks? Yet, what did we do to support them? In our current mood, how do we profit by organizing demonstrations, delivering enthusiastic speeches and shutting up our shops on the basis of absurd rumours spread by the ill-intentioned or the thoughtless? If equality refers only to legal equality and if we do not join our compatriots in [espousing] equality in sacrifice, things will take a different turn ... A nation [the Turkish nation] that has spilt its blood and given its soul for the motherland, cannot be considered alien on the territory where it has fought in order to defend its flag. Only if we remain loyal to the extent of not evading the ultimate sacrifice for our motherland, will we enjoy approval and respect.[30]

Emmanouilidis's support for CUP interests in Parliament would be rewarded with his re-election in 1912. On 4 October of the same year, following the outbreak of the Balkan wars, Emmanouilidis delivered a speech defending Turkey's territorial integrity as well as the rights of its citizens at a meeting held in Sultan Ahmet square, in front of the Aghia Sophia mosque in Istanbul and attended by high-ranking members of the CUP.[31] His stance infuriated the Athenian newspapers, which unleashed a fierce polemic, calling him a 'traitor' once again.[32]

In 1922, after the defeat of the Greeks in the Greek-Turkish War, Emmanouilidis fled to Greece. There he published his memoirs concerning his political activities in a volume entitled *The Last Years of the Ottoman Empire*. The manuscript was ready in August 1920; it was published, however, only in 1924, after not only the ideology of Ottomanism and the Ottoman Empire but the very possibility of coexistence between Muslims and Christians had vanished.[33] Throughout these controversial years, Emmanouilidis had avoided any reference to the Greek state; indeed, he remained loyal to his Ottomanist idea. After all he was, as we have seen, constantly hounded by the Athenian press. He continued in fact to believe that Hellenism had its natural points of reference in the Ecumenical Patriarchate, and that it could be best protected within the Ottoman Empire.

Concluding remarks: the collapse of the empire and its diasporic networks

In 1917, Carolidis returned to Greece and taught at the university for two years. He was then dismissed from his university post, on account of his pro-monarchist stance, during the clash in Greece known as the 'National Discord' between the prime minister, Eleftherios Venizelos, and King Constantine in 1916–22. He was reappointed in 1920, but retired in 1923, because of the defeat in the war of 1922, known as the 'Asia Minor catastrophe', for which the monarchists were held accountable. His political choices on both shores of the Aegean made it impossible for him to carry on any sort of public activity in any of the cities that had marked his life, Smyrna, Athens or Istanbul. He died in Athens in 1930.

Emmanouilidis escaped to Athens following the defeat of the Greek army in 1922. Not being identified with the monarchists, his skills were immediately acknowledged by the Greek authorities. He already had contacts with high-ranking members of the Liberal Party of Eleftherios Venizelos, who now took over. Thus, in the conditions of turmoil following the compulsory exchange of populations between Greece and Turkey, in 1923, Emmanouilidis was appointed governor of Western Macedonia (Kozani) in Greece, and during that same year he was elected deputy of Athens in the Fourth Constitutional Assembly. He also served as the chair of the Parliamentary committee for the Refugee Question (1923–5), and likewise as the chair of the Political Asia Minor Centre (*Politiko Mikrasiatiko Kentro*). In 1926, 1928 and 1936, Emmanouilidis was re-elected as deputy, this time in the Greek Parliament. He served as a minister of 'social affairs' in Venizelos' Cabinet (1928–31) and died in Athens in 1943.

The Cappadocean networks survived both physically and politically until the end of the empire. Emmanouilidis had retained his position within the Ottoman Parliament until 1919, nor was he alone in this respect. Other

Greek deputies, those from the Black Sea, such as Georgios Ioannidis from Trabzon and Thodoros Arzoglou from Samsun, both of them originating in Cappadocia, Niğde and Enderlük (Carolidis's homeland) respectively, retained their seats until the defeat of the Ottoman Empire in the First World War, in 1918, and the occupation of Istanbul by the Allied forces a year later. After all, the ecumenical patriarch of Constantinople who occupied the throne between 1913 and 1918, Germanos V (1835–1920), was also from Cappadocia. He was forced to abdicate, however, having been accused of collaborationism, after the Ottoman government had signed an armistice in 1918. The networks of the Cappadocean Greek Orthodox would seem not to have outlasted the collapse of the empire. Those who survived were now doomed to pursue a life as refugees in a new world where borders were firmly closed and opportunities for diasporic trajectories indubitably limited. Cappadocean culture, being identified with the use of the Turkish language, was declared alien to the essence of Greekness, at any rate in the guise in which it would be elaborated by intellectuals and politicians in the interwar period.

In his memoirs, Emmanouilidis avoided any reference to the period before 1912, when he had actively supported the party of the Young Turks. After 1912, despite the earlier outrage he had caused among Greeks in Istanbul and Athens, he gained a reputation as the defender of the rights of the Christian populations which had suffered extensive persecution during the First World War. His memoirs recounting this narrative were republished in 2010 and were also translated into Turkish in 2013.[34] The passionate lawyer and Ottoman politician would appear to have succeeded in transmitting his own version of his legacy to posterity, downplaying in the process his earlier activities. Conversely, Carolidis's memoirs were never republished or translated into Turkish. In Greece, Carolidis is remembered as an important historian, although some of his works, relating directly to his Ottomanism, are almost unknown.[35]

At a time when the majority of Greeks were inspired by the dream of the collapse of the Ottoman Empire and their 'liberation' by the Greek nation-state, members of the Cappadocean diaspora, as I have tried to demonstrate, invoked a different brand of Greekness, one more open to cooperation with the Muslim Turks in a constitutional polity, and in this regard no doubt shaped by its origin in a Turkish-speaking Karamanlı milieu. After the empire that had allowed such diasporic networks to flourish collapsed, at the end of the First World War, this brand of Greekness was buried under its ruins, to resurface only recently as a result both of what has been described as the 'imperial turn' in historiography and of the new value attributed by historians to individual experience. Thus, the lives of these controversial figures are reintroduced here to scholarship not with a claim about their political correctness, but rather as cases that shed light upon a world that was more mobile, more flexible, and, indeed, more fascinating than we are often led to believe.

Notes

1   Anatolia is the English translation of the Turkish term *Anadolu* which derives from the Greek term *Anatoli* (East). *Mikra Asia* is the Greek term for Asia Minor which refers to the same geography. In this chapter, *Anatolia* and *Asia Minor* are used interchangeably.

2   The term itself originates from the name of the early Turkish dynasty of the Karamanoğuları which ruled over part of this region and was defeated by the Ottomans in the fifteenth century.

3   Richard Clogg, ' "A millet within the millet": The Karamanlides', in Dimitri Gondicas and Charles Issawi (eds), *Ottoman Greeks in the Age of Nationalism* (Princeton: Princeton University Press, 1999), pp. 115–42.

4   No scholar has done more than Evangelia Balta to introduce the field of *Karamanlı* history to international scholarship. For a personal account on how the field of *Karamanlı* studies was formed see Evangelia Balta, 'Cries and whispers in Karamanlidika books before the doom of silence', in idem and Matthias Kappler (eds), *Cries and Whispers in Karamanlidika Books, Proceedings of the First International Conference on Karamanlidika Studies* (Nicosia, 11–13 September 2008), *Turcologica* 83 (Wiesbaden: Harrassowitz Verlag, 2010), pp. 11–22. See also the recent work by Christos Chatziosif: *Synasos* (Heraklion: Crete University Press, 2005).

5   Celal Bayar, *Bende Yazdım [I Wrote Myself Too]* (Istanbul: Baha Matbaası, 1967), vol. 5, p. 1589.

6   Molly Greene, 'Bankrolling the Sultan: The Career of a Nineteenth Century Greek Patriot', in Jeremy Adelman and Steve Aaron (eds), *Trading Cultures: the Worlds of Western Merchants* (Turnhout: Brepols, 2001), pp. 193–212.

7   Melpo Merlier, 'I ellinikes kinotites sti syghroni Capadocia' [The Greek communities in contemporary Cappadocia], *Deltio Kentrou Mikrasiatikon Spoudon* 1 (1977), pp. 29–74.

8   Ioannis Karachristos, 'Metanastefsi apo Capadokia kai Pisidia pros ti Smyrni, 18os aionas-1922: Metanasteftikes stratigikes kai praktikes diahirisis tis metanasteftikis empirias' [Migration from Cappadocia and Pisidia to Smyrna, 18th c-1922: Migrational strategies and ways of dealing with migrants' experience], in Ioannis Karachristos and Paraskevas Potiropoulos (eds), *Proceedings of the International Congress 'Smyrna: The development of a metropolis in the Eastern Mediterrenean'* (Athens: Academy of Athens, 2015, forthcoming).

9   Sia Anagnostopoulou, *Mikra Asia 19os ai-1919 I Ellinorthodoxes kinotites: apo to millet ton Romion sto Elliniko Ethnos [Asia Minor, The Greek-Orthodox Communities. From Rum Millet to the Greek Nation]* (Athens: Ellinika Grammata, 1998), pp. 14–19 and 340–1. See also Ayşe Ozil, *Orthodox Christians in the Late Ottoman Empire: A Study of Communal Relations in Anatolia* (London-New York: Routledge, 2013), pp. 22–8.

10 Vangelis Kechriotis, 'Educating the Nation: Migration and Acculturation on the two Shores of the Aegean at the Turn of the Twentieth Century' in Meltem Toksöz and Biray Kulluoğlu (eds), *Cities of the Mediterranean: From the*

Ottomans to the Present Day (London: IB Tauris, 2010), pp. 139–56, especially pp. 145–6.

11 Anagnostopoulou, *Mikra Asia*, pp. 341–2.

12 Vassilios Metropolitan of Smyrna to Carolidis, 10 June 1900. Carolidis archive, ELIA (Hellenic Literary and Historical Archive), Athens.

13 Nikos Milioris, 'O Syllogos ton Mikrasiaton i 'Anatoli' [The association of Mikrasiates *Anatoli*], *Mikrasiatika Hronika* 12 (1965), pp. 337–67.

14 Haris Exertzoglou, ' "Shifting boundaries": Language, community and the "non-Greek speaking Greeks" ', *Historein* 1 (1999), pp. 75–92.

15 Kechriotis, 'Educating the nation', pp. 148–9.

16 Ilias Anagnostakis and Evangelia Balta, *La découverte de la Cappadoce au dix-neuvième siècle* (Istanbul: Eren kitapevi, 1994), pp. 17–74.

17 Pavlos Carolidis, *Cappadocica iti Pragmatia Istoriki kai Arheologiki peri Kappadokias* [*Cappadokika or a Historical and Archeological Treatise on Cappadocia*] (Constantinople: Evangelinos Misailidis, 1874), p. vi.

18 Caterina Boura, 'The Greek Millet in Turkish Politics: Greeks in the Ottoman Parliament (1908–1918)', in Gondicas and Issawi, *Ottoman Greeks*, pp. 193–206.

19 Pavlos Carolidis, *Logi kai Ypomnimata* [*Discourses and Memoranda*] (Athens: P.A. Petrakou, 1913), pp. 15–16.

20 Ibid., p. 10.

21 Ibid., p. 101.

22 Pavlos Carolidis, 'Ethni kai Fylai', *Athinon Parartima*, no. 1, November 1907, 17–24. For further information see Elli Skopetea, 'Oi Ellines kai oi ehthroi tous: I katastasi tou ethnous stis arhes tou 20ou ai' [The Greeks and their enemies: the state of the nation on the turn of the 20th c.], *Istoria tis Ellados tou 20ou ai, Oi Aparhes 1900–1922* [*History of Greece of the 20th c., the beginnings 1900–1922*], vol. I, part I, pp 12–13. To a large extent Carolidis took up the legacy of Constantinos Paparigopoulos (1815–91), the leading figure of Greek historiography, the scholar who laid the foundations for a scheme according to which Hellenism could boast of 3,000 years of uninterrupted history, which could themselves be divided into five distinct periods: Ancient, Macedonian, Christian, Medieval and Contemporary. Where Carolidis deviated from the pattern established by the founder of the Chair for the History of the Greek Nation at the University of Athens (which Carolidis also held) was in the emphasis he gave to the contribution of Anatolia and Christianity to the qualities of the Greek nation as well as to the importance of the Ottoman legacy.

23 Johan Strauss, 'The Millets and the Ottoman Language: The Contribution of Ottoman Greeks to Ottoman Letters (19th–20th Centuries)', *Die Welt des Islams* 35/2 (November 1995), pp. 189–249, especially pp. 232–5.

24 Stelios Tsalouchos, *Istoria tis orthodoxou kinotitos Smyrnis* [*History of the Orthodox Community of Smyrna*] (Athens, 1908), p. 23.

25 Ibid., p. 26. The use of the ending -*oglou*, which many among those who had originated from Kayseri had replaced with the more Greek -*idis*, is used here in a derogatory manner, in other words, in order to depict him as a Turk.

26 Carolidis, *Speeches and Memoranda*, p. 232. See also Aykut Kansu, *Politics in Post-revolutionary Turkey: 1908–1913* (Leiden: Brill, 2000), p. 30.

27 Meclis-I Mebusan Zabıt Ceridesi (Minutes of the Parliament), I/IV/2, 3 October, 1327/16 October 1911, 1, p. 15.

28 Emmanouilidis' Ottomanist ideas in this context are also discussed in Vangelis Kechriotis, 'On the margins of national historiography: The Greek İttihatçı Emmanouil Emmanouilidis – Opportunist or Ottoman patriot?' in Amy Singer, Christoph K. Neumann and S. Aksin Somel (eds), *Untold Histories of the Middle East: Recovering Voices from the 19th and 20th Centuries* (London: Routledge, 2011), pp. 124–42.

29 Vangelis Kechriotis, 'The enthusiasm turns to fear: everyday life relations between Christians and Muslims in Izmir in the aftermath of the Young Turk Revolution', in *'L'ivresse de la liberté': le révolution de 1908 dans l'Empire ottomane, Collection Turcica*, vol. XVII (Paris: Peteers, 2012), pp. 295–316.

30 *Ittihad*, 'Her şeyden ikdam vazife' [Persistence is our utmost duty], 17 Teşrinievvel (16 October) 1908.

31 *Tanın*, 'Dünkü Büyük nümaişler: Harb! Harb! Sultan Ahmed' te – Harbiye Nezaretinde – Türbe-ı Fatih' te' [Yesterday's large demonstrations: War! War! At Sultan Ahmet (Mosque), at the Ministry of War, at Fatih's tomb], 22 September 1328/5 October 1912.

32 Carolidis defended his political peer, claiming that these did not affect a large part of the Greek Orthodox community in Smyrna where Emmanouilidis was already well known as a lawyer and a patriot. Carolidis, *Speeches and Memoranda*, pp. 233–4.

33 Emmanouil Emmanouilidis, *Ta telefaia eti tis Othomanikis Aftokratorias* [*The Last Years of the Ottoman Empire*] (Athens: G.I. Kallergi, 1924).

34 Their publication in Greek was due to the New Circle of Constantinopolitans and the Association for the Propagation of Useful Books in Athens. The Turkish translation was published by Belge Yayınları in Istanbul.

35 As, for example, the fact that he was the first to translate and publish in 1912 the complete, unabridged biography of Sultan Mehmet II authored by the fifteenth-century Byzantine bureaucrat Kritovoulos and glorifying the Ottoman ruler. See Vangelis Kechriotis, 'A Cappadocian in Athens, an Athenian in Smyrna and a parliamentary in Istanbul: the multiple personae and loyalties of Pavlos Carolidis', in Kent Schull and Christine Isom-Verhaaren (eds), *Living in the Ottoman Realm: Sultans, Subjects, and Elites* (Indiana: Indiana University Press, 2015, forthcoming).

Afterword:

Writing Mediterranean Diasporas After the Transnational Turn

Thomas W. Gallant

At first glance, the informed reader noticing the title, *Mediterranean Diasporas*, will probably think, what can this volume possibly add to the rich body of literature on the topic? Home to three of the great diasporic cultures in world history – Greeks, Jews and Armenians – the Mediterranean has for a long time been a central locus for the study of population dispersement and settlement. If we add in the Iberian and Italian diasporas, then, the Mediterranean could arguably be considered the most diasporic region in the world. Not surprisingly over the years, scholars have examined a wide range of topics from the perspective of Mediterranean diasporas. Recently, however, the concept of diaspora has come under question and has, to some extent, fallen out of favour with greater emphasis being placed upon two related concepts: transnationalism and cosmopolitanism.

Transnationalism has always been an element in defining a diaspora. Indeed, the subtitle of *Diaspora*, previously the premier academic periodical on this topic, was *A Journal of Transnational Studies* and this suggests just how tightly interconnected the two terms were. That the journal has not published under this rubric since 2008 indicates that something important has changed. A partial explanation for this shift may be found in the statement of purpose for the journal, which stated that it was 'dedicated to the multidisciplinary study of the history, culture, social structure, politics and economics of both the traditional diasporas – Armenian, Greek, and Jewish – and those transnational dispersions which in the past three decades [before 1991] have chosen to identify themselves as "diasporas" '. As various formulations of terms foregrounding 'trans-', such as transnational, transimperial and transregional, obtained greater autonomous ontological status, the concept of diaspora increasingly fell out of favour.[1] In part this was because the concept was so closely tied to the mass migration and settlement abroad of a few specific groups and this legacy came to be seen as too analytically limiting. What diaspora leaves out and what transnational encompasses are a whole variety of movements of various peoples and things across time and through space. With the 'transnational turn', then, historians have turned their gaze to examining numerous different topical areas relating to various modalities and flows.[2] One of the most important contributions this book makes is to add intellectual history to the list of topics analysed transnationally.

An approach that has emerged as one of the most important in transnational history is biography. A number of scholars have shown the analytical utility of tracing the careers and movements of individuals, families and groups, such as financiers, merchants or soldiers, so as to uncover broader historical processes like imperialism or the spread of capitalism.[3] The chapters in this volume fall squarely within this paradigm. Each of them deals with men who lived some or all of their lives mostly outside of the boundaries of the place that either was or would become their 'national' homeland. The revolutionary refugees, itinerant intellectuals and displaced politicians discussed here migrated and settled in locales across the Mediterranean and beyond. They became key pieces of a multinodal transnational intellectual network that, because they shared a similar ideological orientation, made them part of a 'liberal international'. But were they in and of themselves a diaspora? Or were they a migration stream embedded in broader, more national diasporas? They were certainly a 'transnational dispersion', to borrow the language employed by *Diaspora*, but did they self-consciously identify themselves as a diaspora? The case studies presented here clearly indicate that they were aware that they were connected to a broader network, even though they did not refer to themselves as a coherent diaspora. In the way that they frame the volume, Isabella and Zanou contribute to the redefinition of diaspora after the transnational turn.

Another factor in the waning of diaspora as an important analytical category has been the emergence of cosmopolitanism. Whereas diaspora, in its traditional sense, referred to the members of a national group who had emigrated to a new land and settled there as a group within a group, cosmopolitanism, as it has been reconceptualized in recent years, leads us to examine the cultural heterogeneity and hybridity not just of elites, as it had in the past, but of numerous groups and sectors of society.[4] This development has led scholars to refer to a host of cosmopolitanisms, such as working-class cosmopolitanism, as I discuss in a forthcoming piece. The essays in this volume, I submit, contribute to what we might call 'intellectual cosmopolitanism'. The sojourners whose tales fill the pages of this book became members of diverse and heterogeneous intellectual communities that were in the broadest sense cosmopolitan.

This book, then, contributes to a major revision of three critically important conceptual fields: those being diaspora, transnationalism, and cosmopolitanism. It also adds another piece to the ongoing revitalization of the fields of intellectual history and the history of ideas. And it does so by tracing the transnational circulation of men and ideas around the Mediterranean and Europe.

Some years ago, the late Eric Hobsbawm deployed the phrase 'the Age of Revolution' to describe the period in European history from 1789 to 1848.[5] And he was absolutely correct in doing so, at least in regard to Western Europe. An era that began with the overthrow of the archetypical *ancien régime* polity, Bourbon France, ended with a virtual tsunami of liberal and nationalist uprisings that transformed the face of Europe. In the Mediterranean, however, a slightly different periodization pertained. While the region witnessed numerous and important insurrections during the first half of the nineteenth century, the revolutionary impulse continued to throb into the twentieth. Every Age of Revolution generates revolutionaries. Whether it be global and globe-trotting jihadists now or liberal insurrectionists then, men from various parts of the world have travelled from afar to join like-minded causes. To date, most of the literature has focused on men who travelled abroad to join revolutionary armies as fighters. That there was a Mediterranean-wide connection among armed warriors has been well-documented.[6] In an excellent new book, the late Richard Stites adopted a transnational biographical approach similar to the one employed by many of the studies in this volume to track the careers of four major revolutionary figures: Colonel Rafael Riego, General Guglielmo Pepe, General Alexander Ipsilantis and Colonel Surgei Muraviev-Apostol.[7] So, we know a great deal about itinerant revolutionary warriors. What has been left out of the story, however, are the men whose ideas were the foundation for revolutionary action. This volume fills that lacuna.

Five of the ten essays in this volume focus on the period from the early nineteenth century until 1848. As well they should, because this was, after all, the time of liberal insurrections and uprisings around the globe. Since almost all of these uprisings failed, the losers quickly took their place among the ranks of political refugees who fled abroad to continue their revolutionary activities. The chapters by Simal, Paquette, Bron, Isabella and Zanou all focus on the critical decade of the 1820s, and all but one concentrate on what we can call 'dimensions of the liberal international'. The one exception is Zanou. She shows that many of the leading Greek or philhellenic activists in the Russian Empire, who embraced many liberal ideas and ideals, were conservative regarding how social and political change should occur, as well as being deeply religious. What men like Ioannis Kapodistrias and Alexandre Stourdza shared with liberal revolutionaries was that they were also part of a diasporic intellectual network. Their developmental trajectory spanned Russia, obviously, as well as the Mediterranean and Europe. Deeply imbued with nationalism, conservative intellectuals faced the dilemma of how to achieve the goal of national liberation while retaining the core principles of Restoration-period conservatism. Foregrounded in their discussions of the intellectual ferment during the Age of Revolution was the struggle between liberalism and conservatism and between those who espoused revolutionary change and those who opted for reformist evolution.

The remaining essays in the book span the nineteenth century with two of them covering the period up to 1848, while the other three discuss various developments during the second half of the century. If the revolutions of 1848 represented the 'springtime for the people', then the 1830s and early 1840s was the winter of their discontent. These were the years when alternative paths to modernity other than revolution began to be explored. Coller, for example, shows through a discussion of Hassuna D'Ghies's brief career how the ideology of 'New Ottomanism' developed out of the fruitful exchange between young Muslim intellectuals and European Christian thinkers as a new way to reform the empire. The chapters that deal with the second half of the nineteenth century confront, as they must, Romantic nationalism. One, by Puto and Isabella, shows how it influenced the development of late-forming nationalisms, in this case that of Albanians. The other two sketch out the complicated responses that Romantic nationalism elicited. Kechriotis demonstrates how even in the face of the virulent, radical nationalism that developed in the Greek world during the late nineteenth century,[8] some groups, in this case the Turkish-speaking *Karamanlı*, still embraced an identity and espoused a political perspective that harkened back to an imperial past rather than a national future.

In closing, there are four important and interrelated conclusions that emerge from the chapters in this volume. The first of these is that modern scholarship has placed so much emphasis on nationalism that it has distracted us from examining other possibilities for political change. Many of the diaspora intellectuals discussed in this book are rightly considered among the founding fathers of their respective countries. And indeed many of them played critically important roles in developing their respective nationalisms and in delineating the physical space of their imagined communities. What has been under-appreciated, as shown in some of these chapters, is that many of them did not necessarily see the nation-state as the ultimate goal of revolutionary action. That a nation could easily and happily flourish in a multi-national empire was certainly an idea that had resonance, with the proviso that national rights were recognized and protected in a participatory constitutional system.

A second, related conclusion is that diaspora intellectuals, more so than their indigenous brethren, were engaged in acts of imagination. That the nation was an imaginary community is a conclusion that has been around for a long time. What set diaspora intellectuals apart was that they were involved in a double act of imagination; not only did they contribute to the construction of an imaginary human community but also to the delineation of the national space. Much of the literature in diaspora studies has shown how expatriates and immigrants abroad fabricate an imaginary homeland. Sometimes it was as a utopian and sometimes a dystopian space but it was always an act of imagination tinged by nostalgia. Just as the confrontation with cultural others while abroad helps to shape the diaspora intellectual's national identity, so too does living in a different physical space play a critical role in defining how he perceives the national homeland.

The third major conclusion of this book is to help define the processes by which ideas moved and circulated. Two things stood out for me. The first was that diaspora intellectuals were connected to knowledge networks that spanned the Mediterranean and Europe. It was along the lines of these networks that ideas about freedom, liberty, revolutionary organization and liberalism generally flowed. There was truly a European-Mediterranean liberal international that played a critically important role in the intellectual production of the ideas that shaped the nineteenth century. The book also shows that in strictly national terms the flow of ideas and influences was not necessarily from the 'homeland' to the diaspora but the other way around. If the first point emphasizes multi-directionality in the circulation of ideas, the second points to there having been a bidirectional flow within specific national contexts.

The fourth and final conclusion I would point to is that we need to see the Mediterranean world as not being peripheral or marginal to the major political and ideological developments of the nineteenth century. As these chapters show, the Mediterranean was in many and important ways at the centre of revolutionary trends and was a crucial node in the liberal international network that spanned not just Europe but much of the globe as well.

In sum, then, it will be hard to think about nineteenth-century liberalism, nationalism and the revolutions that they spawned without factoring in the key role played by diasporic Mediterranean intellectuals. Not only did these transnational and cosmopolitan refugees and migrants contribute significantly to modern state- and nation-building in the Mediterranean but they were vitally important actors in movements that helped to shape the very foundations of the modern world.

Notes

1   In the remainder of this brief chapter, I use transnational or transnationalism as short-hand reference for the various categories of the 'trans'.

2   Patricia Clavin, 'Defining Transnationalism', *Contemporary European History* 14/4 (2005), pp. 421–39; idem, 'Time, Manner, Place: Writing Modern European History in Global, Transnational and International Contexts', *European History Quarterly* 40/4 (2010), pp. 624–40.

3   Christopher H. Johnson, David Warren Sabean, Simon Teuscher and Trivellato Francesca (eds), *Transregional and Transnational Families in Europe and*

Beyond: Experiences Since the Middle Ages (New York: Berghan Books, 2011); Natalie Rothman, *Brokering Empire: Trans-imperial Subjects Between Venice and Istanbul* (Ithaca: Cornell University Press, 2012); Emma Rothschild, *The Inner Life of Empires: an Eighteenth-century History* (Princeton: Princeton University Press, 2011).

4   Thomas W. Gallant, 'Tales From the Dark Side: Transnational Migration, the Underworld and The "Other" Greeks of the Diaspora', in Dimitris Tziovas (ed.), *Greek Diaspora and Migration Since 1700: Society, Politics and Culture* (London: Ashgate Publishing, 2009), pp. 17–29; idem, 'All Unquiet on the Waterfront: Eastern Mediterranean Port-cities as Sites of Working-class Cosmopolitanism', *Mediterranean Historical Review*, under review (2015), pp. 1–28.

5   Eric Hobsbawm, *The Age of Revolution, 1789–1848* (London: Weidenfeld & Nicholson, 1962).

6   See, for example, Gilles Pécout, 'Philhellenism in Italy: Political Friendship and the Italian Volunteers in the Mediterranean in the Nineteenth Century', *Journal of Modern Italian Studies* 9/4 (2004), pp. 405–27.

7   Richard Stites, *The Four Horsemen: Riding to Liberty in Post-Napoleonic Europe* (New York: Oxford University Press, 2014).

8   Thomas W. Gallant, *The Edinburgh History of the Greeks, 1768 to 1913 the Long Nineteenth Century* (Edinburgh: Edinburgh University Press, 2015), p. 293.

INDEX